MARVEL KNIGHTS
X-MEN

MARVEL KNIGHTS

X-MEN

HAUNTED

STORY & ART
BRAHM REVEL

COLOR ARTIST
CRISTIANE PETER

LETTERER
VC'S JOE SABINO

COVER ARTISTS
BRAHM REVEL & CRISTIANE PETER

ASSISTANT EDITOR
DEVIN LEWIS

EDITOR
SANA AMANAT

COLLECTION EDITOR: JENNIFER GRÜNWALD **ASSOCIATE MANAGING EDITOR:** ALEX STARBUCK
EDITOR, SPECIAL PROJECTS: MARK D. BEAZLEY **SENIOR EDITOR, SPECIAL PROJECTS:** JEFF YOUNGQUIST
SVP PRINT, SALES & MARKETING: DAVID GABRIEL **BOOK DESIGNER:** RODOLFO MURAGUCHI

EDITOR IN CHIEF: AXEL ALONSO **CHIEF CREATIVE OFFICER:** JOE QUESADA
PUBLISHER: DAN BUCKLEY **EXECUTIVE PRODUCER:** ALAN FINE

MARVEL KNIGHTS: X-MEN — HAUNTED. Contains material originally published in magazine form as MARVEL KNIGHTS X-MEN #1-5. First printing 2014. ISBN# 978-0-7851-8546-8. Published by MARVEL WORLDWIDE INC., a subsidiary of MARVEL ENTERTAINMENT, LLC. OFFICE OF PUBLICATION: 135 West 50th Street, New York, NY 10020. Copyright © 2013 and 2014 Marvel Characters, Inc. All rights reserved. All characters featured in this issue and the distinctive names and likenesses thereof, and all related indicia are trademarks of Marvel Characters, Inc. No similarity between any of the names, characters, persons, and/or institutions in this magazine with those of any living or dead person or institution is intended, and any such similarity which may exist is purely coincidental. **Printed in Canada.** ALAN FINE, EVP - Office of the President, Marvel Worldwide, Inc. and EVP & CMO Marvel Characters B.V.; DAN BUCKLEY, Publisher & President - Print, Animation & Digital Divisions; JOE QUESADA, Chief Creative Officer; TOM BREVOORT, SVP of Publishing; DAVID BOGART, SVP of Operations & Procurement, Publishing; C.B. CEBULSKI, SVP of Creator & Content Development; DAVID GABRIEL, SVP Print, Sales & Marketing; JIM O'KEEFE, VP of Operations & Logistics; DAN CARR, Executive Director of Publishing Technology; SUSAN CRESPI, Editorial Operations Manager; ALEX MORALES, Publishing Operations Manager; STAN LEE, Chairman Emeritus. For information regarding advertising in Marvel Comics or on Marvel.com, please contact Niza Disla, Director of Marvel Partnerships, at ndisla@marvel.com. For Marvel subscription inquiries, please call 800-217-9158. **Manufactured between 3/21/2014 and 4/28/2014 by SOLISCO PRINTERS, SCOTT, QC, CANADA.**

10 9 8 7 6 5 4 3 2 1

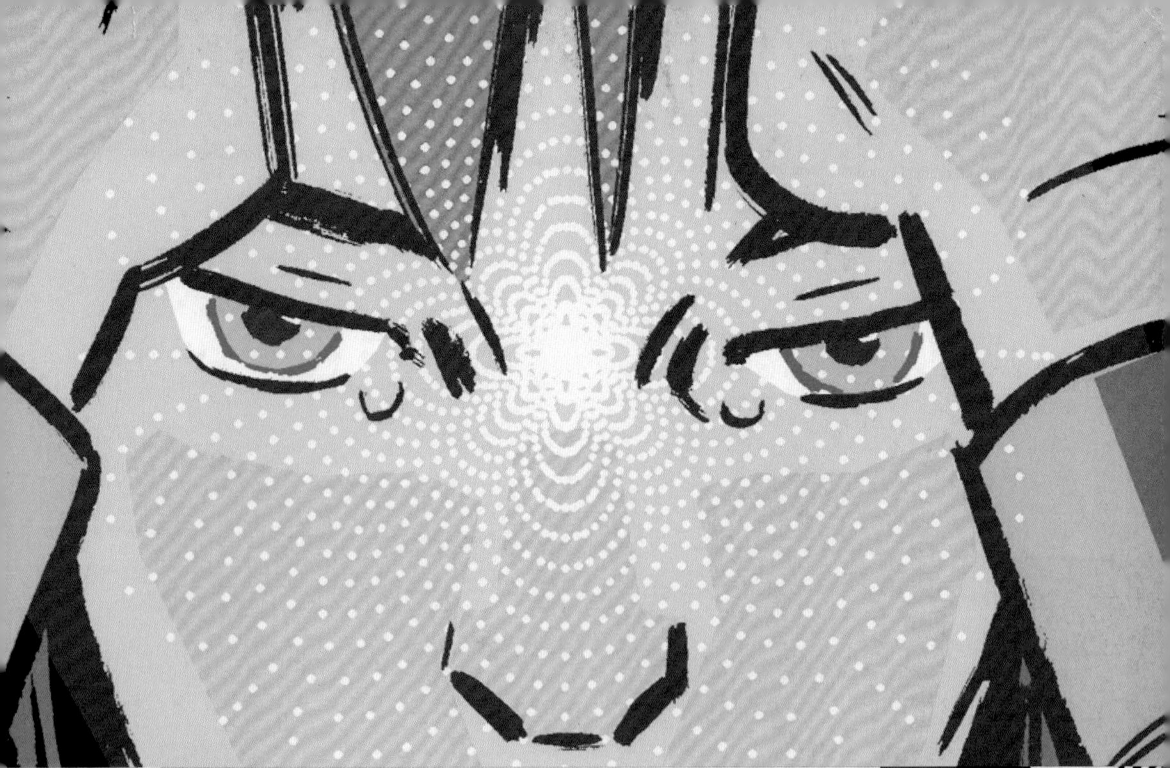

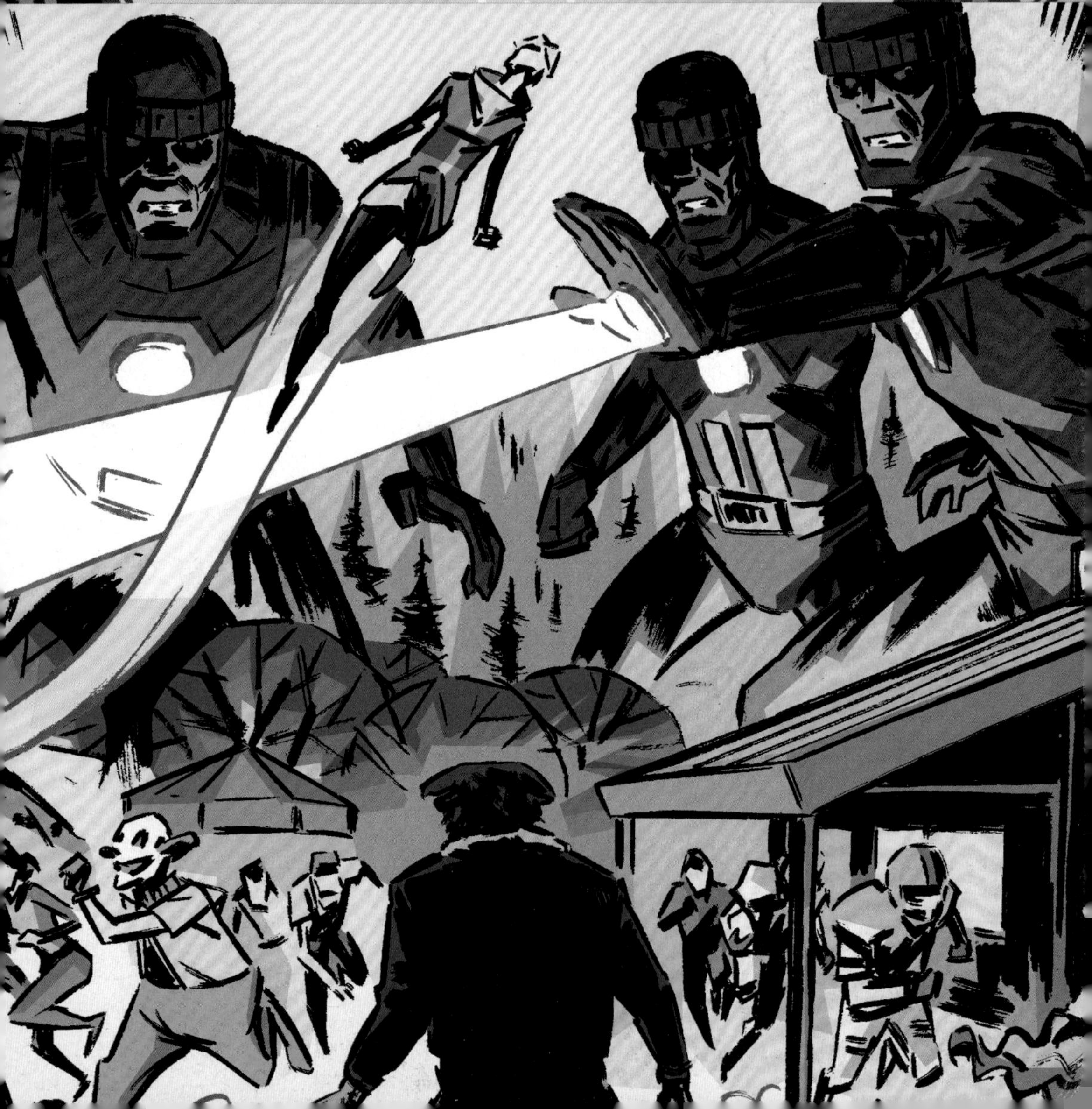

1

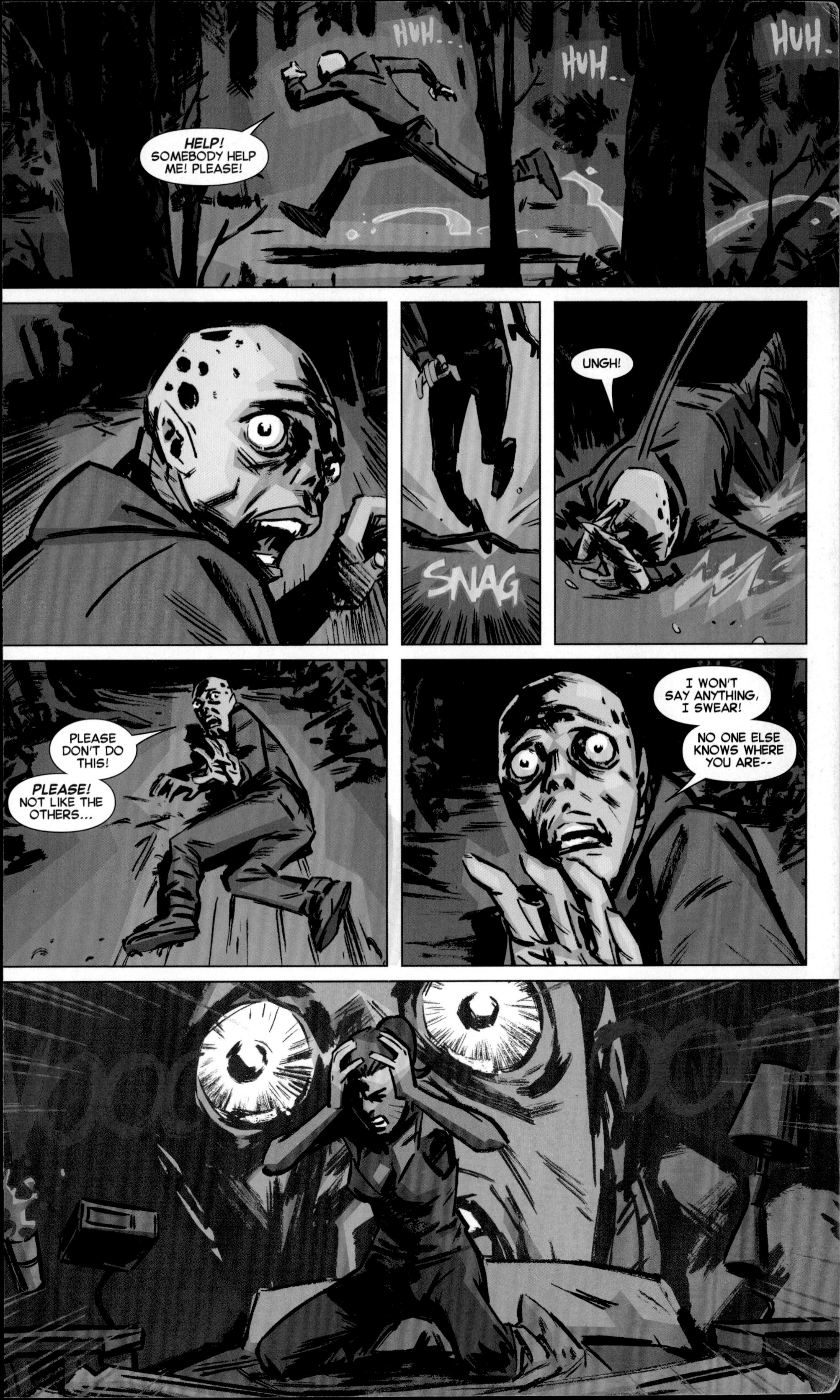
HUH...
HUH...
HUH...
HELP! SOMEBODY HELP ME! PLEASE!
SNAG
UNGH!
PLEASE DON'T DO THIS!
PLEASE! NOT LIKE THE OTHERS...
I WON'T SAY ANYTHING, I SWEAR!
NO ONE ELSE KNOWS WHERE YOU ARE--

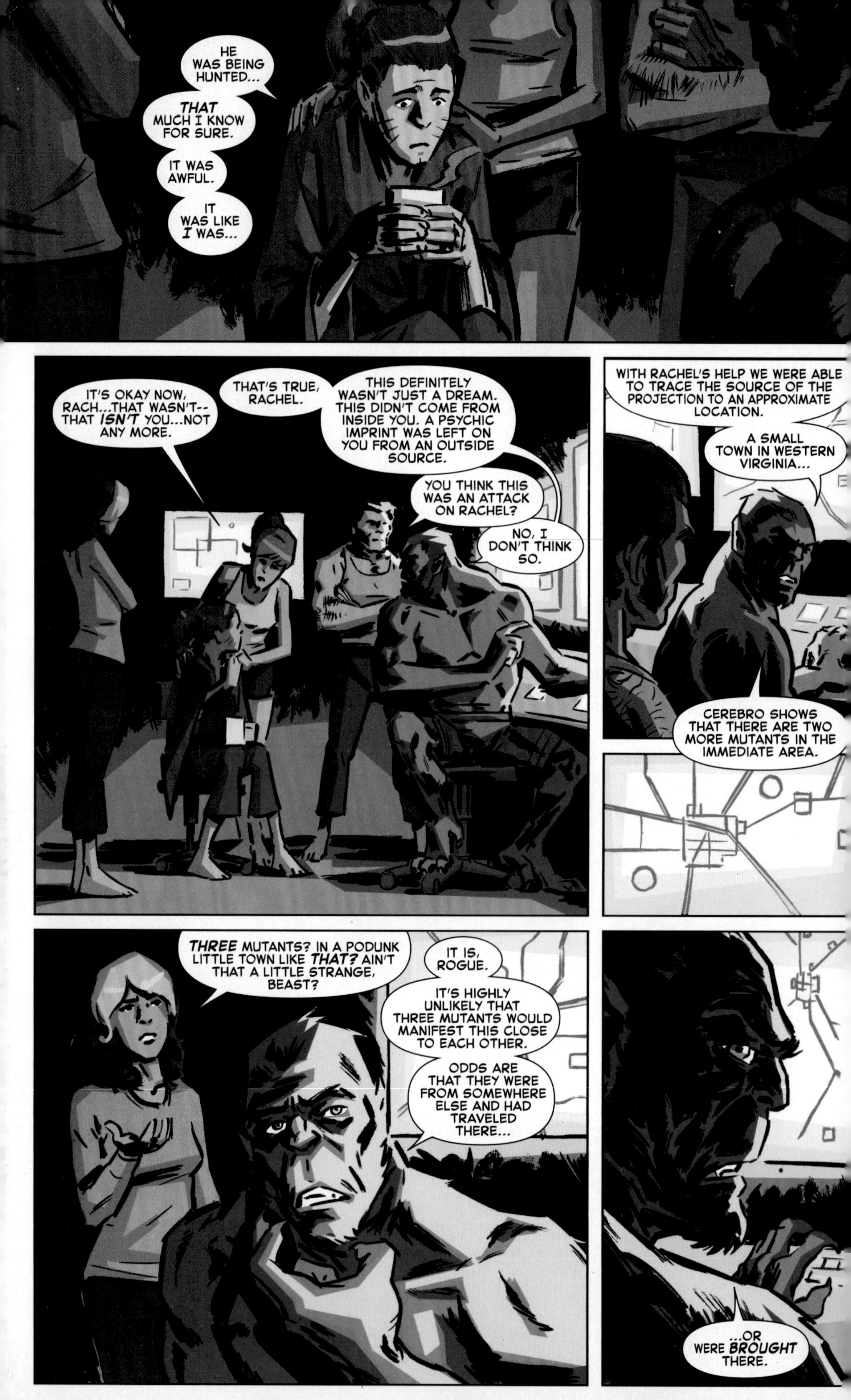
HE WAS BEING HUNTED...
THAT MUCH I KNOW FOR SURE.
IT WAS AWFUL.
IT WAS LIKE I WAS...
IT'S OKAY NOW, RACH...THAT WASN'T--THAT ISN'T YOU...NOT ANY MORE.
THAT'S TRUE, RACHEL.
THIS DEFINITELY WASN'T JUST A DREAM. THIS DIDN'T COME FROM INSIDE YOU. A PSYCHIC IMPRINT WAS LEFT ON YOU FROM AN OUTSIDE SOURCE.
YOU THINK THIS WAS AN ATTACK ON RACHEL?
NO, I DON'T THINK SO.
WITH RACHEL'S HELP WE WERE ABLE TO TRACE THE SOURCE OF THE PROJECTION TO AN APPROXIMATE LOCATION.
A SMALL TOWN IN WESTERN VIRGINIA...
CEREBRO SHOWS THAT THERE ARE TWO MORE MUTANTS IN THE IMMEDIATE AREA.
THREE MUTANTS? IN A PODUNK LITTLE TOWN LIKE THAT? AIN'T THAT A LITTLE STRANGE, BEAST?
IT IS, ROGUE.
IT'S HIGHLY UNLIKELY THAT THREE MUTANTS WOULD MANIFEST THIS CLOSE TO EACH OTHER.
ODDS ARE THAT THEY WERE FROM SOMEWHERE ELSE AND HAD TRAVELED THERE...
...OR WERE BROUGHT THERE.

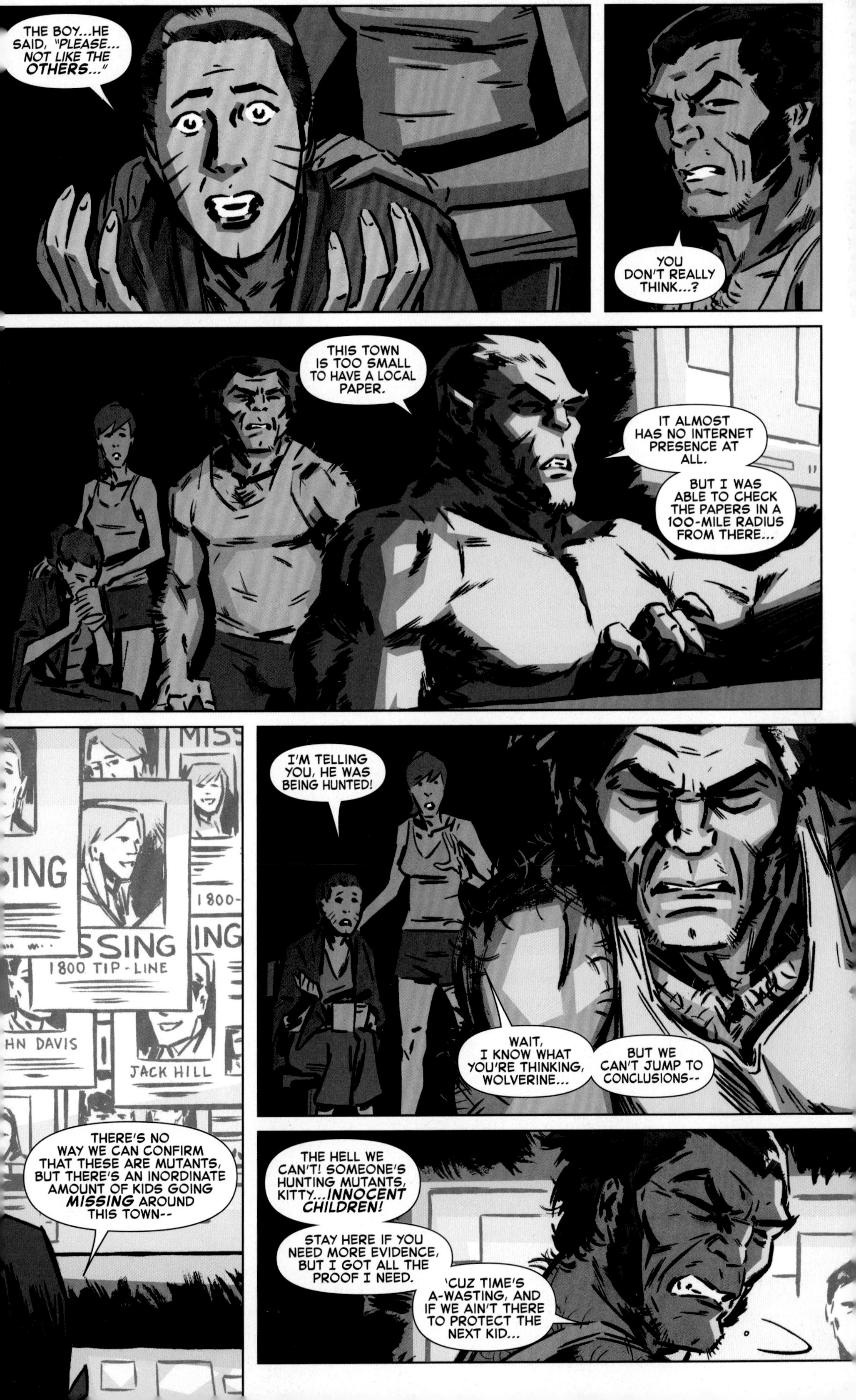

THE BOY...HE SAID, "PLEASE... NOT LIKE THE OTHERS..."
YOU DON'T REALLY THINK...?
THIS TOWN IS TOO SMALL TO HAVE A LOCAL PAPER.
IT ALMOST HAS NO INTERNET PRESENCE AT ALL.
BUT I WAS ABLE TO CHECK THE PAPERS IN A 100-MILE RADIUS FROM THERE...
MISS
SING
1800-
ING
SSING
1800 TIP-LINE
HN DAVIS
JACK HILL
THERE'S NO WAY WE CAN CONFIRM THAT THESE ARE MUTANTS, BUT THERE'S AN INORDINATE AMOUNT OF KIDS GOING MISSING AROUND THIS TOWN--
I'M TELLING YOU, HE WAS BEING HUNTED!
WAIT, I KNOW WHAT YOU'RE THINKING, WOLVERINE...
BUT WE CAN'T JUMP TO CONCLUSIONS--
THE HELL WE CAN'T! SOMEONE'S HUNTING MUTANTS, KITTY...INNOCENT CHILDREN!
STAY HERE IF YOU NEED MORE EVIDENCE, BUT I GOT ALL THE PROOF I NEED.
'CUZ TIME'S A-WASTING, AND IF WE AIN'T THERE TO PROTECT THE NEXT KID...

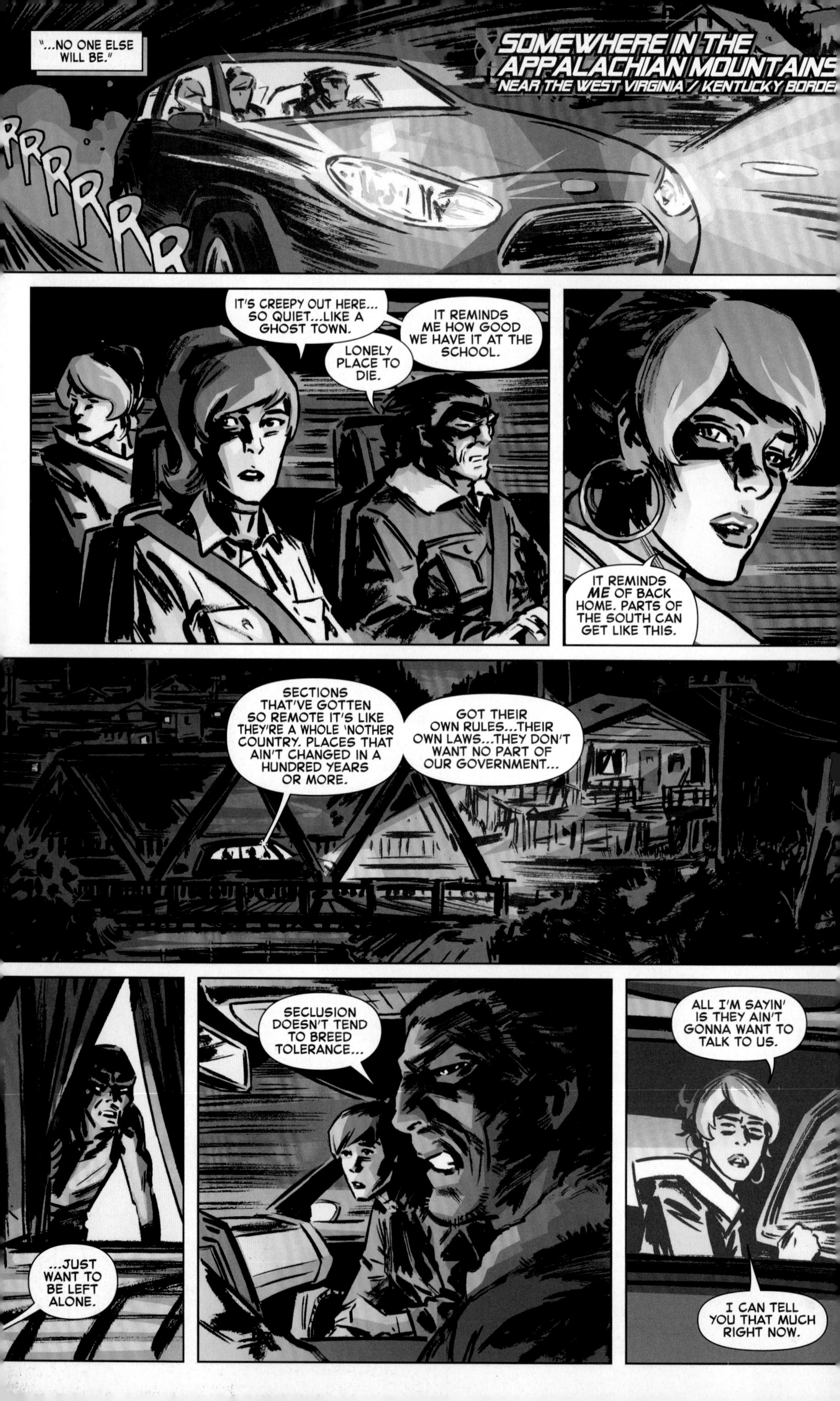

"...NO ONE ELSE WILL BE."
SOMEWHERE IN THE APPALACHIAN MOUNTAINS
NEAR THE WEST VIRGINIA / KENTUCKY BORDE
RRRRRRR
IT'S CREEPY OUT HERE... SO QUIET...LIKE A GHOST TOWN.
IT REMINDS ME HOW GOOD WE HAVE IT AT THE SCHOOL.
LONELY PLACE TO DIE.
IT REMINDS ME OF BACK HOME. PARTS OF THE SOUTH CAN GET LIKE THIS.
SECTIONS THAT'VE GOTTEN SO REMOTE IT'S LIKE THEY'RE A WHOLE 'NOTHER COUNTRY. PLACES THAT AIN'T CHANGED IN A HUNDRED YEARS OR MORE.
GOT THEIR OWN RULES...THEIR OWN LAWS...THEY DON'T WANT NO PART OF OUR GOVERNMENT...
...JUST WANT TO BE LEFT ALONE.
SECLUSION DOESN'T TEND TO BREED TOLERANCE...
ALL I'M SAYIN' IS THEY AIN'T GONNA WANT TO TALK TO US.
I CAN TELL YOU THAT MUCH RIGHT NOW.

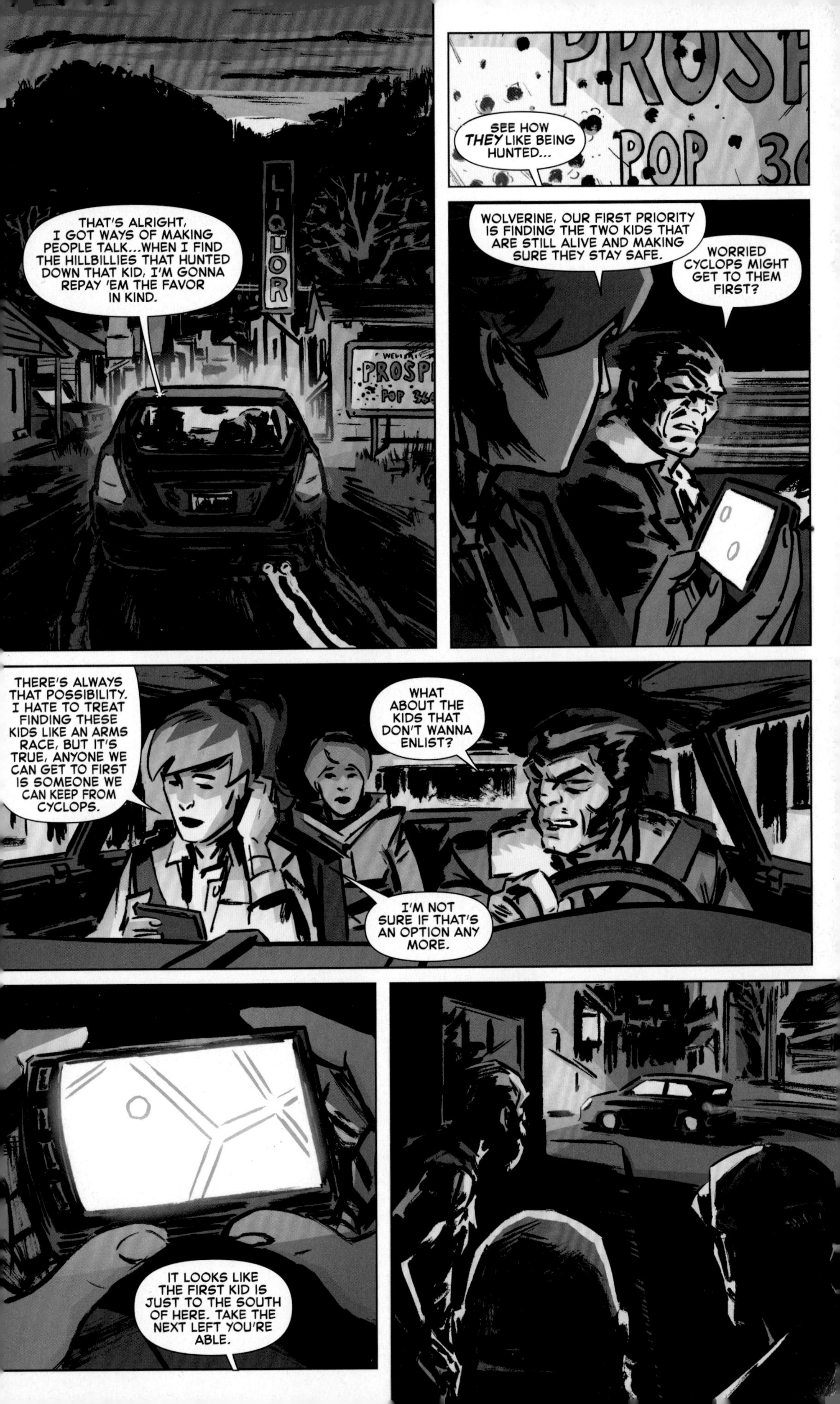
LIQUOR
PROSP
POP 36
THAT'S ALRIGHT, I GOT WAYS OF MAKING PEOPLE TALK...WHEN I FIND THE HILLBILLIES THAT HUNTED DOWN THAT KID, I'M GONNA REPAY 'EM THE FAVOR IN KIND.
PROSP
POP 36
SEE HOW THEY LIKE BEING HUNTED...
WOLVERINE, OUR FIRST PRIORITY IS FINDING THE TWO KIDS THAT ARE STILL ALIVE AND MAKING SURE THEY STAY SAFE.
WORRIED CYCLOPS MIGHT GET TO THEM FIRST?
THERE'S ALWAYS THAT POSSIBILITY. I HATE TO TREAT FINDING THESE KIDS LIKE AN ARMS RACE, BUT IT'S TRUE, ANYONE WE CAN GET TO FIRST IS SOMEONE WE CAN KEEP FROM CYCLOPS.
WHAT ABOUT THE KIDS THAT DON'T WANNA ENLIST?
I'M NOT SURE IF THAT'S AN OPTION ANY MORE.
IT LOOKS LIKE THE FIRST KID IS JUST TO THE SOUTH OF HERE. TAKE THE NEXT LEFT YOU'RE ABLE.

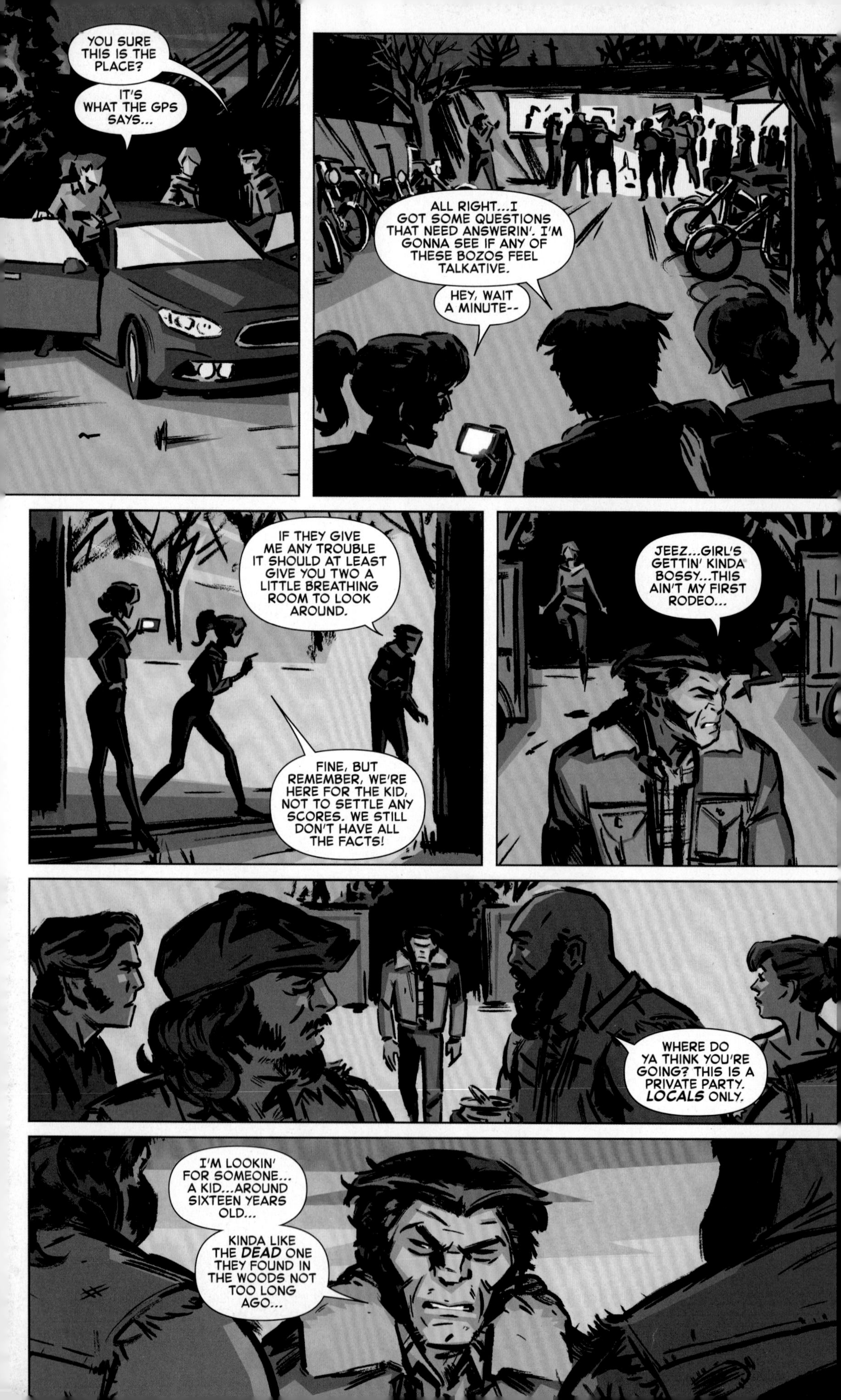

YOU SURE THIS IS THE PLACE?
IT'S WHAT THE GPS SAYS...
ALL RIGHT...I GOT SOME QUESTIONS THAT NEED ANSWERIN'. I'M GONNA SEE IF ANY OF THESE BOZOS FEEL TALKATIVE.
HEY, WAIT A MINUTE--
IF THEY GIVE ME ANY TROUBLE IT SHOULD AT LEAST GIVE YOU TWO A LITTLE BREATHING ROOM TO LOOK AROUND.
FINE, BUT REMEMBER, WE'RE HERE FOR THE KID, NOT TO SETTLE ANY SCORES. WE STILL DON'T HAVE ALL THE FACTS!
JEEZ...GIRL'S GETTIN' KINDA BOSSY...THIS AIN'T MY FIRST RODEO...
WHERE DO YA THINK YOU'RE GOING? THIS IS A PRIVATE PARTY. *LOCALS* ONLY.
I'M LOOKIN' FOR SOMEONE... A KID...AROUND SIXTEEN YEARS OLD...
KINDA LIKE THE *DEAD* ONE THEY FOUND IN THE WOODS NOT TOO LONG AGO...

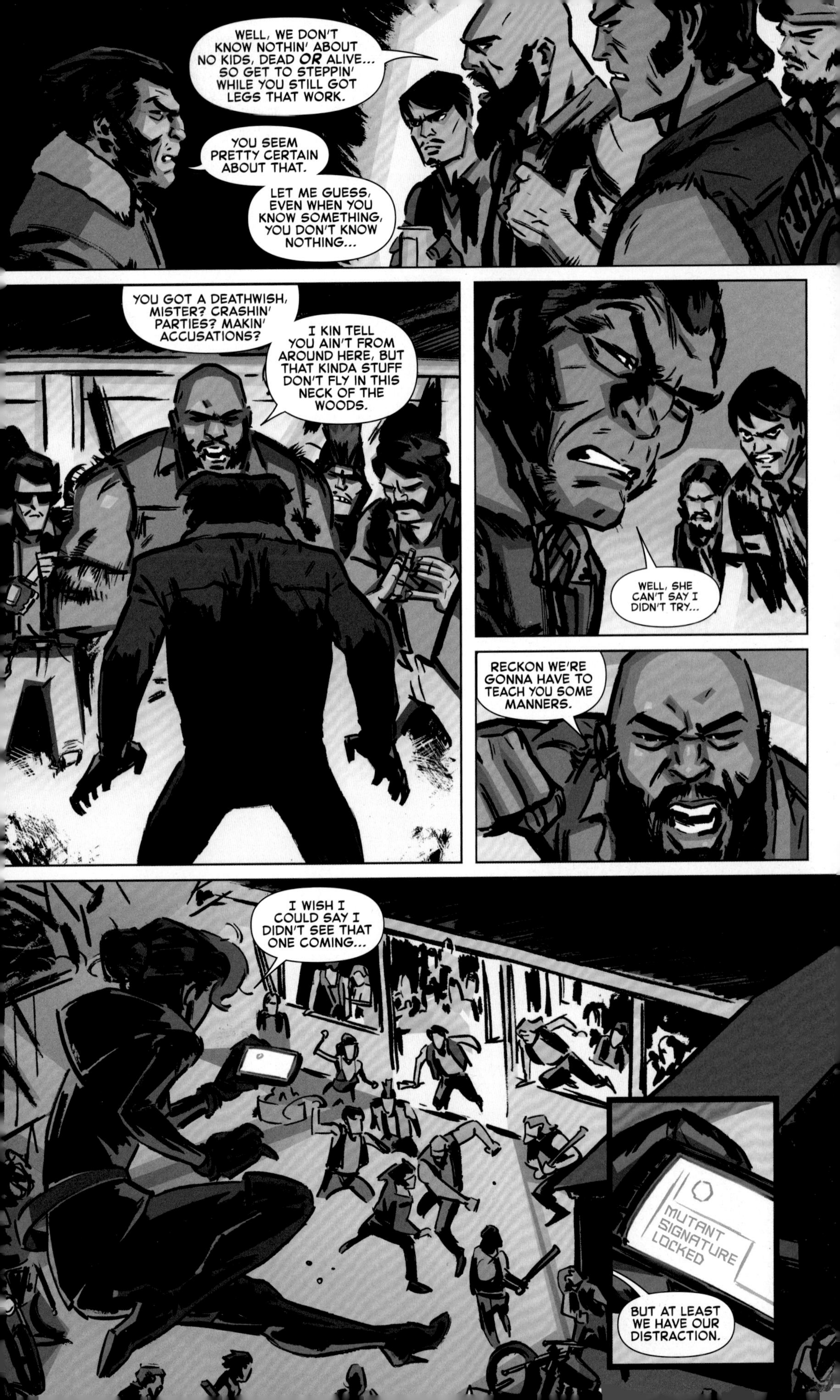
WELL, WE DON'T KNOW NOTHIN' ABOUT NO KIDS, DEAD *OR* ALIVE... SO GET TO STEPPIN' WHILE YOU STILL GOT LEGS THAT WORK.
YOU SEEM PRETTY CERTAIN ABOUT THAT.
LET ME GUESS, EVEN WHEN YOU KNOW SOMETHING, YOU DON'T KNOW NOTHING...
YOU GOT A DEATHWISH, MISTER? CRASHIN' PARTIES? MAKIN' ACCUSATIONS?
I KIN TELL YOU AIN'T FROM AROUND HERE, BUT THAT KINDA STUFF DON'T FLY IN THIS NECK OF THE WOODS.
WELL, SHE CAN'T SAY I DIDN'T TRY...
RECKON WE'RE GONNA HAVE TO TEACH YOU SOME MANNERS.
I WISH I COULD SAY I DIDN'T SEE THAT ONE COMING...
MUTANT SIGNATURE LOCKED
BUT AT LEAST WE HAVE OUR DISTRACTION.

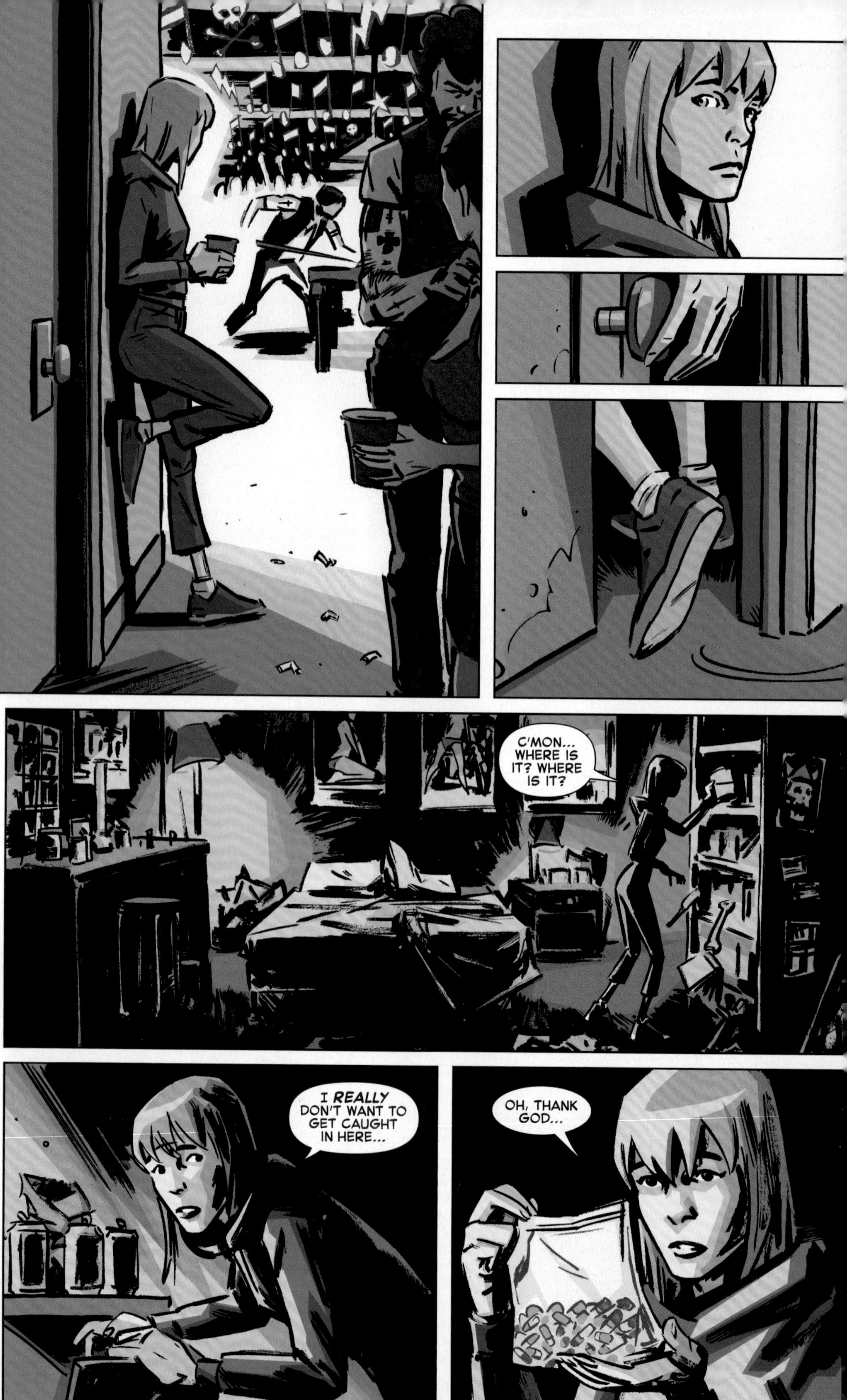
C'MON... WHERE IS IT? WHERE IS IT?
I REALLY DON'T WANT TO GET CAUGHT IN HERE...
OH, THANK GOD...

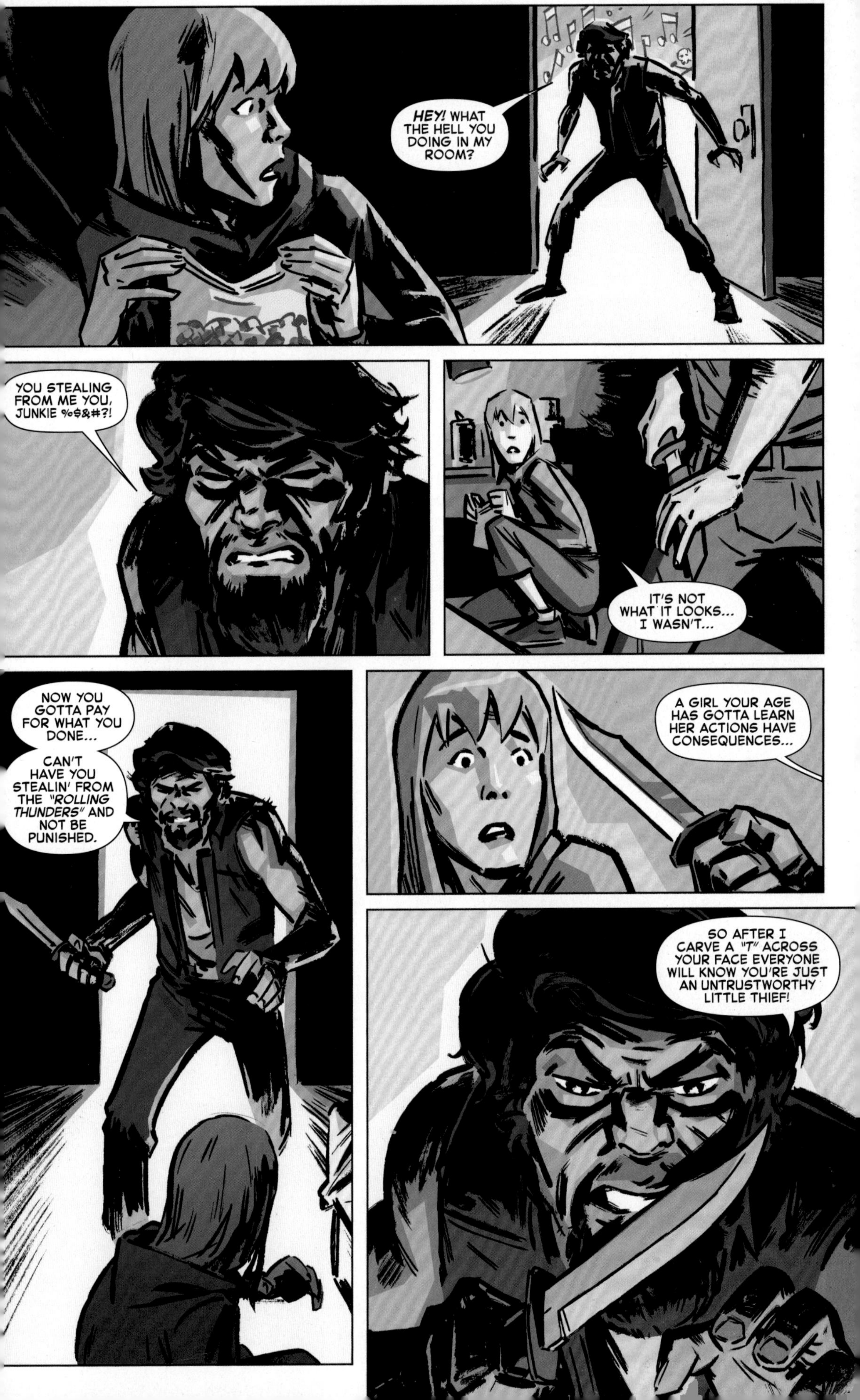

HEY! WHAT THE HELL YOU DOING IN MY ROOM?
YOU STEALING FROM ME YOU, JUNKIE %$&#?!
IT'S NOT WHAT IT LOOKS... I WASN'T...
NOW YOU GOTTA PAY FOR WHAT YOU DONE...
CAN'T HAVE YOU STEALIN' FROM THE "ROLLING THUNDERS" AND NOT BE PUNISHED.
A GIRL YOUR AGE HAS GOTTA LEARN HER ACTIONS HAVE CONSEQUENCES...
SO AFTER I CARVE A "T" ACROSS YOUR FACE EVERYONE WILL KNOW YOU'RE JUST AN UNTRUSTWORTHY LITTLE THIEF!

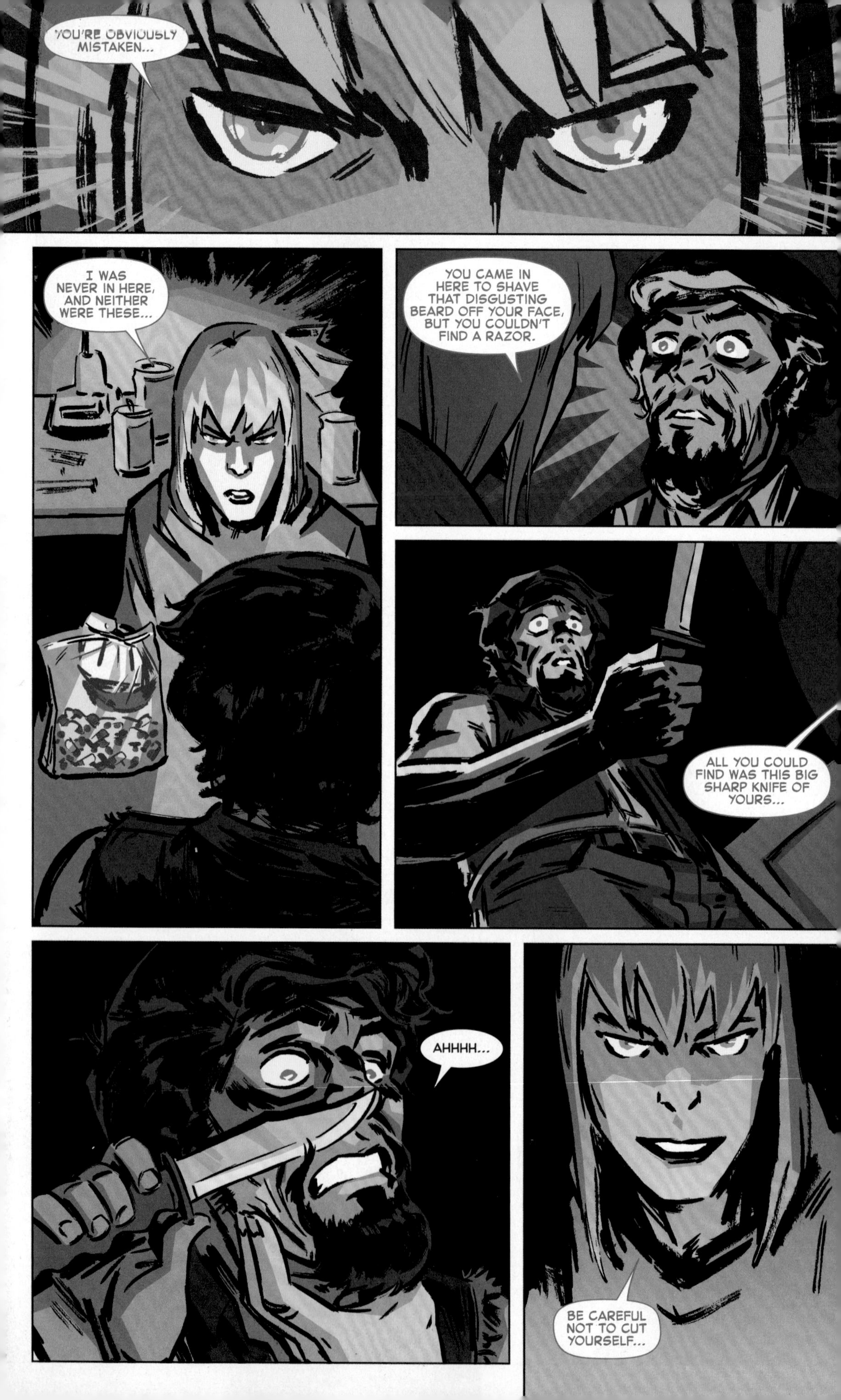
YOU'RE OBVIOUSLY MISTAKEN...
I WAS NEVER IN HERE, AND NEITHER WERE THESE...
YOU CAME IN HERE TO SHAVE THAT DISGUSTING BEARD OFF YOUR FACE, BUT YOU COULDN'T FIND A RAZOR.
ALL YOU COULD FIND WAS THIS BIG SHARP KNIFE OF YOURS...
AHHHH...
BE CAREFUL NOT TO CUT YOURSELF...

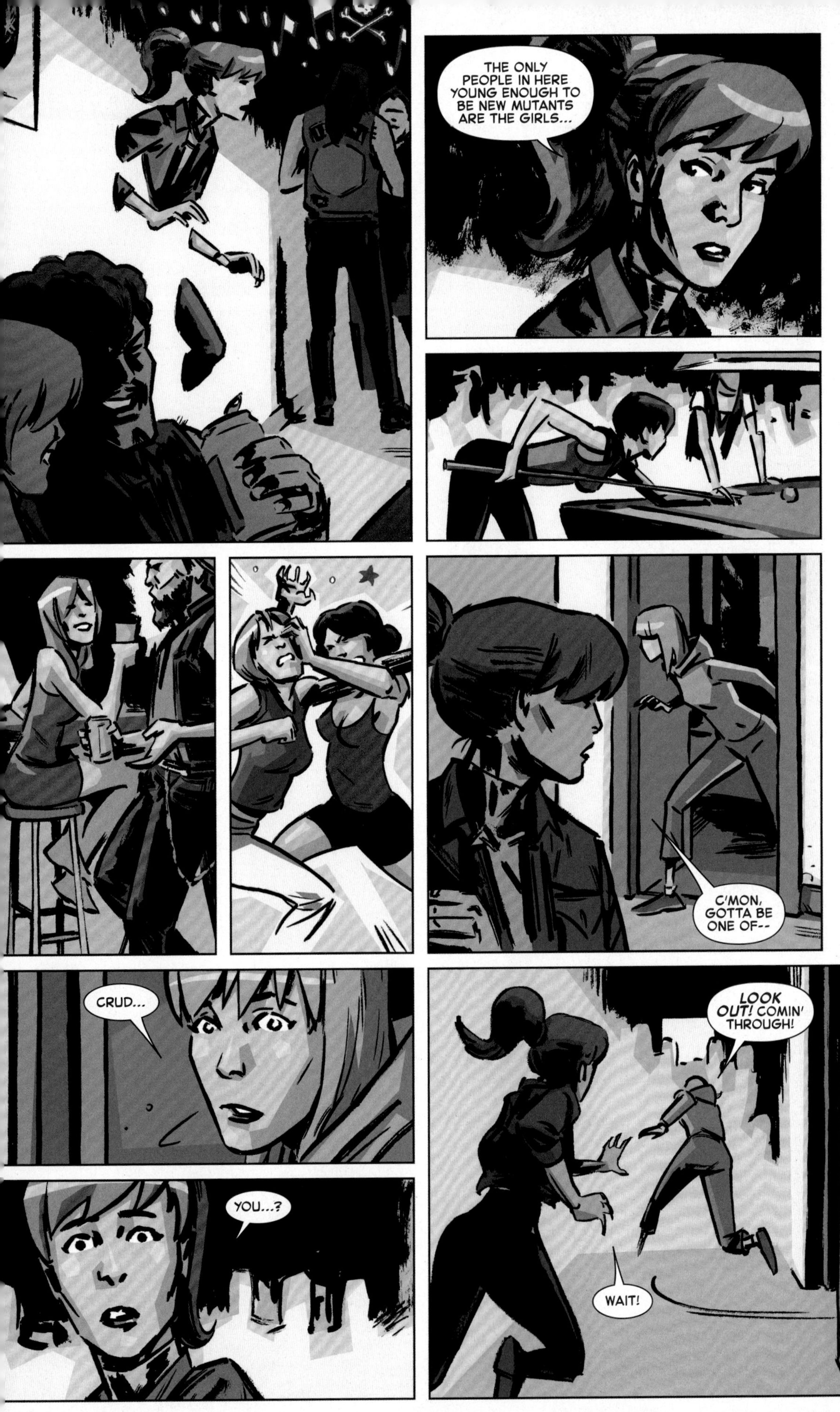
THE ONLY PEOPLE IN HERE YOUNG ENOUGH TO BE NEW MUTANTS ARE THE GIRLS...
C'MON, GOTTA BE ONE OF--
CRUD...
YOU...?
LOOK OUT! COMIN' THROUGH!
WAIT!

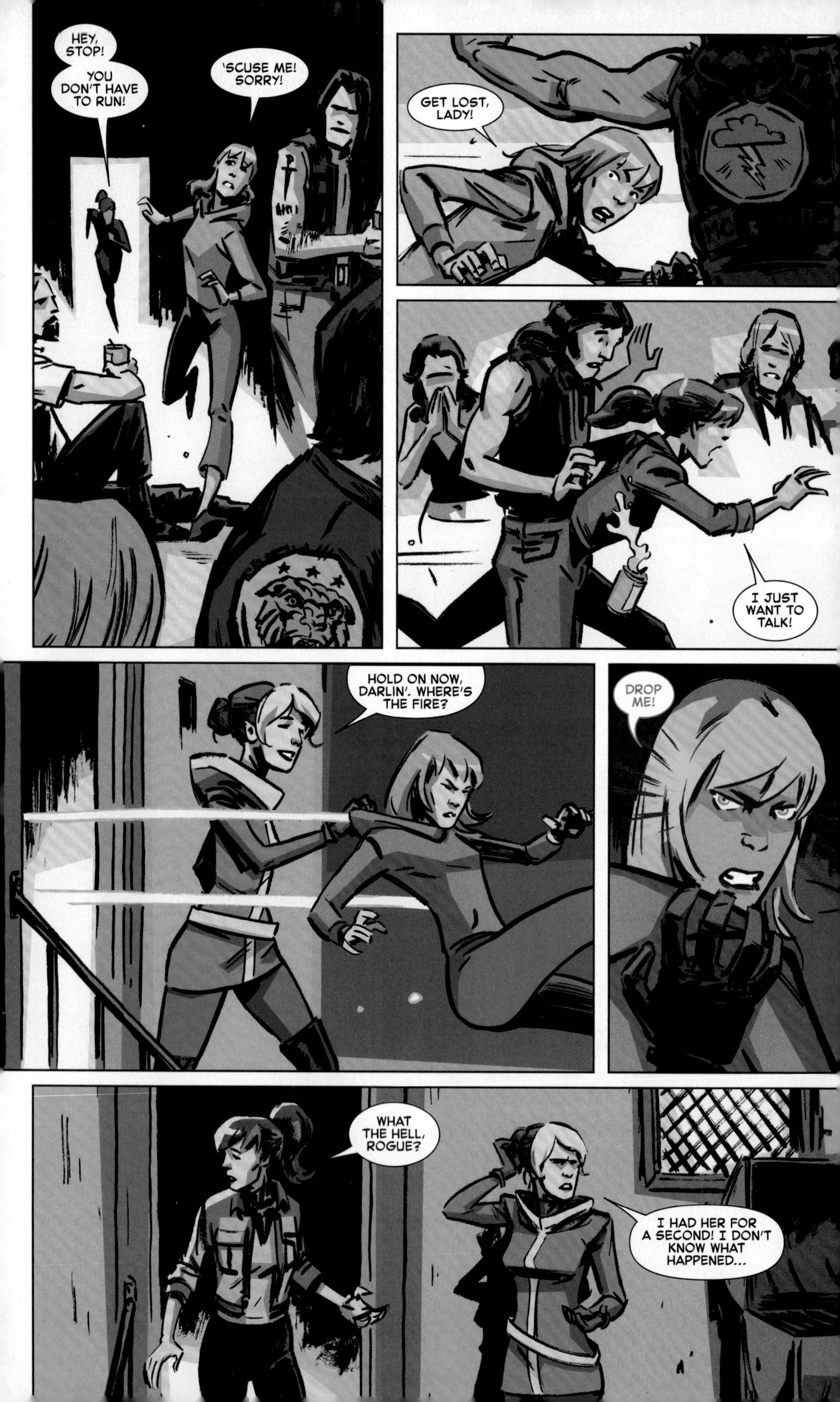
HEY, STOP!
YOU DON'T HAVE TO RUN!
'SCUSE ME! SORRY!
GET LOST, LADY!
I JUST WANT TO TALK!
HOLD ON NOW, DARLIN'. WHERE'S THE FIRE?
DROP ME!
WHAT THE HELL, ROGUE?
I HAD HER FOR A SECOND! I DON'T KNOW WHAT HAPPENED...

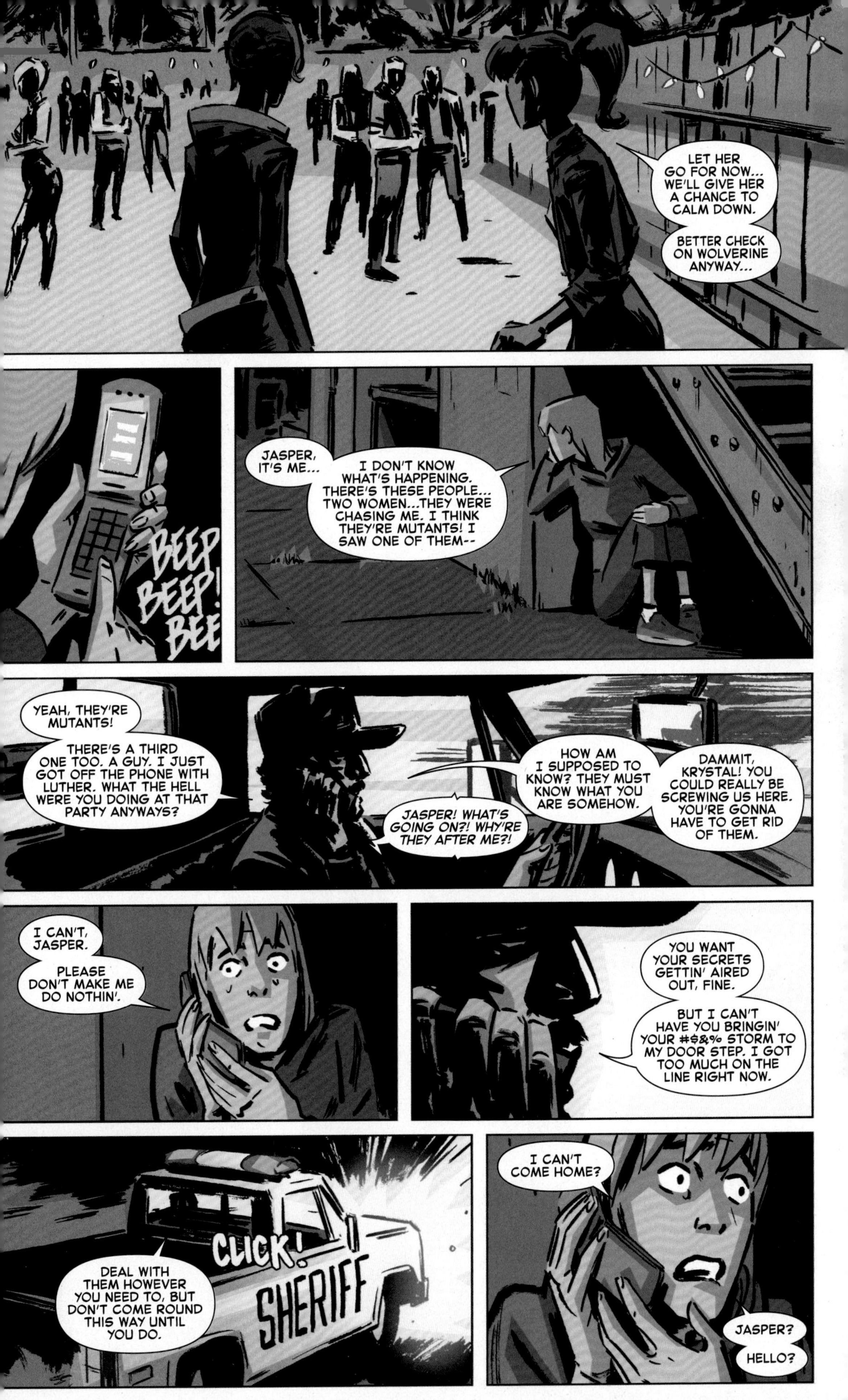
LET HER GO FOR NOW... WE'LL GIVE HER A CHANCE TO CALM DOWN.
BETTER CHECK ON WOLVERINE ANYWAY...
BEEP BEEP! BEE
JASPER, IT'S ME...
I DON'T KNOW WHAT'S HAPPENING. THERE'S THESE PEOPLE... TWO WOMEN...THEY WERE CHASING ME. I THINK THEY'RE MUTANTS! I SAW ONE OF THEM--
YEAH, THEY'RE MUTANTS!
THERE'S A THIRD ONE TOO. A GUY. I JUST GOT OFF THE PHONE WITH LUTHER. WHAT THE HELL WERE YOU DOING AT THAT PARTY ANYWAYS?
JASPER! WHAT'S GOING ON?! WHY'RE THEY AFTER ME?!
HOW AM I SUPPOSED TO KNOW? THEY MUST KNOW WHAT YOU ARE SOMEHOW.
DAMMIT, KRYSTAL! YOU COULD REALLY BE SCREWING US HERE. YOU'RE GONNA HAVE TO GET RID OF THEM.
I CAN'T, JASPER.
PLEASE DON'T MAKE ME DO NOTHIN'.
YOU WANT YOUR SECRETS GETTIN' AIRED OUT, FINE.
BUT I CAN'T HAVE YOU BRINGIN' YOUR #$&% STORM TO MY DOOR STEP. I GOT TOO MUCH ON THE LINE RIGHT NOW.
DEAL WITH THEM HOWEVER YOU NEED TO, BUT DON'T COME ROUND THIS WAY UNTIL YOU DO.
CLICK!
SHERIFF
I CAN'T COME HOME?
JASPER?
HELLO?

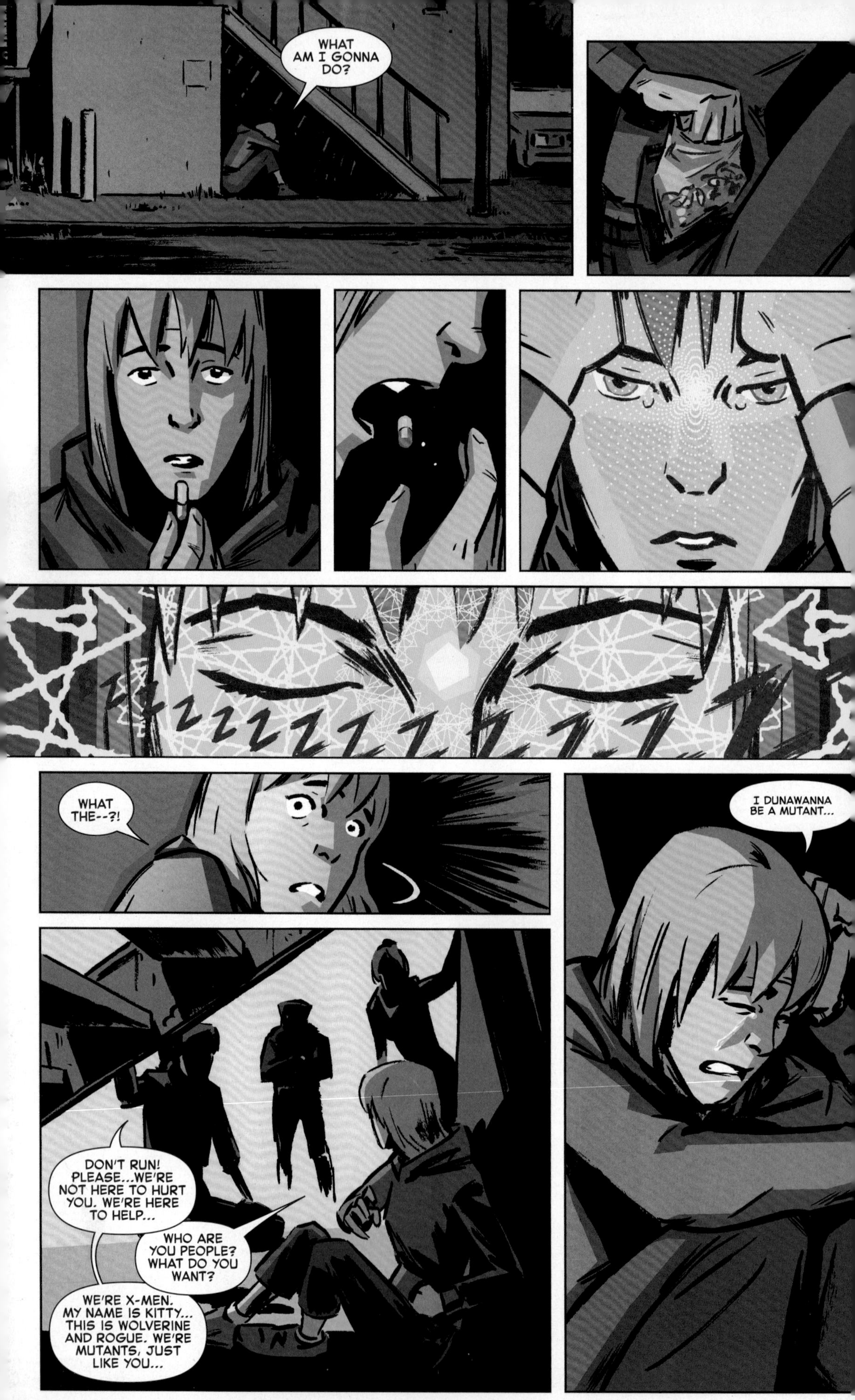
WHAT AM I GONNA DO?
ZZZZZZZZZZZ
WHAT THE--?!
I DUNAWANNA BE A MUTANT...
DON'T RUN! PLEASE...WE'RE NOT HERE TO HURT YOU. WE'RE HERE TO HELP...
WHO ARE YOU PEOPLE? WHAT DO YOU WANT?
WE'RE X-MEN. MY NAME IS KITTY... THIS IS WOLVERINE AND ROGUE. WE'RE MUTANTS, JUST LIKE YOU...

OH, SWEETHEART, IT'S NOTHING TO BE ASHAMED OF.

WHAT'S YOUR NAME, DARLIN'?

KRYSTAL...

KRYSTAL, I KNOW WHAT IT'S LIKE TO BE DIFFERENT IN A SMALL TOWN. HOW DESPERATE THE NEED TO FIT IN IS. I BEEN THERE...BUT YOU CAN'T BEAT YOURSELF UP LIKE THIS. IT GETS BETTER...

WHAT DO YOU WANT FROM ME?

KILLED? WHAT--WHAT DO YOU MEAN, KILLED?

A MUTANT'S RECENTLY BEEN KILLED IN THESE PARTS.

AND WE HAVE REASONS TO BELIEVE HE MIGHT BE THE FIRST OF MANY.

WE MEAN MURDERED.

YOU COULD BE IN REAL DANGER, KRYSTAL.

IT'S A DANGEROUS TIME FOR MUTANTS EVERYWHERE BUT WE CAN HELP YOU IF YOU'LL LET US.

MURDERED...?

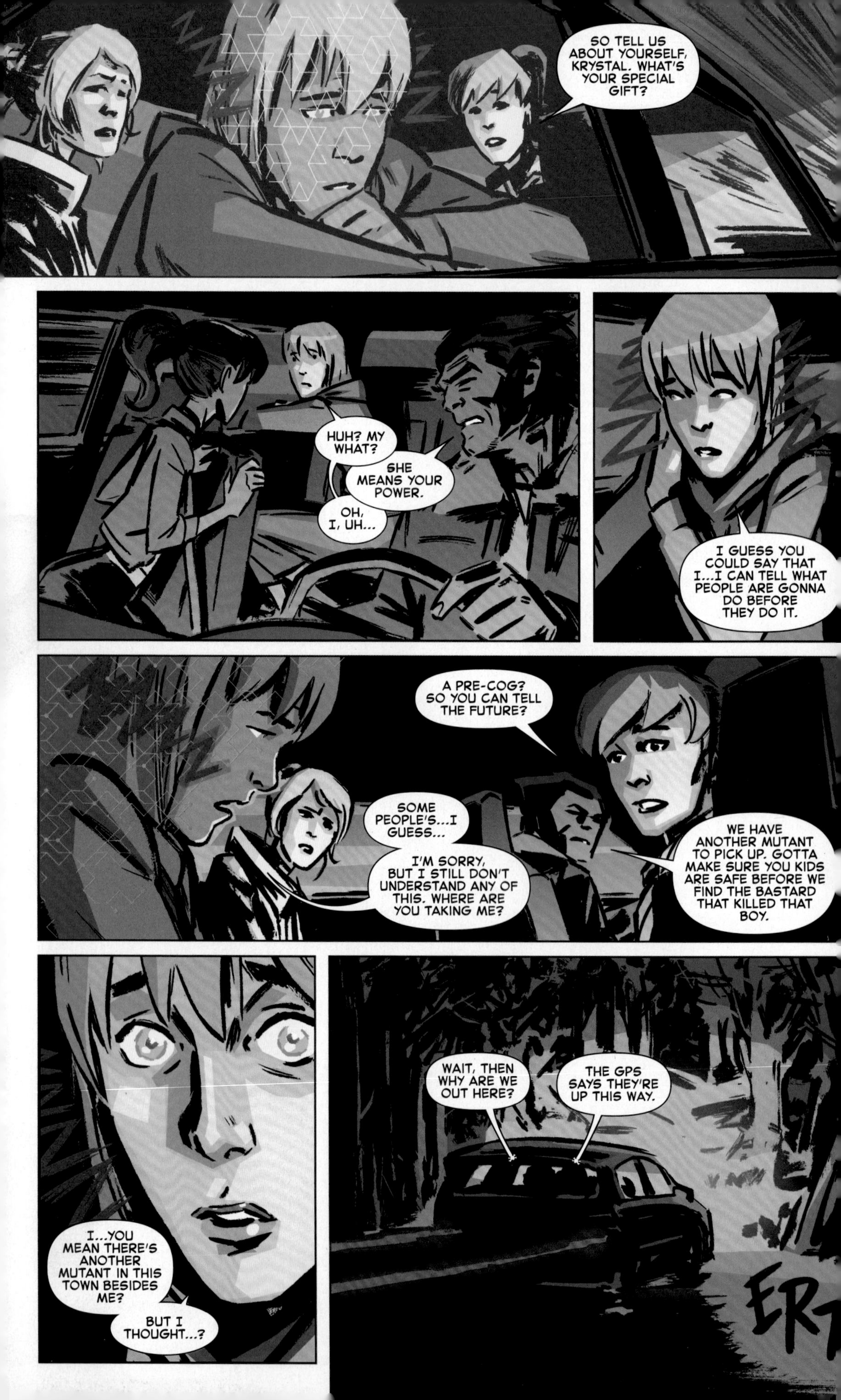

SO TELL US ABOUT YOURSELF, KRYSTAL. WHAT'S YOUR SPECIAL GIFT?
HUH? MY WHAT?
SHE MEANS YOUR POWER.
OH, I, UH...
I GUESS YOU COULD SAY THAT I...I CAN TELL WHAT PEOPLE ARE GONNA DO BEFORE THEY DO IT.
A PRE-COG? SO YOU CAN TELL THE FUTURE?
SOME PEOPLE'S...I GUESS...
I'M SORRY, BUT I STILL DON'T UNDERSTAND ANY OF THIS. WHERE ARE YOU TAKING ME?
WE HAVE ANOTHER MUTANT TO PICK UP. GOTTA MAKE SURE YOU KIDS ARE SAFE BEFORE WE FIND THE BASTARD THAT KILLED THAT BOY.
I...YOU MEAN THERE'S ANOTHER MUTANT IN THIS TOWN BESIDES ME?
BUT I THOUGHT...?
WAIT, THEN WHY ARE WE OUT HERE?
THE GPS SAYS THEY'RE UP THIS WAY.

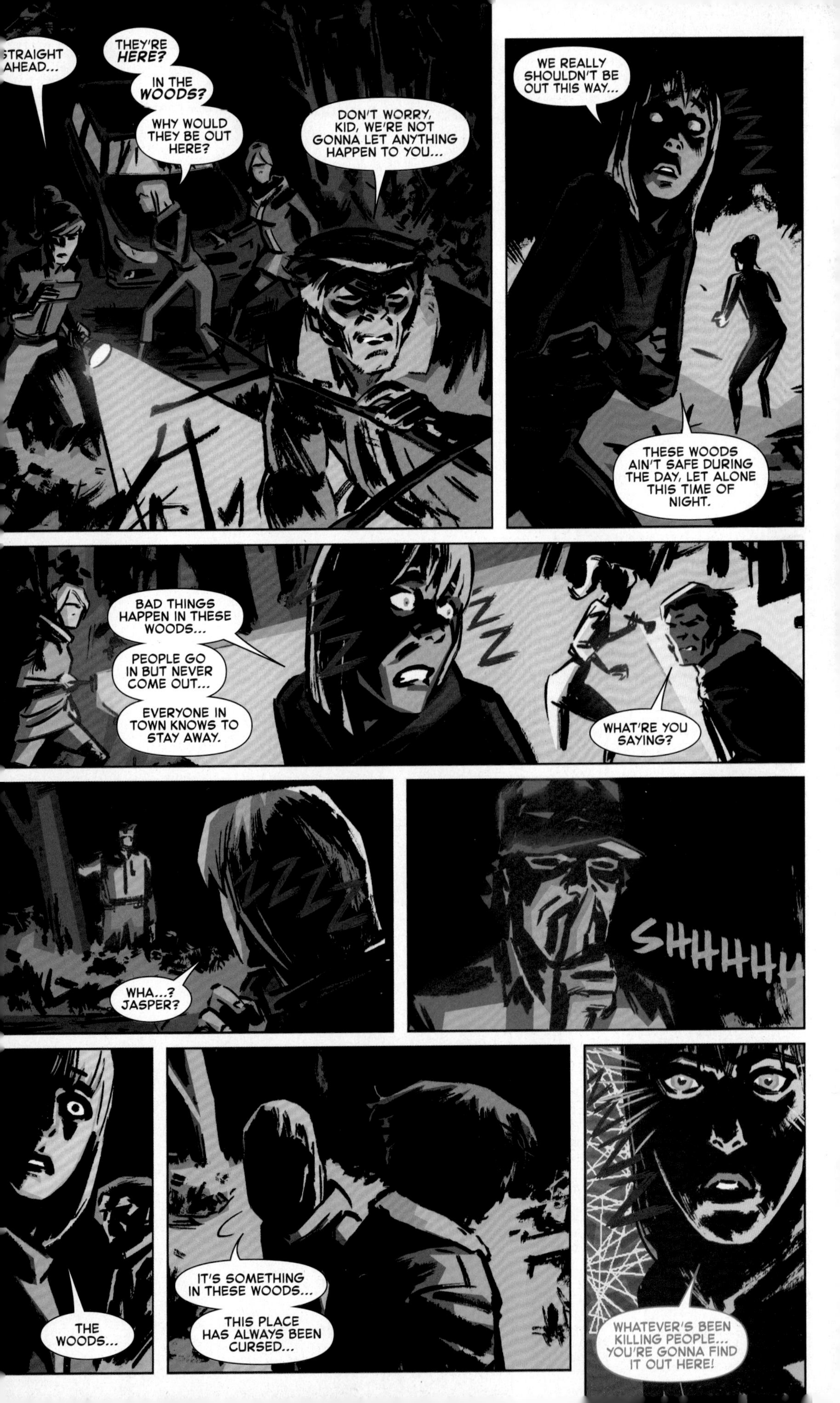
STRAIGHT AHEAD...
THEY'RE HERE?
IN THE WOODS?
WHY WOULD THEY BE OUT HERE?
DON'T WORRY, KID, WE'RE NOT GONNA LET ANYTHING HAPPEN TO YOU...
WE REALLY SHOULDN'T BE OUT THIS WAY...
THESE WOODS AIN'T SAFE DURING THE DAY, LET ALONE THIS TIME OF NIGHT.
BAD THINGS HAPPEN IN THESE WOODS...
PEOPLE GO IN BUT NEVER COME OUT...
EVERYONE IN TOWN KNOWS TO STAY AWAY.
WHAT'RE YOU SAYING?
WHA...? JASPER?
SHHHHH
THE WOODS...
IT'S SOMETHING IN THESE WOODS...
THIS PLACE HAS ALWAYS BEEN CURSED...
WHATEVER'S BEEN KILLING PEOPLE... YOU'RE GONNA FIND IT OUT HERE!

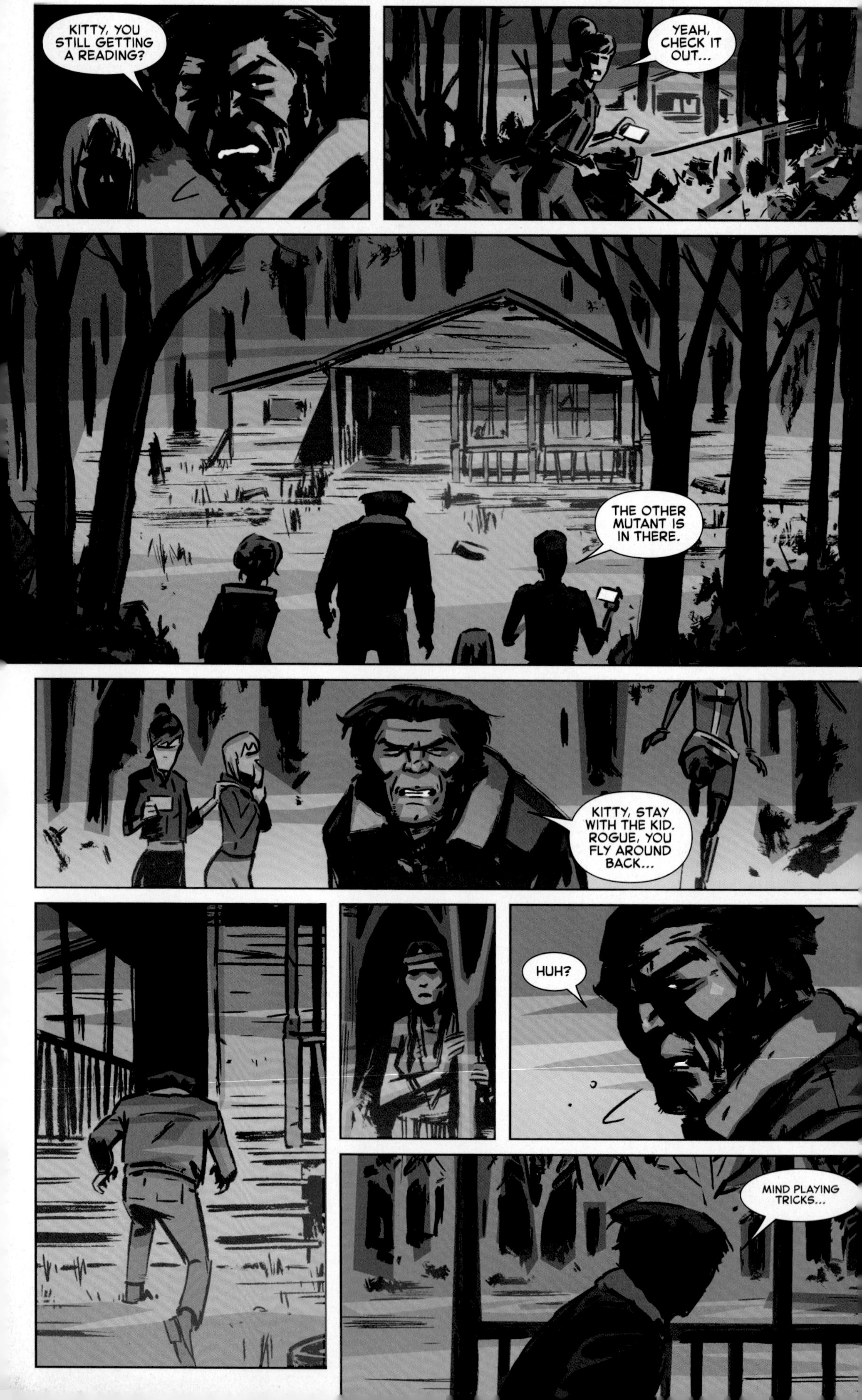
KITTY, YOU STILL GETTING A READING?
YEAH, CHECK IT OUT...
THE OTHER MUTANT IS IN THERE.
KITTY, STAY WITH THE KID. ROGUE, YOU FLY AROUND BACK...
HUH?
MIND PLAYING TRICKS...

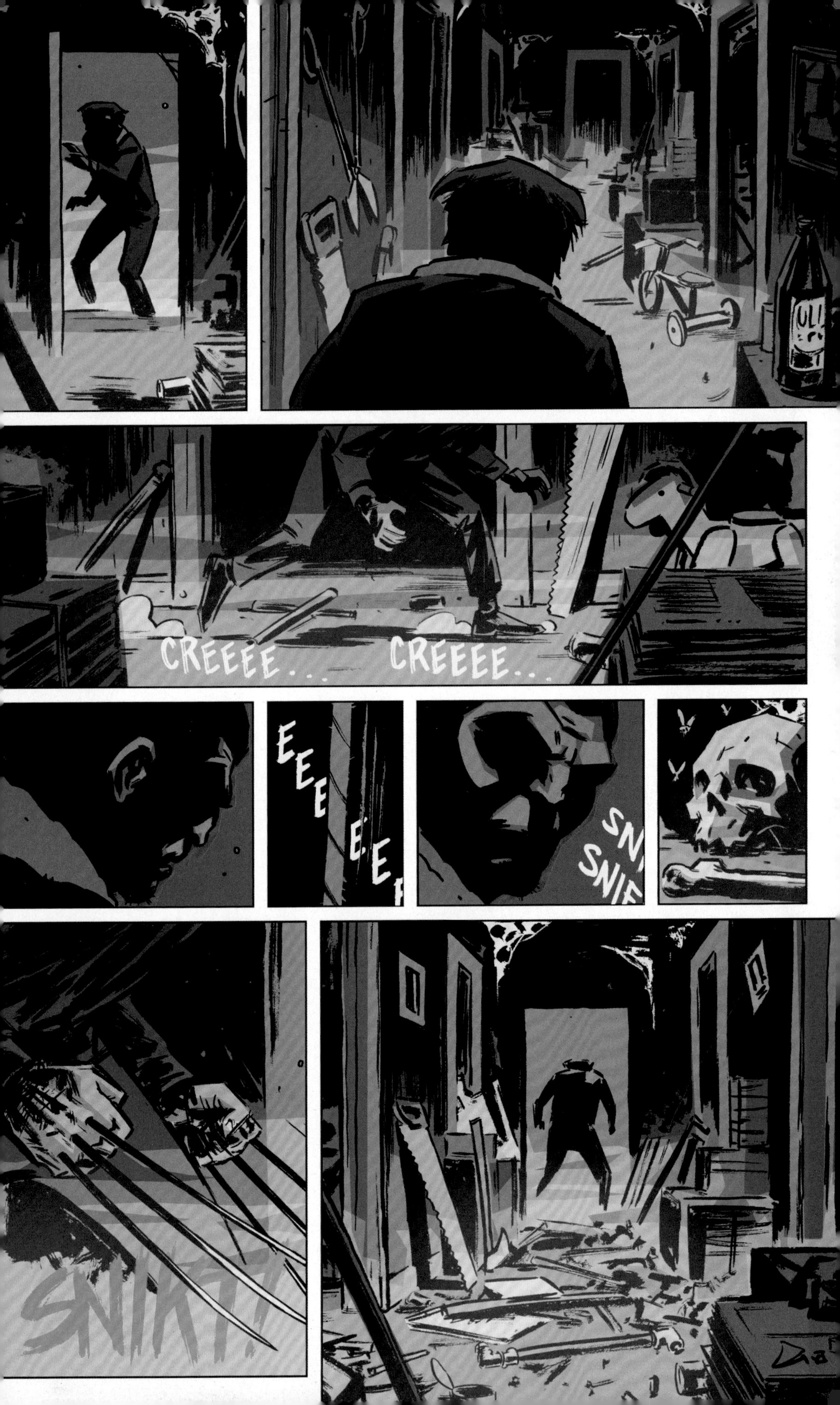
CREEEE... CREEEE...
EEEE
EEEE
SNI
SNIF
SNIKT!

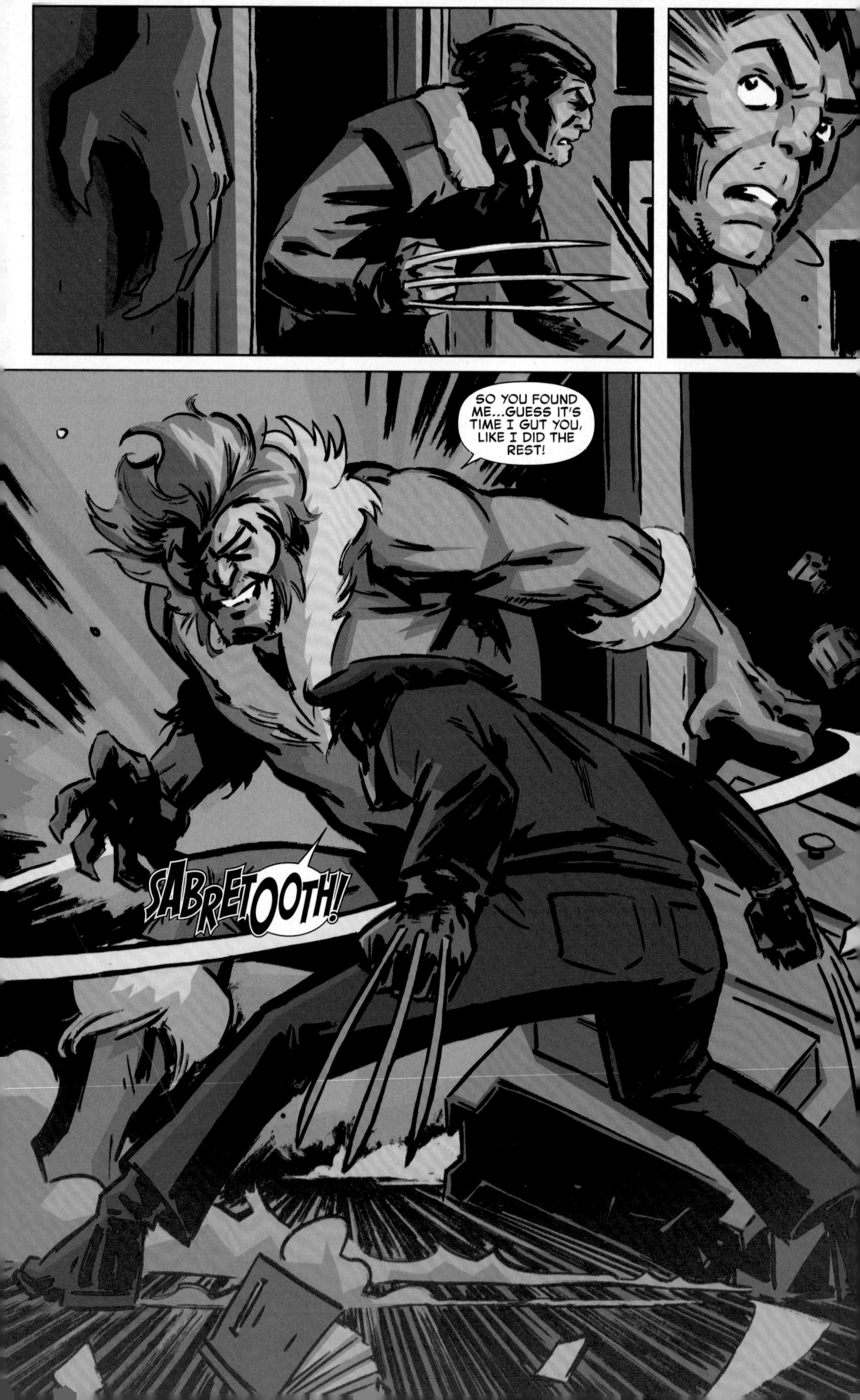
SO YOU FOUND ME...GUESS IT'S TIME I GUT YOU, LIKE I DID THE REST!
SABRETOOTH!

2

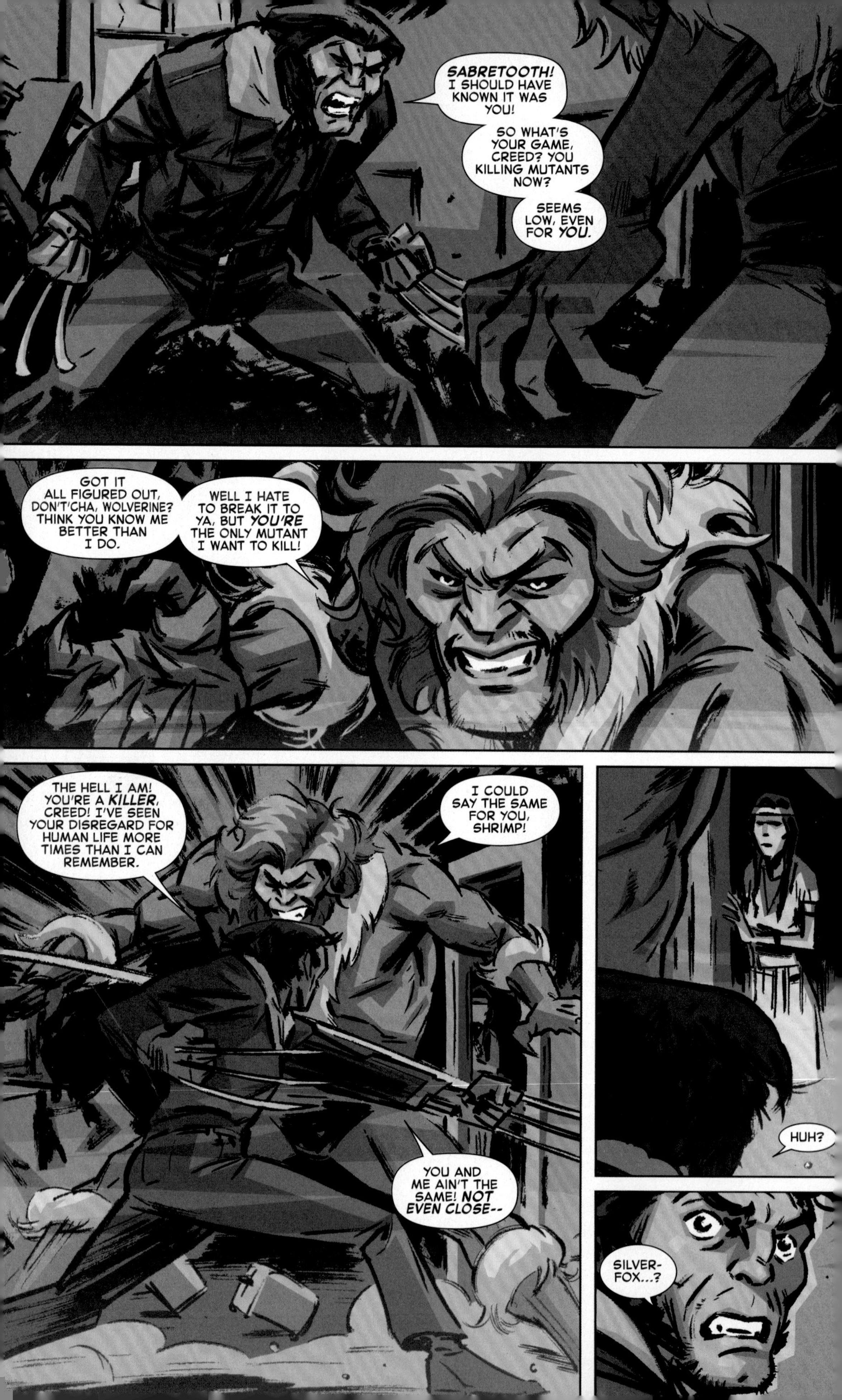
SABRETOOTH! I SHOULD HAVE KNOWN IT WAS YOU!
SO WHAT'S YOUR GAME, CREED? YOU KILLING MUTANTS NOW?
SEEMS LOW, EVEN FOR YOU.
GOT IT ALL FIGURED OUT, DON'T'CHA, WOLVERINE? THINK YOU KNOW ME BETTER THAN I DO.
WELL I HATE TO BREAK IT TO YA, BUT YOU'RE THE ONLY MUTANT I WANT TO KILL!
THE HELL I AM! YOU'RE A KILLER, CREED! I'VE SEEN YOUR DISREGARD FOR HUMAN LIFE MORE TIMES THAN I CAN REMEMBER.
I COULD SAY THE SAME FOR YOU, SHRIMP!
YOU AND ME AIN'T THE SAME! NOT EVEN CLOSE--
HUH?
SILVER-FOX...?

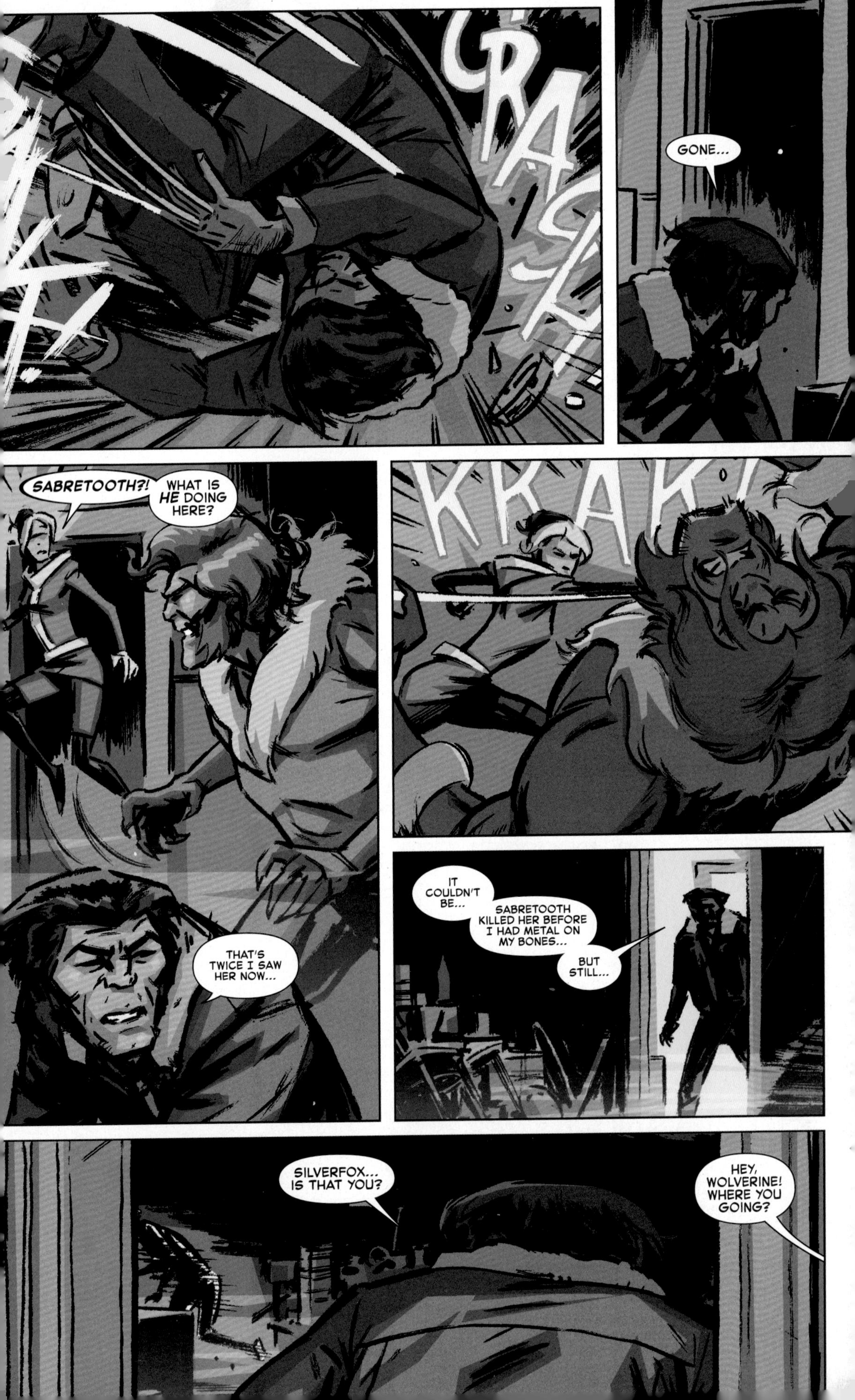
CRACK!
GONE...
SABRETOOTH?!
WHAT IS HE DOING HERE?
KRAK!
THAT'S TWICE I SAW HER NOW...
IT COULDN'T BE...
SABRETOOTH KILLED HER BEFORE I HAD METAL ON MY BONES...
BUT STILL...
SILVERFOX... IS THAT YOU?
HEY, WOLVERINE! WHERE YOU GOING?

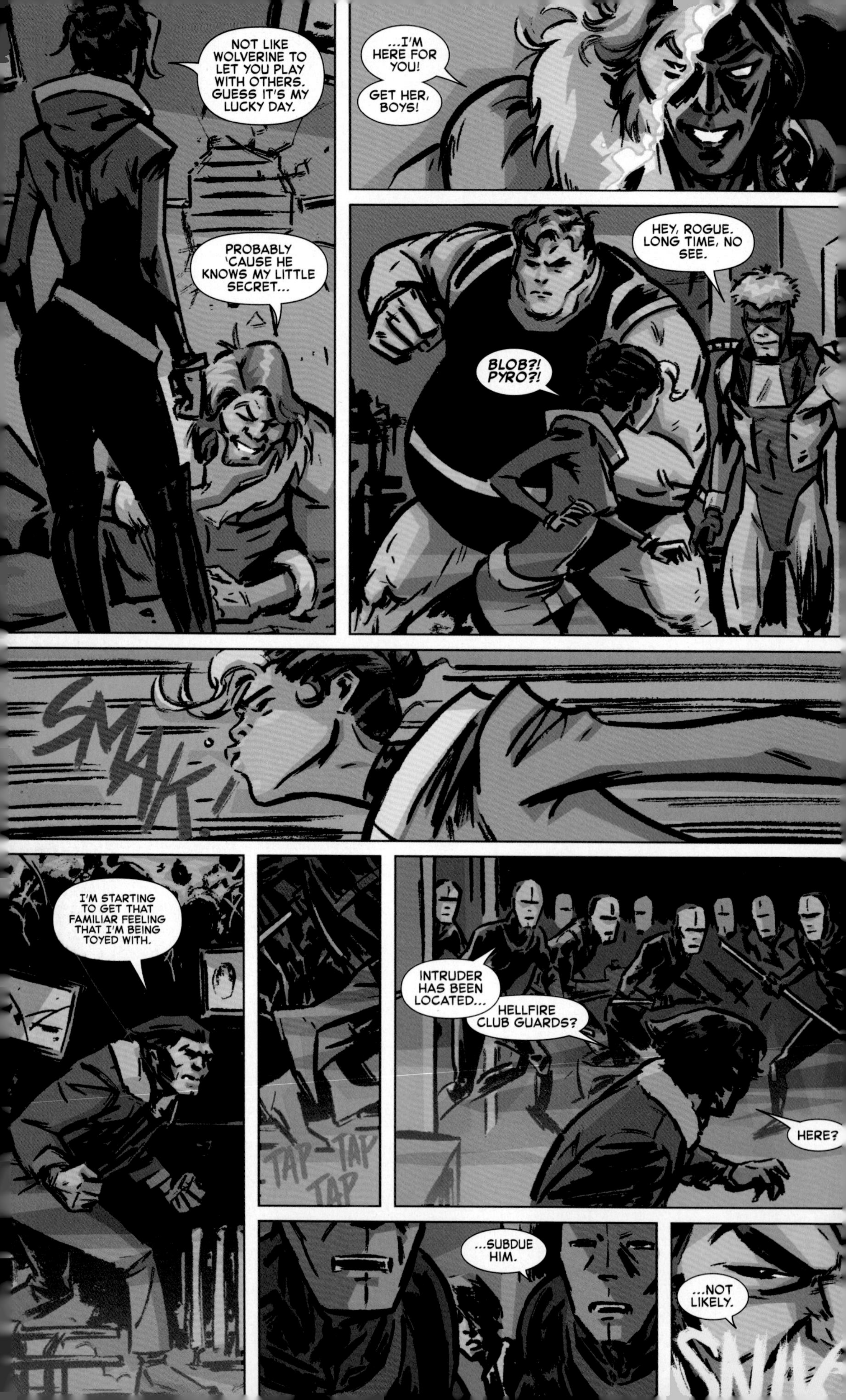
NOT LIKE WOLVERINE TO LET YOU PLAY WITH OTHERS. GUESS IT'S MY LUCKY DAY.
PROBABLY 'CAUSE HE KNOWS MY LITTLE SECRET...
...I'M HERE FOR YOU!
GET HER, BOYS!
HEY, ROGUE. LONG TIME, NO SEE.
BLOB?! PYRO?!
SMAK!
I'M STARTING TO GET THAT FAMILIAR FEELING THAT I'M BEING TOYED WITH.
TAP TAP TAP
INTRUDER HAS BEEN LOCATED...
HELLFIRE CLUB GUARDS?
HERE?
...SUBDUE HIM.
...NOT LIKELY.

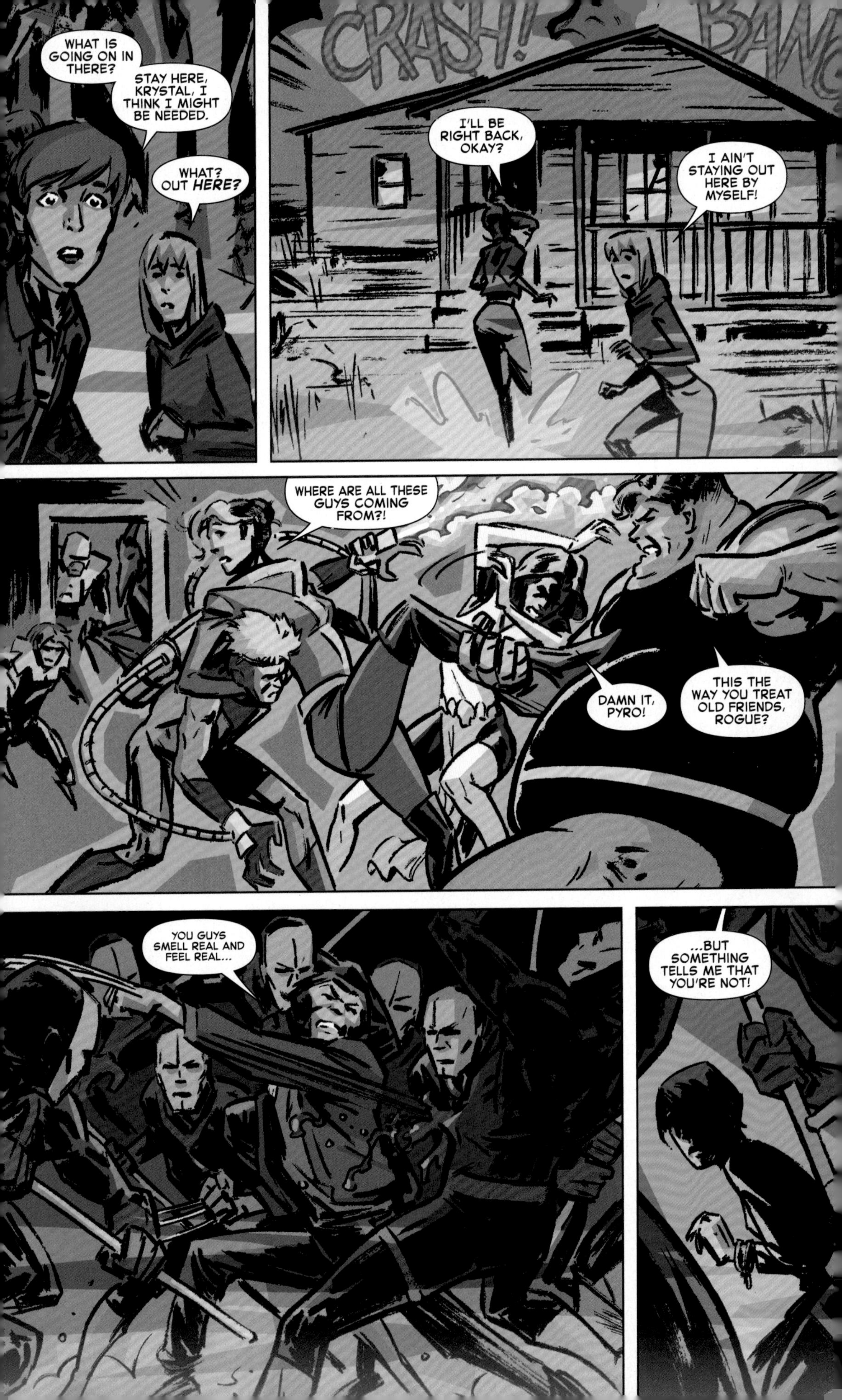
WHAT IS GOING ON IN THERE?
STAY HERE, KRYSTAL, I THINK I MIGHT BE NEEDED.
WHAT? OUT HERE?
CRASH!
BAWO
I'LL BE RIGHT BACK, OKAY?
I AIN'T STAYING OUT HERE BY MYSELF!
WHERE ARE ALL THESE GUYS COMING FROM?!
DAMN IT, PYRO!
THIS THE WAY YOU TREAT OLD FRIENDS, ROGUE?
YOU GUYS SMELL REAL AND FEEL REAL...
...BUT SOMETHING TELLS ME THAT YOU'RE NOT!

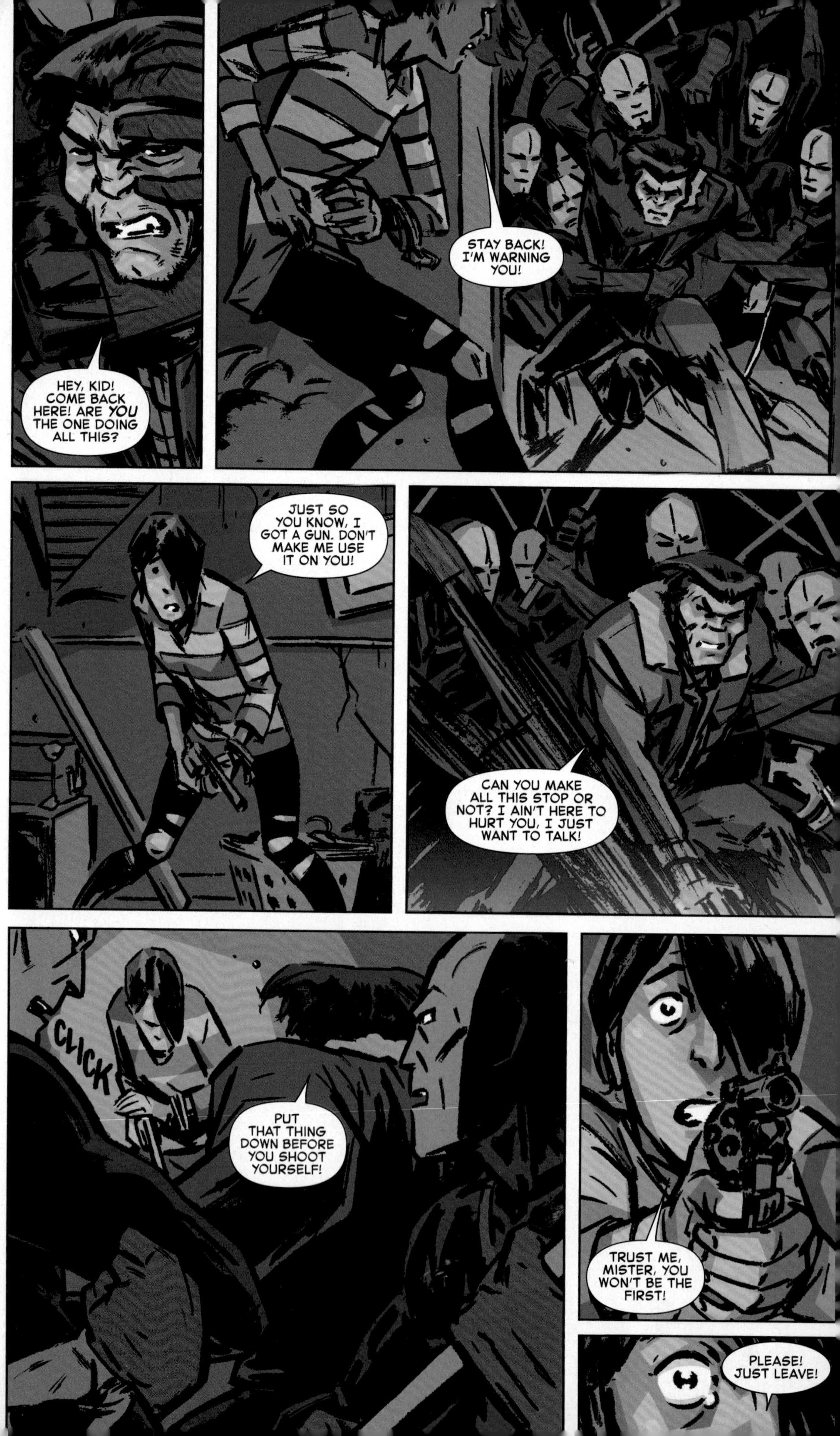
HEY, KID! COME BACK HERE! ARE YOU THE ONE DOING ALL THIS?
STAY BACK! I'M WARNING YOU!
JUST SO YOU KNOW, I GOT A GUN. DON'T MAKE ME USE IT ON YOU!
CAN YOU MAKE ALL THIS STOP OR NOT? I AIN'T HERE TO HURT YOU, I JUST WANT TO TALK!
CLICK
PUT THAT THING DOWN BEFORE YOU SHOOT YOURSELF!
TRUST ME, MISTER, YOU WON'T BE THE FIRST!
PLEASE! JUST LEAVE!

OH MY GOD! I DIDN'T MEAN...

WOLVERINE! WHAT THE HELL IS GOING ON IN HERE?

I GOT THIS, KITTY...

YOU SEE WHAT HAPPENS WHEN YOU PLAY WITH GUNS, KID?

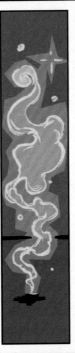

WHAT THE HELL ARE YOU?

PLEEAASE!

DON'T KILL ME! I WON'T SAY ANYTHING! I SWEAR!

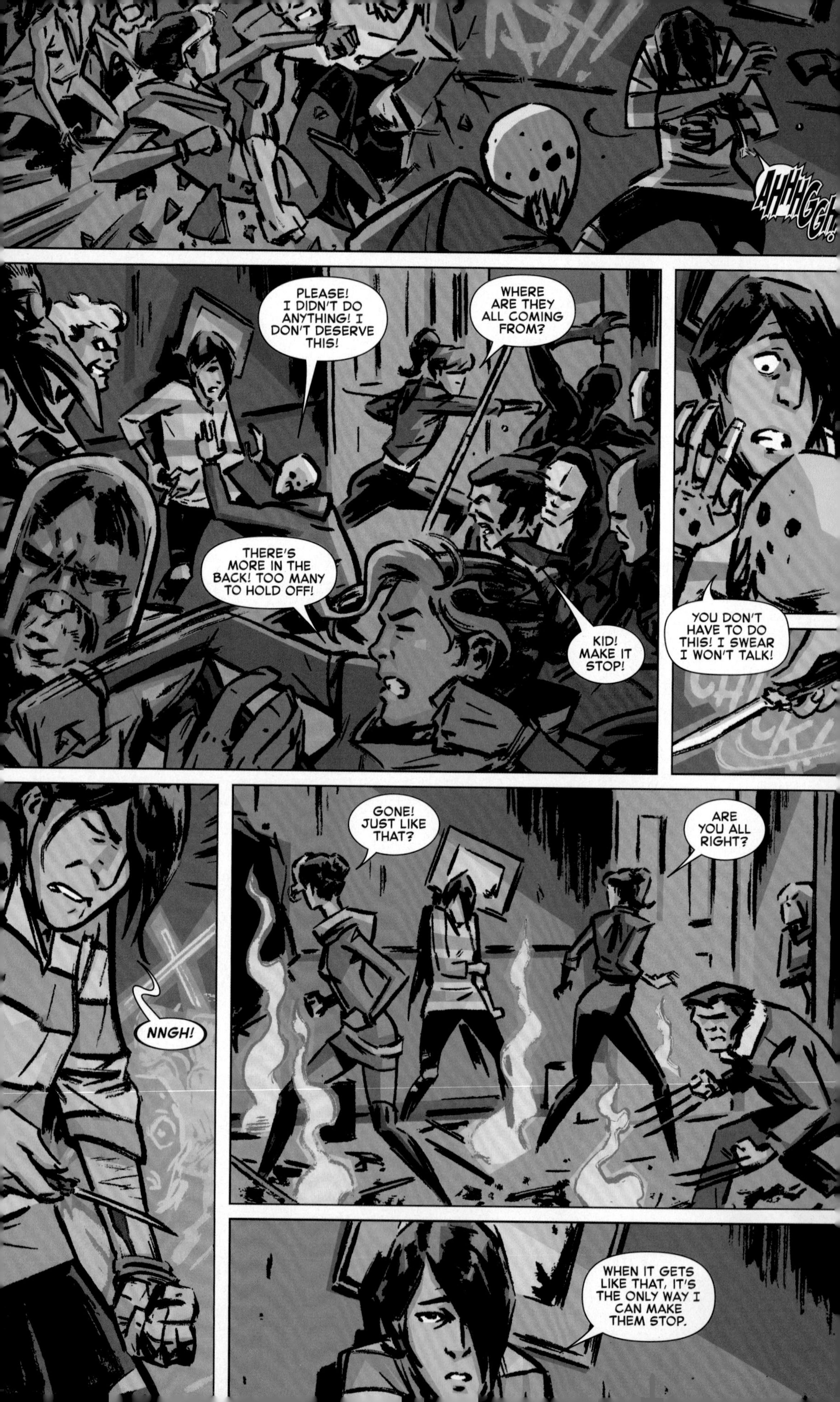

AHHHGG!!
PLEASE! I DIDN'T DO ANYTHING! I DON'T DESERVE THIS!
WHERE ARE THEY ALL COMING FROM?
THERE'S MORE IN THE BACK! TOO MANY TO HOLD OFF!
KID! MAKE IT STOP!
YOU DON'T HAVE TO DO THIS! I SWEAR I WON'T TALK!
NNGH!
GONE! JUST LIKE THAT?
ARE YOU ALL RIGHT?
WHEN IT GETS LIKE THAT, IT'S THE ONLY WAY I CAN MAKE THEM STOP.

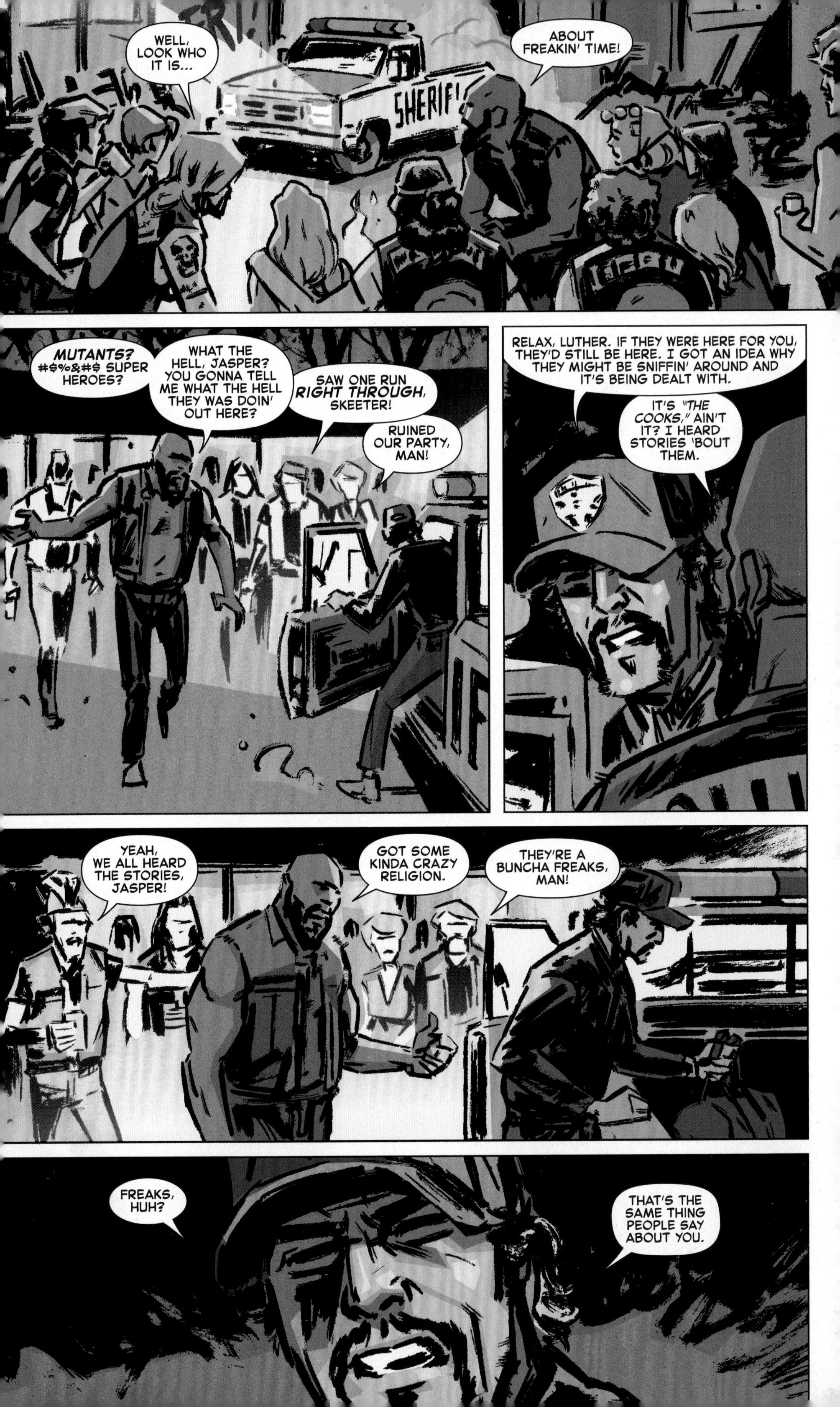
WELL, LOOK WHO IT IS...
ABOUT FREAKIN' TIME!
MUTANTS? #$%&#$ SUPER HEROES?
WHAT THE HELL, JASPER? YOU GONNA TELL ME WHAT THE HELL THEY WAS DOIN' OUT HERE?
SAW ONE RUN RIGHT THROUGH, SKEETER!
RUINED OUR PARTY, MAN!
RELAX, LUTHER. IF THEY WERE HERE FOR YOU, THEY'D STILL BE HERE. I GOT AN IDEA WHY THEY MIGHT BE SNIFFIN' AROUND AND IT'S BEING DEALT WITH.
IT'S "THE COOKS," AIN'T IT? I HEARD STORIES 'BOUT THEM.
YEAH, WE ALL HEARD THE STORIES, JASPER!
GOT SOME KINDA CRAZY RELIGION.
THEY'RE A BUNCHA FREAKS, MAN!
FREAKS, HUH?
THAT'S THE SAME THING PEOPLE SAY ABOUT YOU.

HEY! WATCH IT!

IT'S TRUE.

BUT IT DON'T STOP ME FROM DOING BUSINESS WITH YOU. WE GOT A GOOD THING GOING HERE, RIGHT?

AIN'T THAT THE BEST STUFF YOU EVER SOLD?

YEAH... IT'S SCARY HOW GOOD IT IS...STUFF SELLS ITSELF.

EXACTLY! YOU GUYS JUST KEEP THOSE GUNS COMING AND WE'LL ALL BE ABLE TO RETIRE EARLY.

MORE GUNS, HUH? THEY CAN'T GET ENOUGH, CAN THEY? THAT MAKES ME UNEASY.

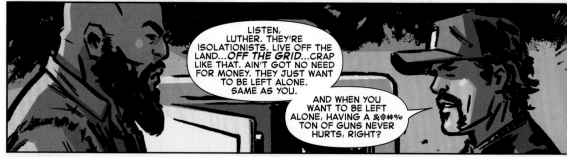

LISTEN, LUTHER. THEY'RE ISOLATIONISTS. LIVE OFF THE LAND...*OFF THE GRID*...CRAP LIKE THAT. AIN'T GOT NO NEED FOR MONEY. THEY JUST WANT TO BE LEFT ALONE. SAME AS YOU.

AND WHEN YOU WANT TO BE LEFT ALONE, HAVING A &$#% TON OF GUNS NEVER HURTS, RIGHT?

HEH... YEAH, THAT'LL DO IT.

SO, IF YOU SEE THESE MUTANTS AGAIN, YOU DO WHAT YOU GOTTA DO TO PUT THEM DOWN.

OTHERWISE, JUST LAY LOW UNTIL THIS ALL BLOWS OVER AND LET ME DEAL WITH I I ALREADY GOT SOMEONE ON THE JOB.

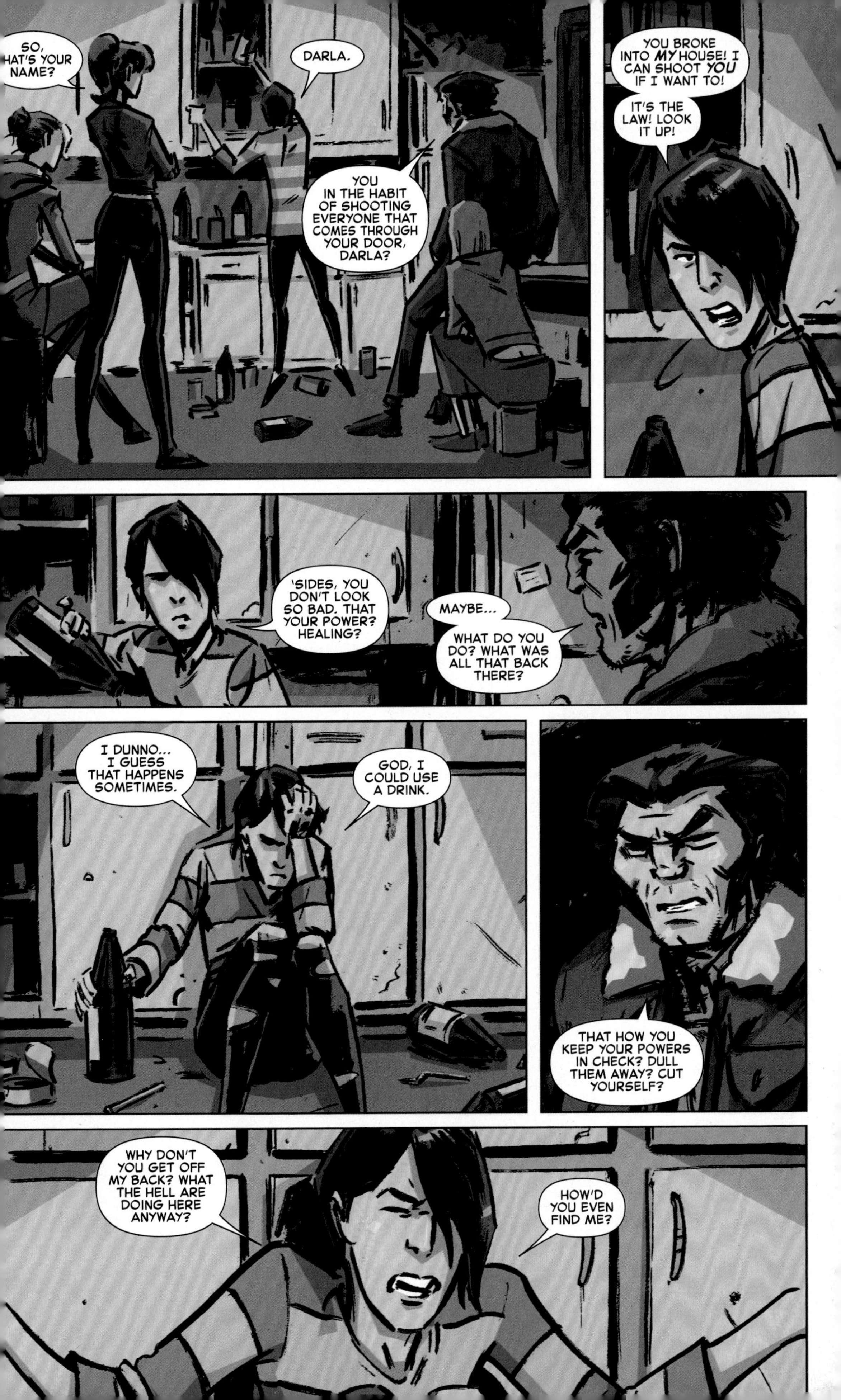

SO, HAT'S YOUR NAME?
DARLA.
YOU IN THE HABIT OF SHOOTING EVERYONE THAT COMES THROUGH YOUR DOOR, DARLA?
YOU BROKE INTO MY HOUSE! I CAN SHOOT YOU IF I WANT TO!
IT'S THE LAW! LOOK IT UP!
'SIDES, YOU DON'T LOOK SO BAD. THAT YOUR POWER? HEALING?
MAYBE...
WHAT DO YOU DO? WHAT WAS ALL THAT BACK THERE?
I DUNNO... I GUESS THAT HAPPENS SOMETIMES.
GOD, I COULD USE A DRINK.
THAT HOW YOU KEEP YOUR POWERS IN CHECK? DULL THEM AWAY? CUT YOURSELF?
WHY DON'T YOU GET OFF MY BACK? WHAT THE HELL ARE DOING HERE ANYWAY?
HOW'D YOU EVEN FIND ME?

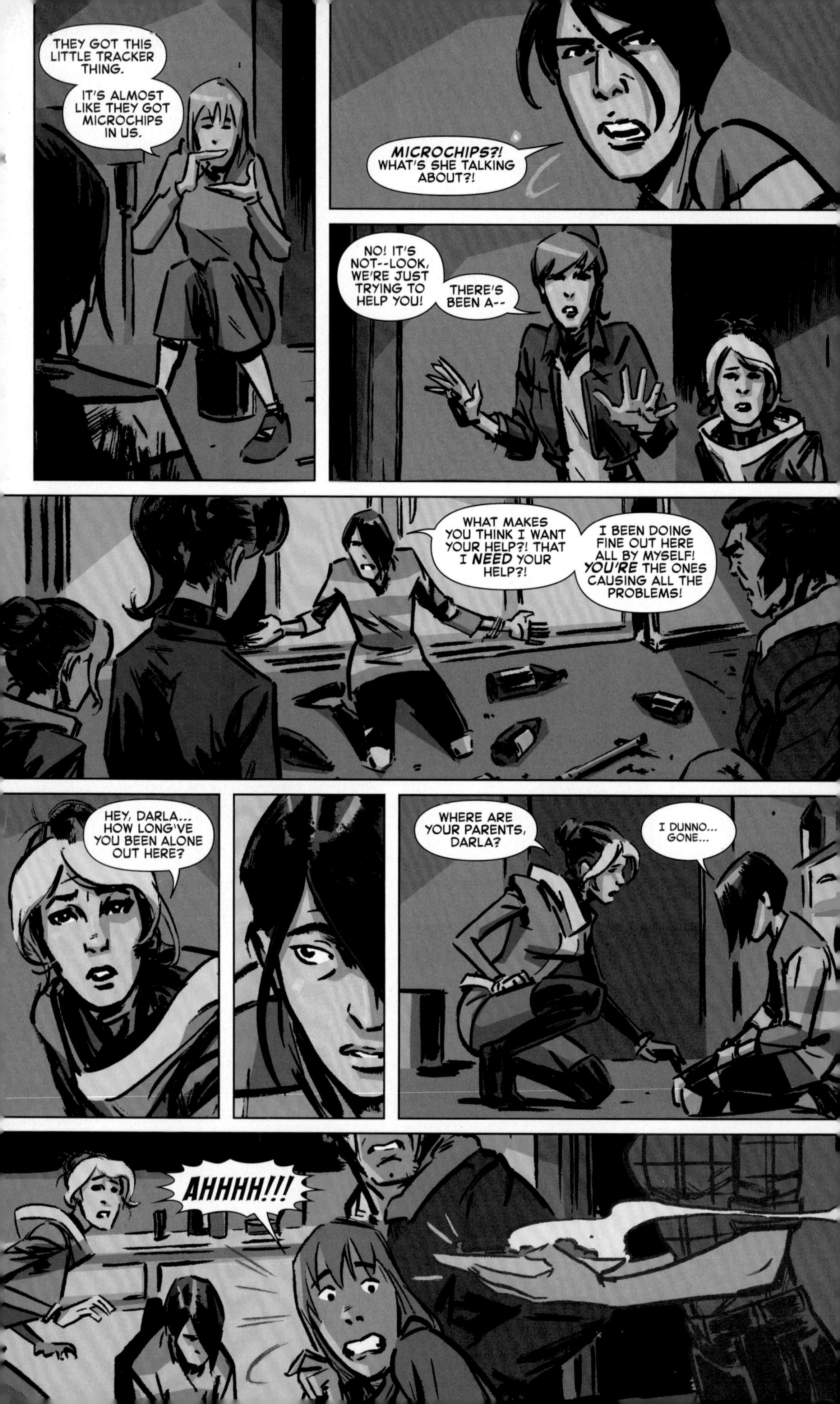

THEY GOT THIS LITTLE TRACKER THING.
IT'S ALMOST LIKE THEY GOT MICROCHIPS IN US.
MICROCHIPS?! WHAT'S SHE TALKING ABOUT?!
NO! IT'S NOT--LOOK, WE'RE JUST TRYING TO HELP YOU!
THERE'S BEEN A--
WHAT MAKES YOU THINK I WANT YOUR HELP?! THAT I NEED YOUR HELP?!
I BEEN DOING FINE OUT HERE ALL BY MYSELF! YOU'RE THE ONES CAUSING ALL THE PROBLEMS!
HEY, DARLA... HOW LONG'VE YOU BEEN ALONE OUT HERE?
WHERE ARE YOUR PARENTS, DARLA?
I DUNNO... GONE...
AHHHH!!!

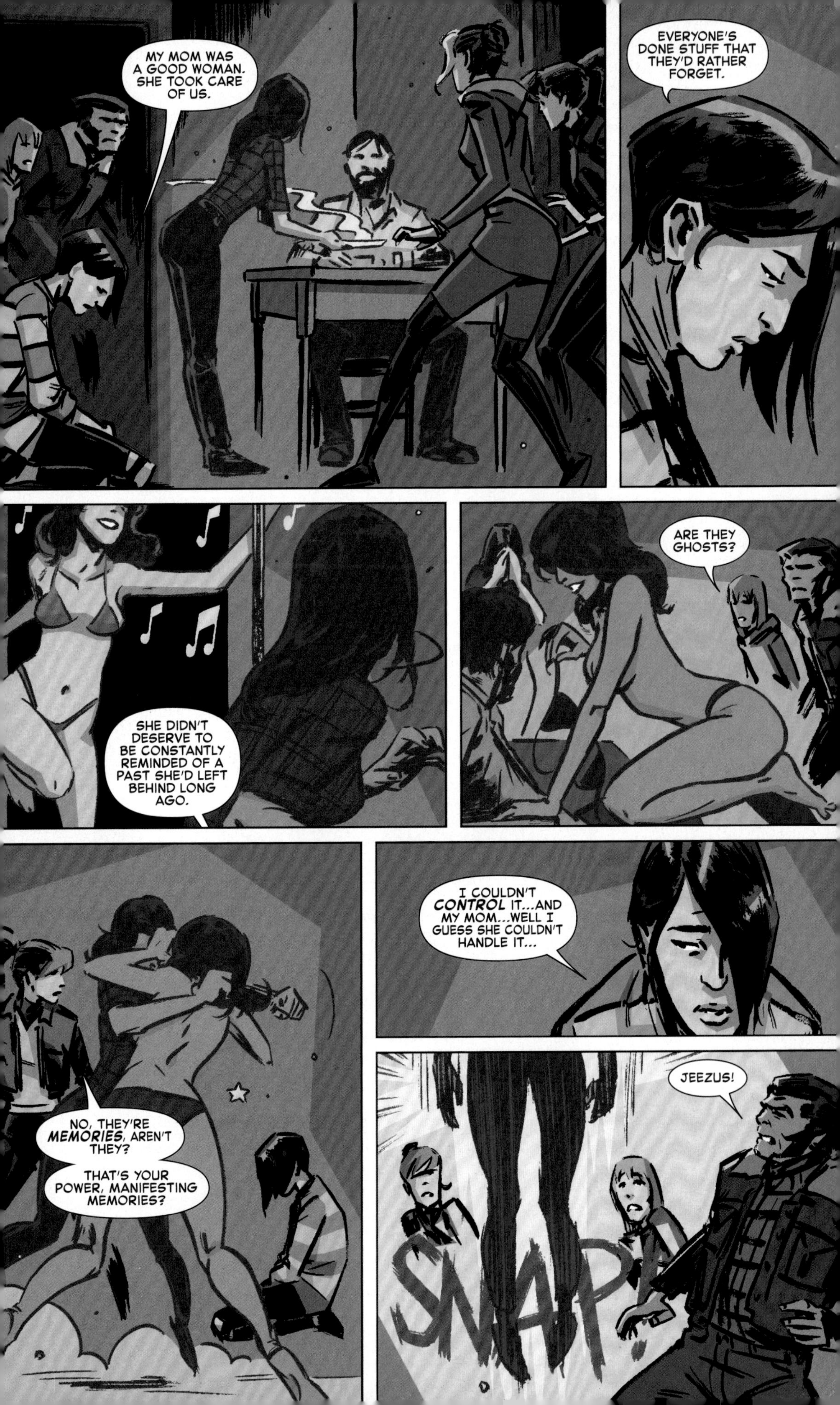
MY MOM WAS A GOOD WOMAN. SHE TOOK CARE OF US.
EVERYONE'S DONE STUFF THAT THEY'D RATHER FORGET.
SHE DIDN'T DESERVE TO BE CONSTANTLY REMINDED OF A PAST SHE'D LEFT BEHIND LONG AGO.
ARE THEY GHOSTS?
NO, THEY'RE MEMORIES, AREN'T THEY?
THAT'S YOUR POWER, MANIFESTING MEMORIES?
I COULDN'T CONTROL IT...AND MY MOM...WELL I GUESS SHE COULDN'T HANDLE IT...
JEEZUS!
SNAP!

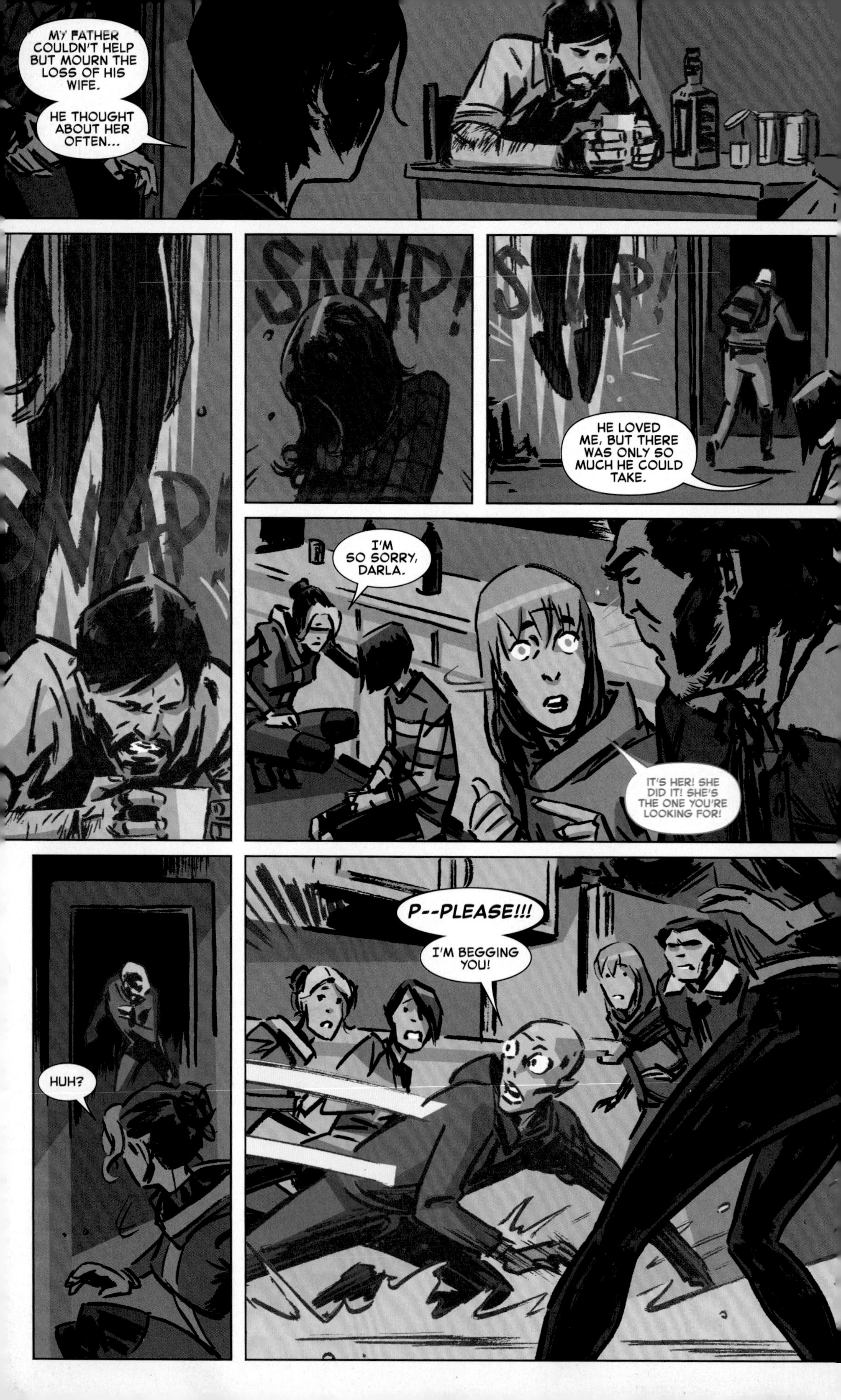

MY FATHER COULDN'T HELP BUT MOURN THE LOSS OF HIS WIFE.
HE THOUGHT ABOUT HER OFTEN...
SNAP!
SNAP!
SNAP!
HE LOVED ME, BUT THERE WAS ONLY SO MUCH HE COULD TAKE.
I'M SO SORRY, DARLA.
IT'S HER! SHE DID IT! SHE'S THE ONE YOU'RE LOOKING FOR!
HUH?
P--PLEASE!!!
I'M BEGGING YOU!

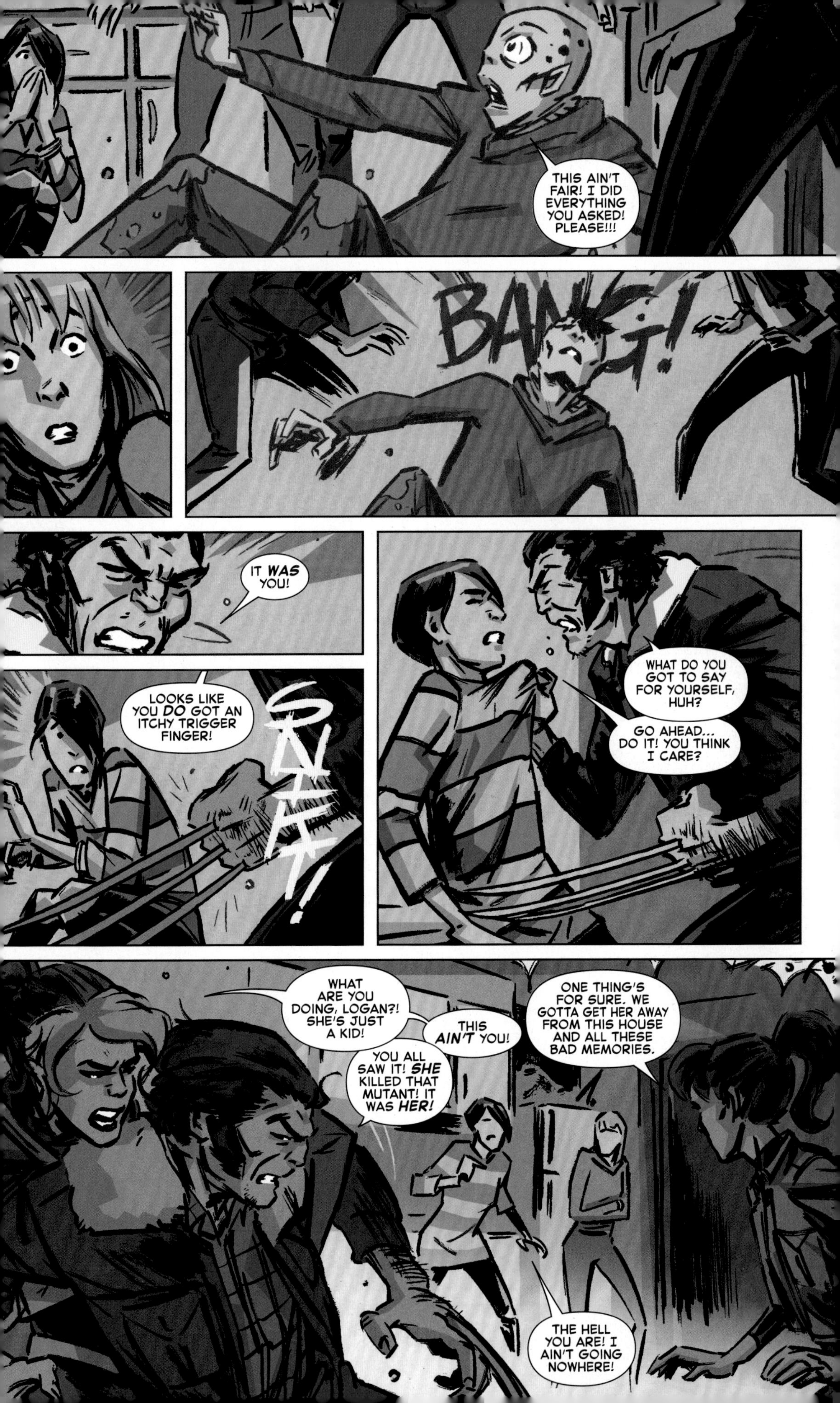
THIS AIN'T FAIR! I DID EVERYTHING YOU ASKED! PLEASE!!!
BANG!
IT *WAS* YOU!
LOOKS LIKE YOU *DO* GOT AN ITCHY TRIGGER FINGER!
SNIKT!
WHAT DO YOU GOT TO SAY FOR YOURSELF, HUH?
GO AHEAD... DO IT! YOU THINK I CARE?
WHAT ARE YOU DOING, LOGAN?! SHE'S JUST A KID!
THIS *AIN'T* YOU!
YOU ALL SAW IT! *SHE* KILLED THAT MUTANT! IT WAS *HER!*
ONE THING'S FOR SURE. WE GOTTA GET HER AWAY FROM THIS HOUSE AND ALL THESE BAD MEMORIES.
THE HELL YOU ARE! I AIN'T GOING NOWHERE!

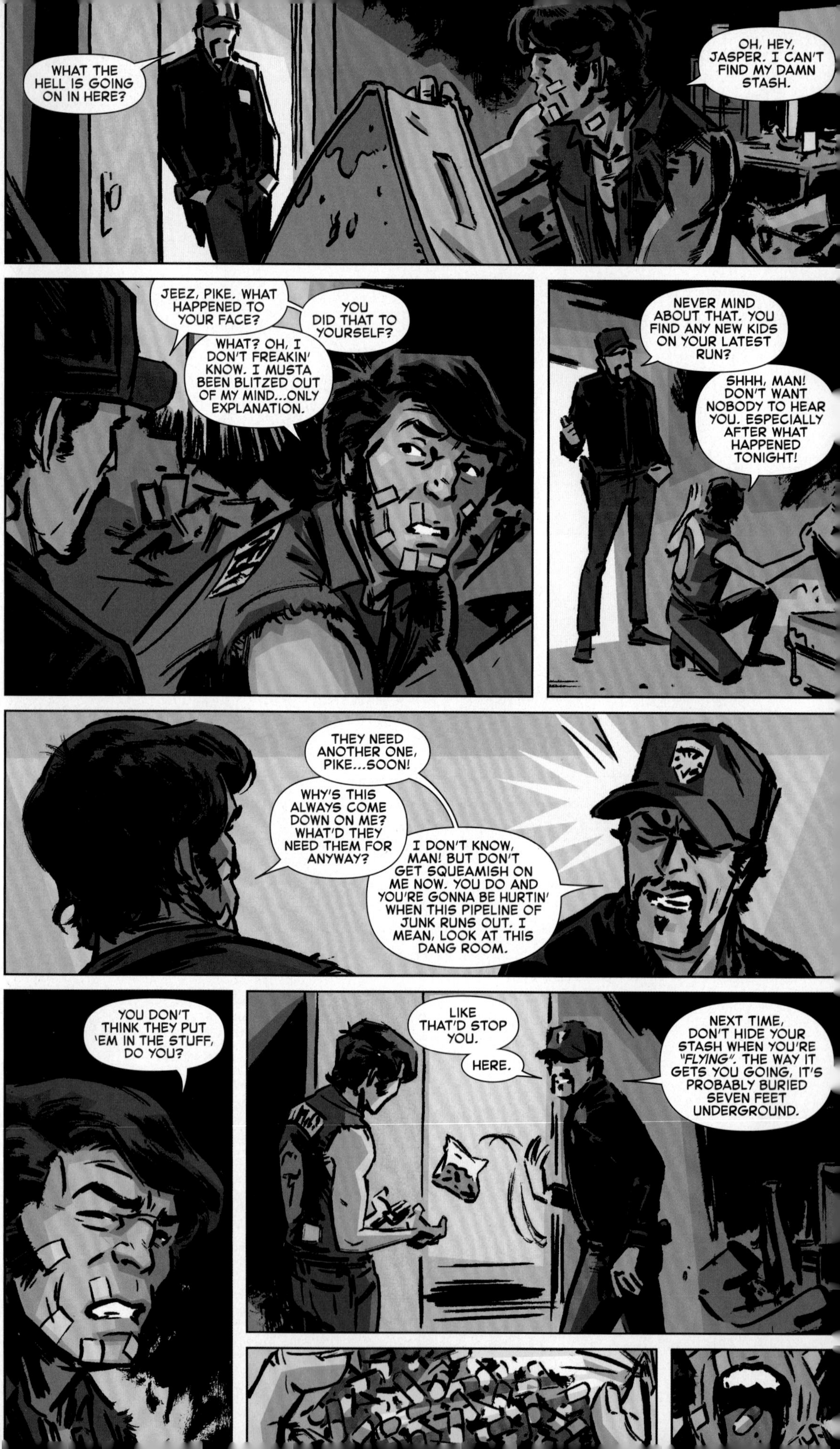
WHAT THE HELL IS GOING ON IN HERE?
OH, HEY, JASPER. I CAN'T FIND MY DAMN STASH.
JEEZ, PIKE. WHAT HAPPENED TO YOUR FACE?
YOU DID THAT TO YOURSELF?
WHAT? OH, I DON'T FREAKIN' KNOW. I MUSTA BEEN BLITZED OUT OF MY MIND...ONLY EXPLANATION.
NEVER MIND ABOUT THAT. YOU FIND ANY NEW KIDS ON YOUR LATEST RUN?
SHHH, MAN! DON'T WANT NOBODY TO HEAR YOU. ESPECIALLY AFTER WHAT HAPPENED TONIGHT!
THEY NEED ANOTHER ONE, PIKE...SOON!
WHY'S THIS ALWAYS COME DOWN ON ME? WHAT'D THEY NEED THEM FOR ANYWAY?
I DON'T KNOW, MAN! BUT DON'T GET SQUEAMISH ON ME NOW. YOU DO AND YOU'RE GONNA BE HURTIN' WHEN THIS PIPELINE OF JUNK RUNS OUT. I MEAN, LOOK AT THIS DANG ROOM.
YOU DON'T THINK THEY PUT 'EM IN THE STUFF, DO YOU?
LIKE THAT'D STOP YOU.
HERE.
NEXT TIME, DON'T HIDE YOUR STASH WHEN YOU'RE "FLYING". THE WAY IT GETS YOU GOING, IT'S PROBABLY BURIED SEVEN FEET UNDERGROUND.

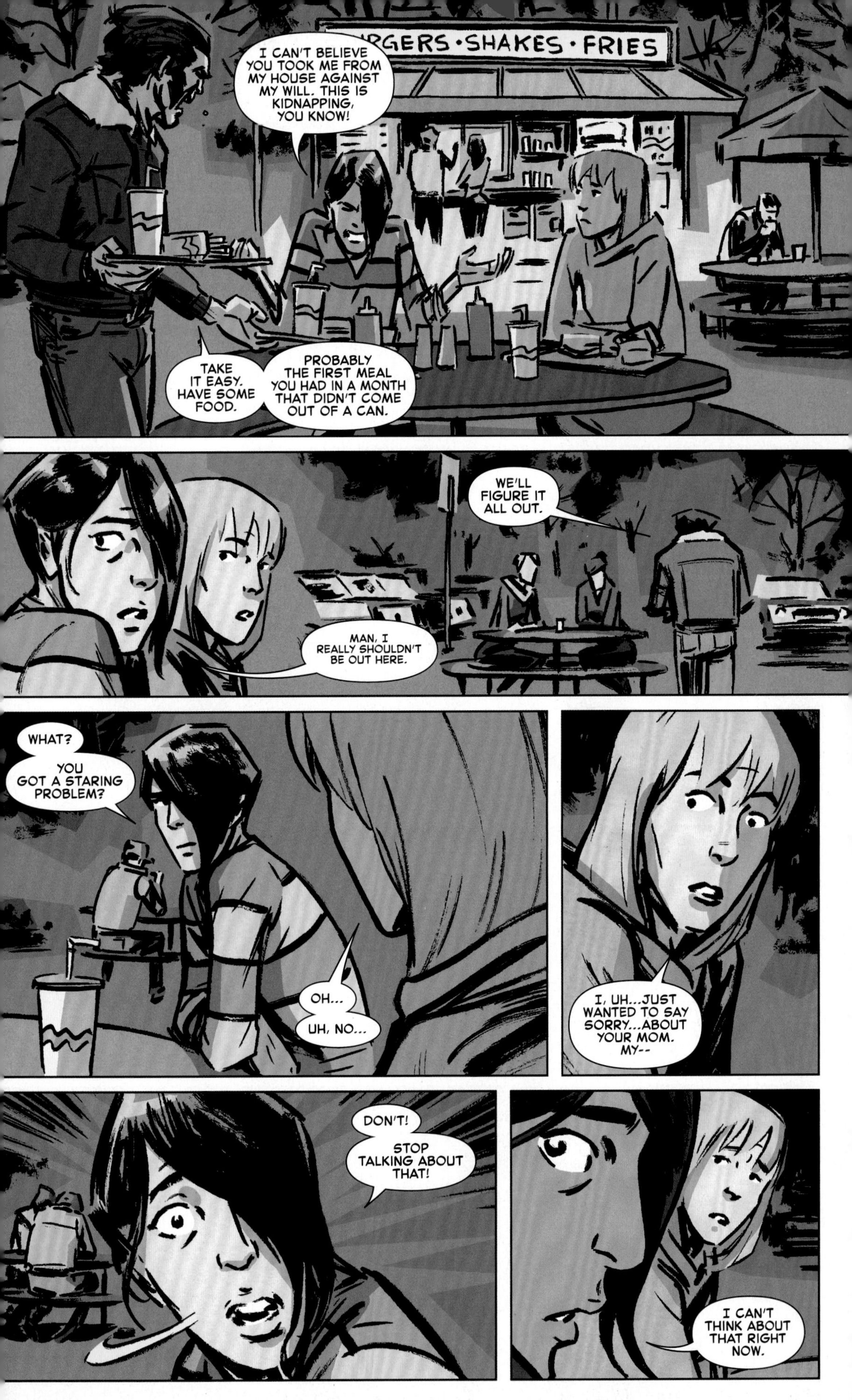
URGERS • SHAKES • FRIES
I CAN'T BELIEVE YOU TOOK ME FROM MY HOUSE AGAINST MY WILL. THIS IS KIDNAPPING, YOU KNOW!
TAKE IT EASY. HAVE SOME FOOD.
PROBABLY THE FIRST MEAL YOU HAD IN A MONTH THAT DIDN'T COME OUT OF A CAN.
WE'LL FIGURE IT ALL OUT.
MAN, I REALLY SHOULDN'T BE OUT HERE.
WHAT?
YOU GOT A STARING PROBLEM?
OH...
UH, NO...
I, UH...JUST WANTED TO SAY SORRY...ABOUT YOUR MOM. MY--
DON'T!
STOP TALKING ABOUT THAT!
I CAN'T THINK ABOUT THAT RIGHT NOW.

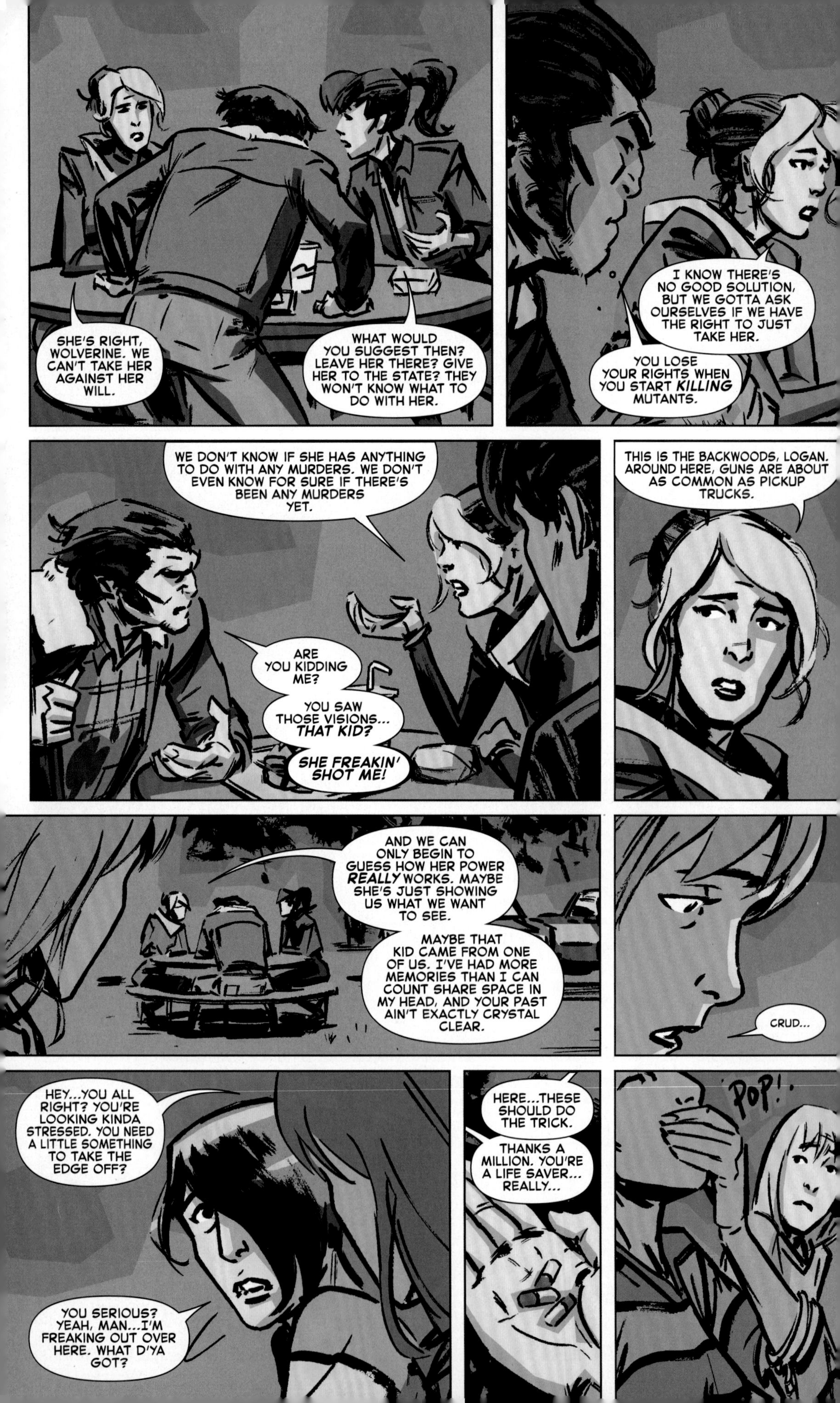
SHE'S RIGHT, WOLVERINE. WE CAN'T TAKE HER AGAINST HER WILL.
WHAT WOULD YOU SUGGEST THEN? LEAVE HER THERE? GIVE HER TO THE STATE? THEY WON'T KNOW WHAT TO DO WITH HER.
I KNOW THERE'S NO GOOD SOLUTION, BUT WE GOTTA ASK OURSELVES IF WE HAVE THE RIGHT TO JUST TAKE HER.
YOU LOSE YOUR RIGHTS WHEN YOU START KILLING MUTANTS.
WE DON'T KNOW IF SHE HAS ANYTHING TO DO WITH ANY MURDERS. WE DON'T EVEN KNOW FOR SURE IF THERE'S BEEN ANY MURDERS YET.
ARE YOU KIDDING ME?
YOU SAW THOSE VISIONS... THAT KID?
SHE FREAKIN' SHOT ME!
THIS IS THE BACKWOODS, LOGAN. AROUND HERE, GUNS ARE ABOUT AS COMMON AS PICKUP TRUCKS.
AND WE CAN ONLY BEGIN TO GUESS HOW HER POWER REALLY WORKS. MAYBE SHE'S JUST SHOWING US WHAT WE WANT TO SEE.
MAYBE THAT KID CAME FROM ONE OF US. I'VE HAD MORE MEMORIES THAN I CAN COUNT SHARE SPACE IN MY HEAD, AND YOUR PAST AIN'T EXACTLY CRYSTAL CLEAR.
CRUD...
HEY...YOU ALL RIGHT? YOU'RE LOOKING KINDA STRESSED. YOU NEED A LITTLE SOMETHING TO TAKE THE EDGE OFF?
YOU SERIOUS? YEAH, MAN...I'M FREAKING OUT OVER HERE. WHAT D'YA GOT?
HERE...THESE SHOULD DO THE TRICK.
THANKS A MILLION. YOU'RE A LIFE SAVER... REALLY...
POP!

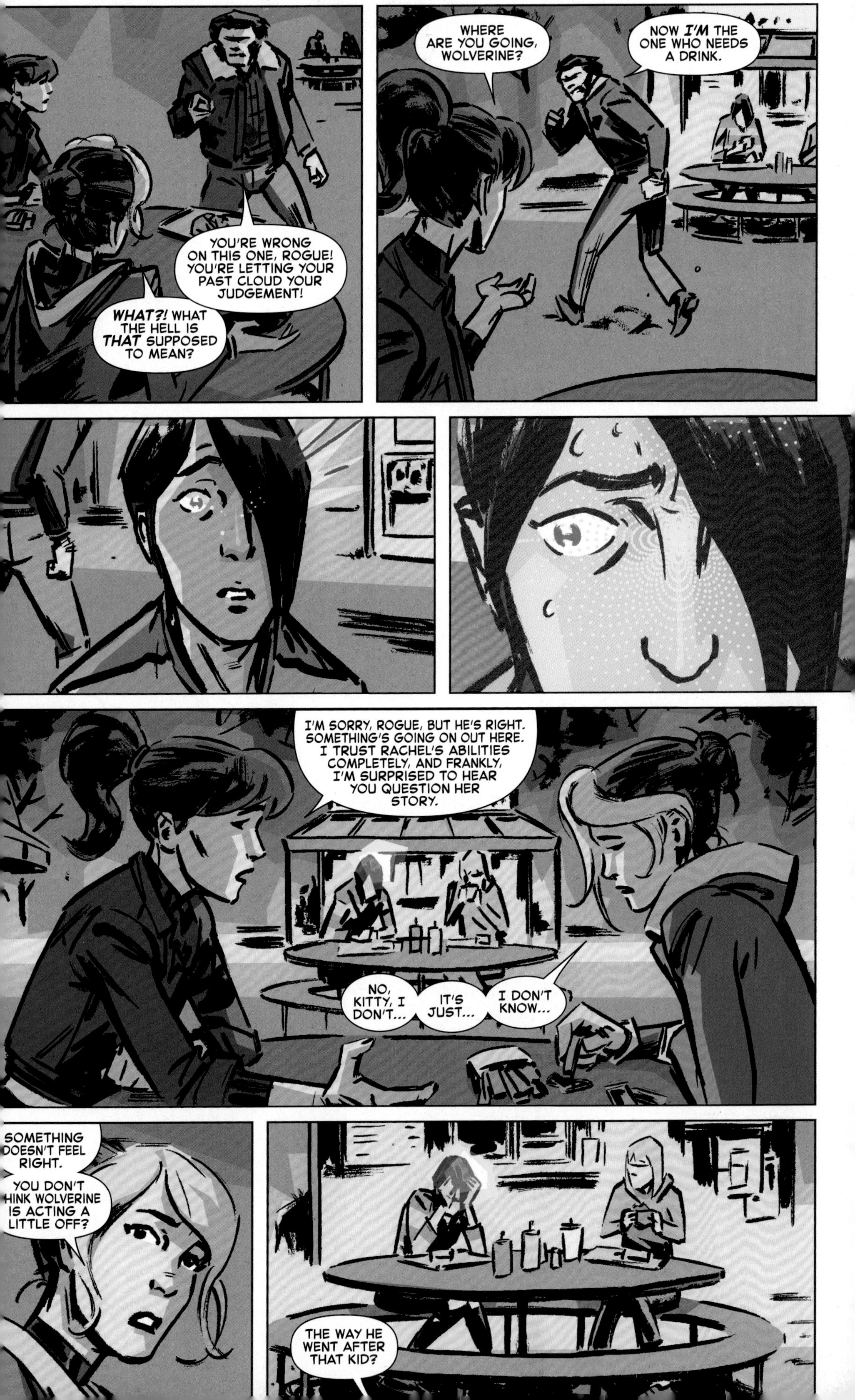
YOU'RE WRONG ON THIS ONE, ROGUE! YOU'RE LETTING YOUR PAST CLOUD YOUR JUDGEMENT!
WHAT?! WHAT THE HELL IS THAT SUPPOSED TO MEAN?
WHERE ARE YOU GOING, WOLVERINE?
NOW I'M THE ONE WHO NEEDS A DRINK.
I'M SORRY, ROGUE, BUT HE'S RIGHT. SOMETHING'S GOING ON OUT HERE. I TRUST RACHEL'S ABILITIES COMPLETELY, AND FRANKLY, I'M SURPRISED TO HEAR YOU QUESTION HER STORY.
NO, KITTY, I DON'T...
IT'S JUST...
I DON'T KNOW...
SOMETHING DOESN'T FEEL RIGHT.
YOU DON'T HINK WOLVERINE IS ACTING A LITTLE OFF?
THE WAY HE WENT AFTER THAT KID?

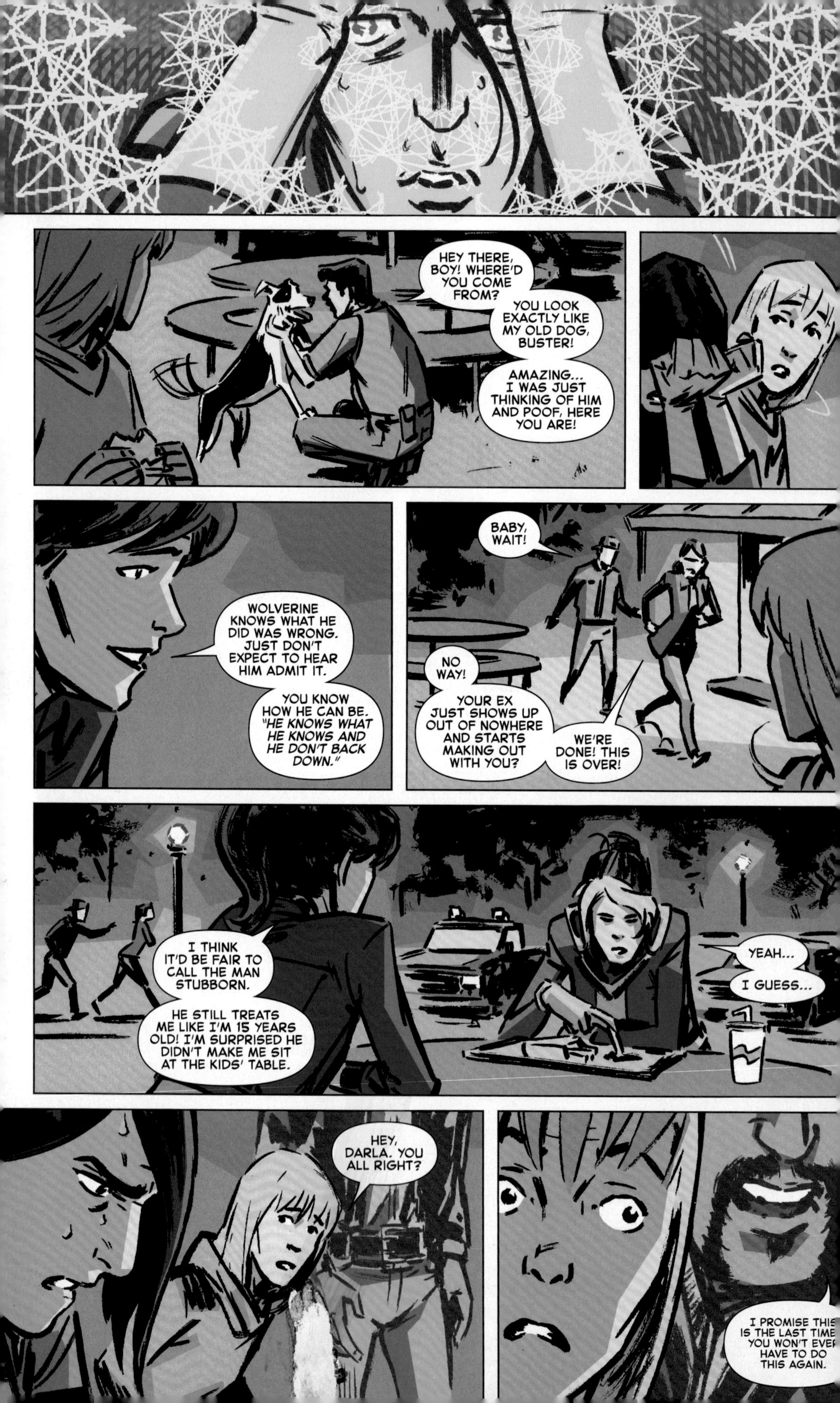
HEY THERE, BOY! WHERE'D YOU COME FROM?
YOU LOOK EXACTLY LIKE MY OLD DOG, BUSTER!
AMAZING... I WAS JUST THINKING OF HIM AND POOF, HERE YOU ARE!
WOLVERINE KNOWS WHAT HE DID WAS WRONG. JUST DON'T EXPECT TO HEAR HIM ADMIT IT.
YOU KNOW HOW HE CAN BE. *"HE KNOWS WHAT HE KNOWS AND HE DON'T BACK DOWN."*
BABY, WAIT!
NO WAY!
YOUR EX JUST SHOWS UP OUT OF NOWHERE AND STARTS MAKING OUT WITH YOU?
WE'RE DONE! THIS IS OVER!
I THINK IT'D BE FAIR TO CALL THE MAN STUBBORN.
HE STILL TREATS ME LIKE I'M 15 YEARS OLD! I'M SURPRISED HE DIDN'T MAKE ME SIT AT THE KIDS' TABLE.
YEAH...
I GUESS...
HEY, DARLA. YOU ALL RIGHT?
I PROMISE THIS IS THE LAST TIME YOU WON'T EVER HAVE TO DO THIS AGAIN.

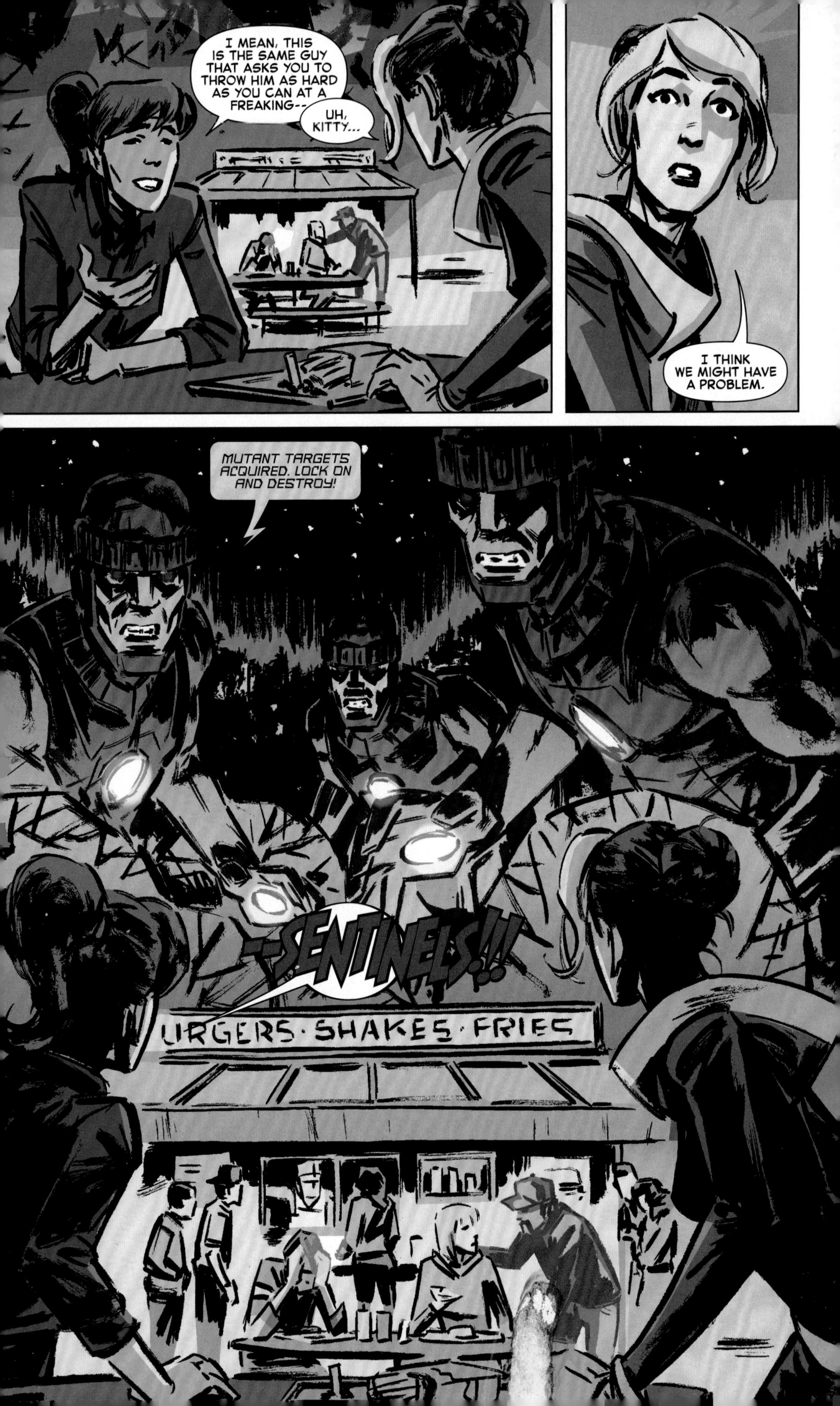

I MEAN, THIS IS THE SAME GUY THAT ASKS YOU TO THROW HIM AS HARD AS YOU CAN AT A FREAKING--
UH, KITTY...
I THINK WE MIGHT HAVE A PROBLEM.
MUTANT TARGETS ACQUIRED. LOCK ON AND DESTROY!
--SENTINELS!!
URGERS · SHAKES · FRIES

3

THE COOKS' COMPOUND.

PLEASE, SHERIFF, SIT DOWN...TO WHAT DO WE OWE THIS UNEXPECTED PLEASURE?

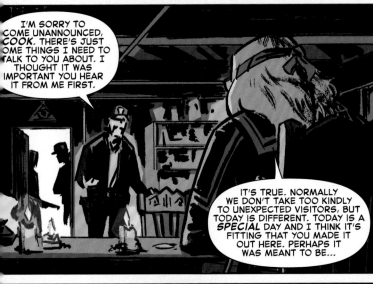

I'M SORRY TO COME UNANNOUNCED, COOK. THERE'S JUST SOME THINGS I NEED TO TALK TO YOU ABOUT. I THOUGHT IT WAS IMPORTANT YOU HEAR IT FROM ME FIRST.

IT'S TRUE. NORMALLY WE DON'T TAKE TOO KINDLY TO UNEXPECTED VISITORS, BUT TODAY IS DIFFERENT. TODAY IS A SPECIAL DAY AND I THINK IT'S FITTING THAT YOU MADE IT OUT HERE. PERHAPS IT WAS MEANT TO BE...

RELAX, JASPER... WE ARE WELL AWARE OF WHAT'S GOING ON IN TOWN...

REALLY...?

YEAH...WELL HERE'S THE THING. WE GOT A FEW MUTANTS SNIFFING AROUND TOWN. AND THESE AIN'T LIKE THE ONES WE SUPPLY YOU GUYS WITH. THESE ARE SOME REAL HEAVY HITTERS...LIKE THE ONES YOU SEE ON TV...

I DON'T KNOW WHAT THEY'RE HERE FOR BUT--

THAT THOSE MUTANTS WERE ABLE TO FIND OUR LITTLE COMMUNITY ALL THE WAY OUT HERE IS A SIGN, JASPER. A SIGN THAT THINGS ARE CHANGING...

JUST BECAUSE WE SECLUDE OURSELVES AWAY IN THESE HILLS, DOESN'T MEAN WE'RE UNAWARE OF WHAT'S HAPPENING DOWN BELOW.

OUR ABILITY TO SEE IS VAST. IN FACT, THERE ISN'T MUCH THAT WE DON'T SEE.

...AND AS A RESULT, CHANGES MUST BE MADE HERE AS WELL.

PLEASE...WE HAVE MUCH TO DISCUSS.

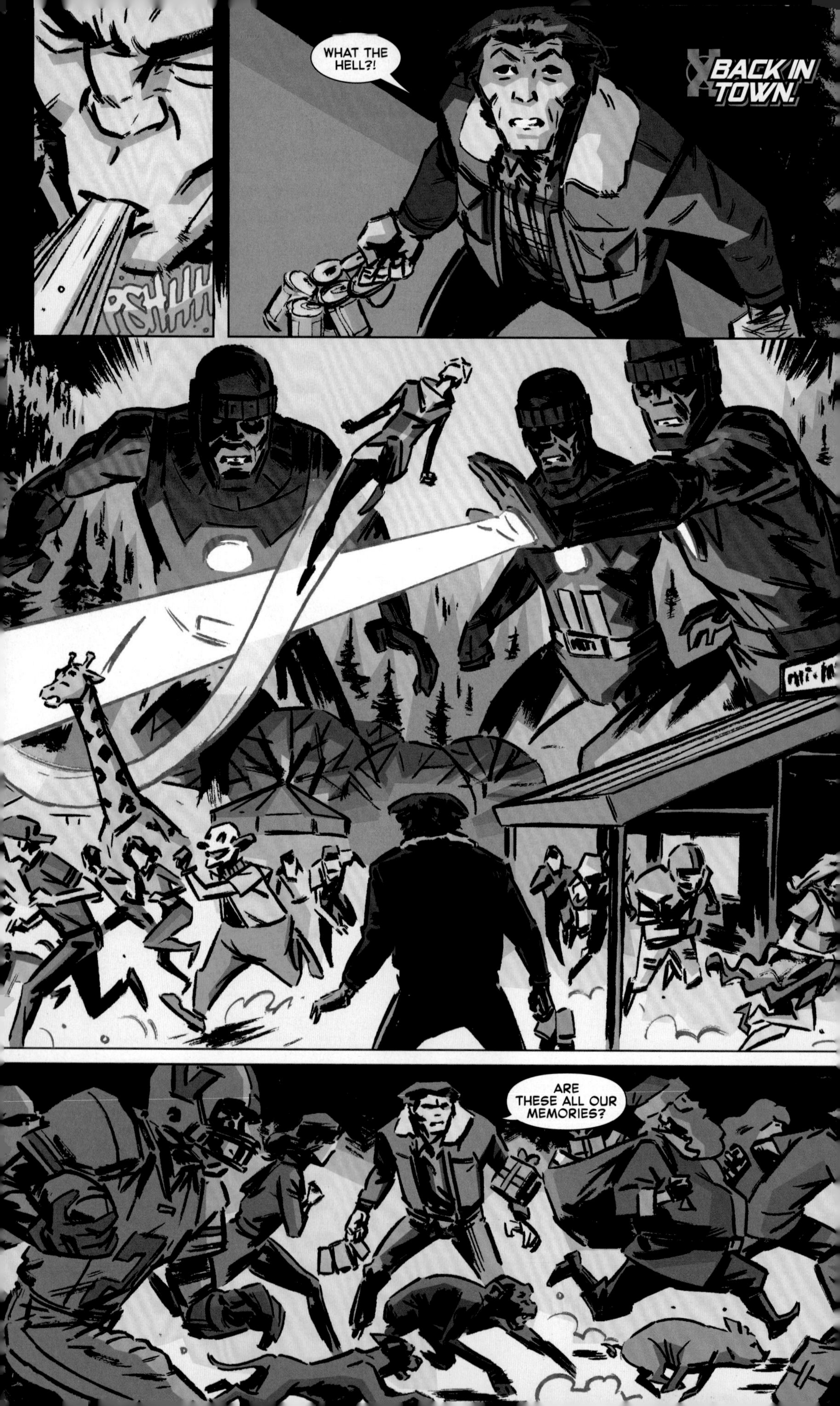
PSHHH
WHAT THE HELL?!
BACK IN TOWN.
ARE THESE ALL OUR MEMORIES?

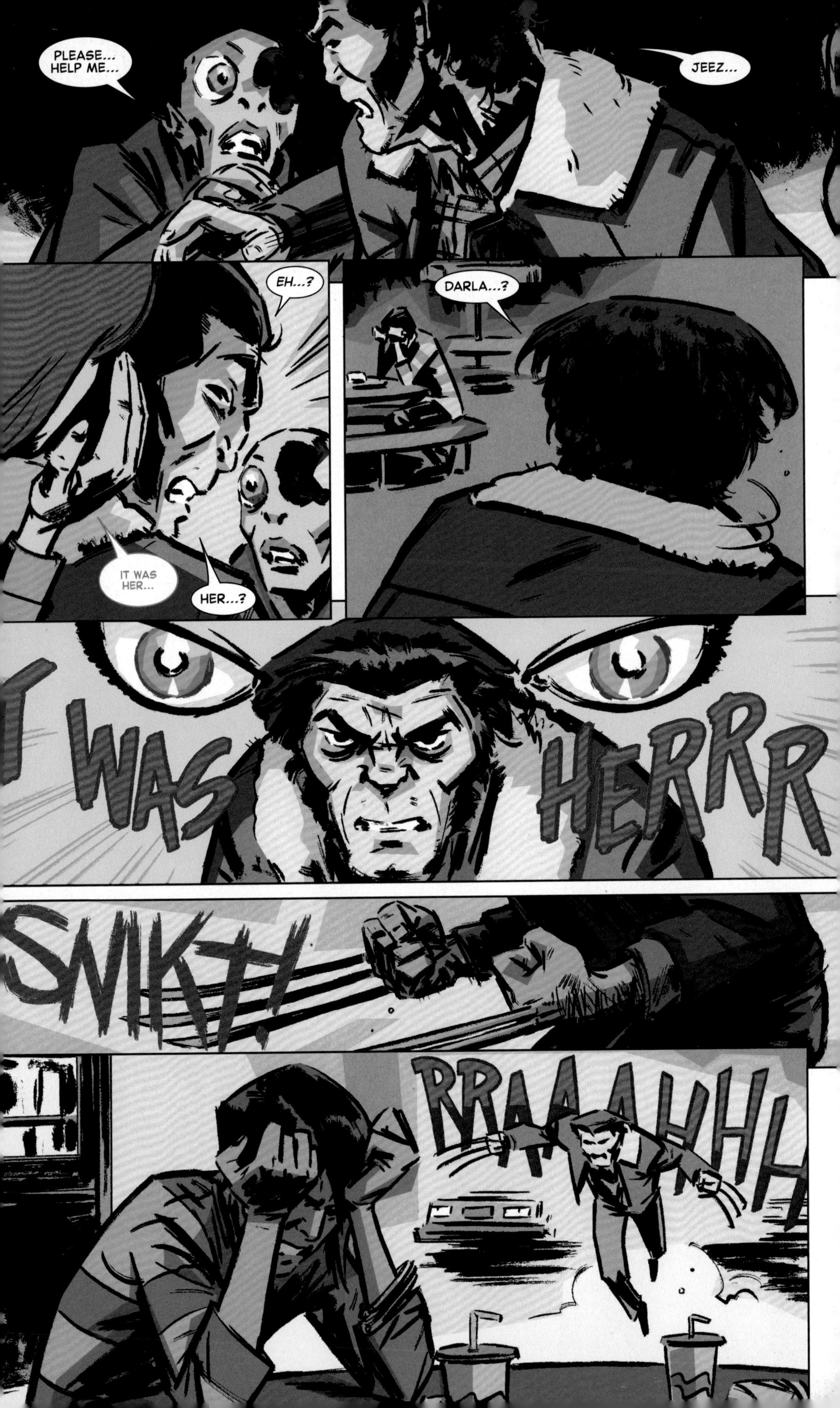

PLEASE... HELP ME...
JEEZ...
EH...?
IT WAS HER...
HER...?
DARLA...?
IT WAS HERRR
SNIKT!
RRAAAHHH

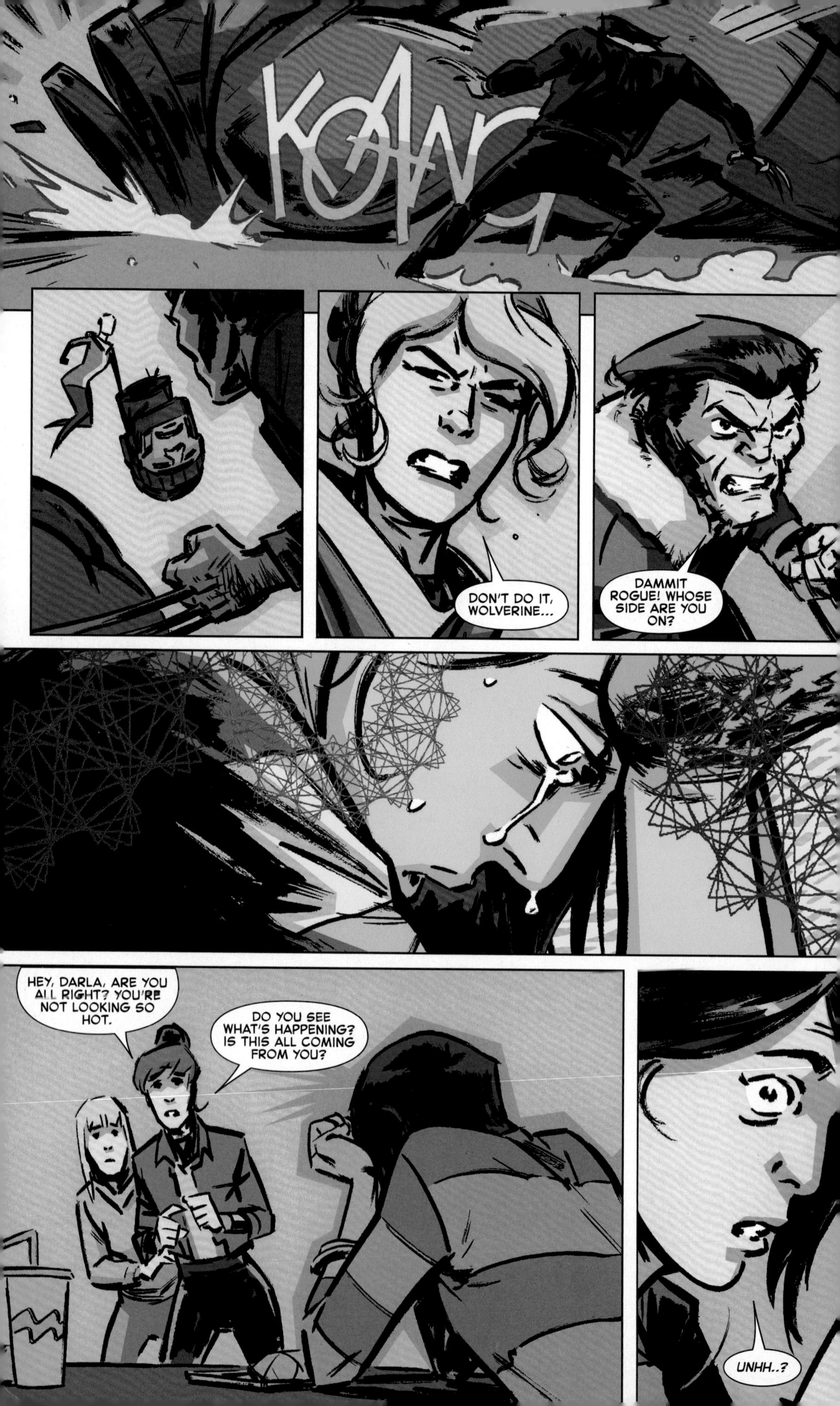
KRANG
DON'T DO IT, WOLVERINE...
DAMMIT ROGUE! WHOSE SIDE ARE YOU ON?
HEY, DARLA, ARE YOU ALL RIGHT? YOU'RE NOT LOOKING SO HOT.
DO YOU SEE WHAT'S HAPPENING? IS THIS ALL COMING FROM YOU?
UNHH..?

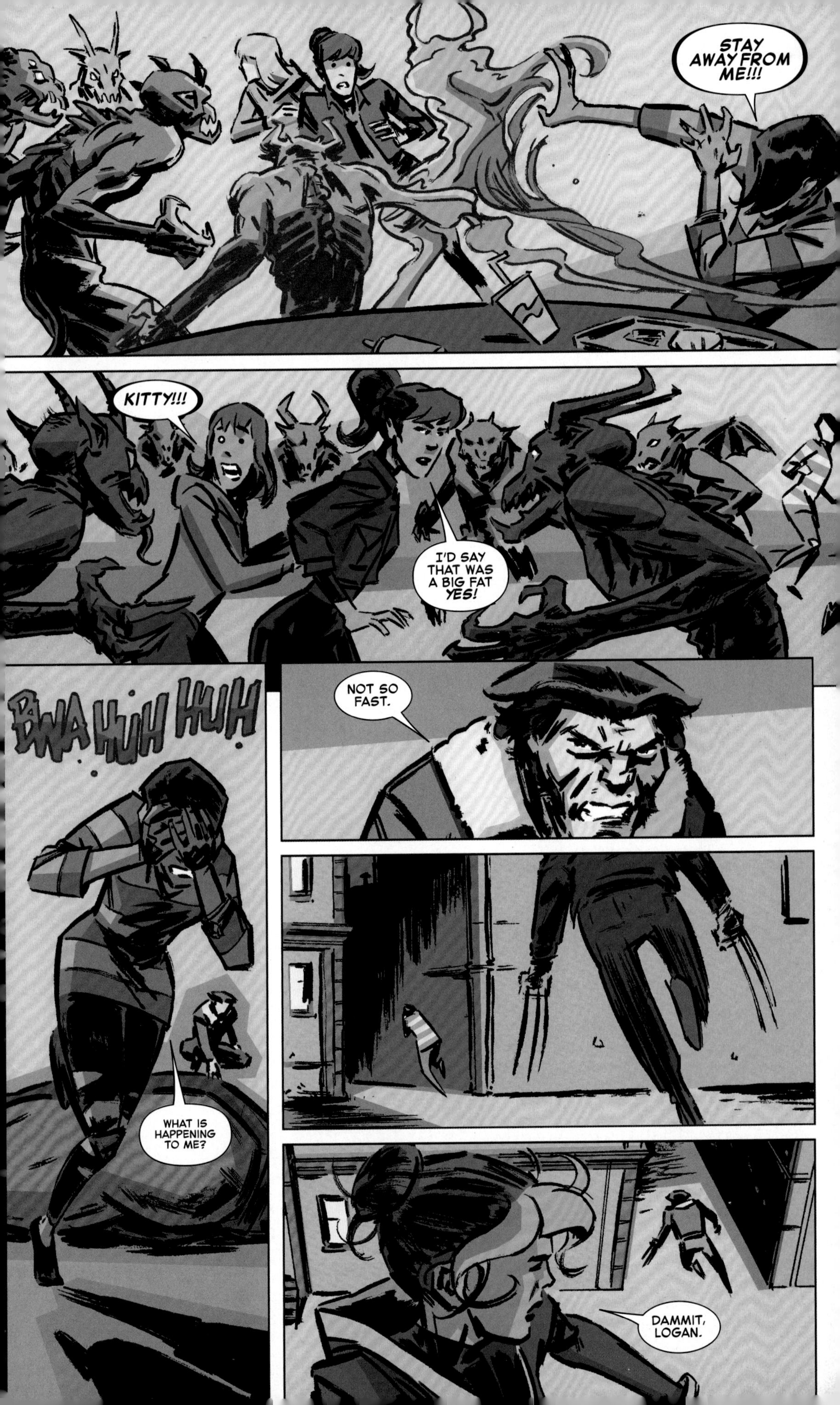
STAY AWAY FROM ME!!!
KITTY!!!
I'D SAY THAT WAS A BIG FAT YES!
BWA HUH HUH
WHAT IS HAPPENING TO ME?
NOT SO FAST.
DAMMIT, LOGAN.

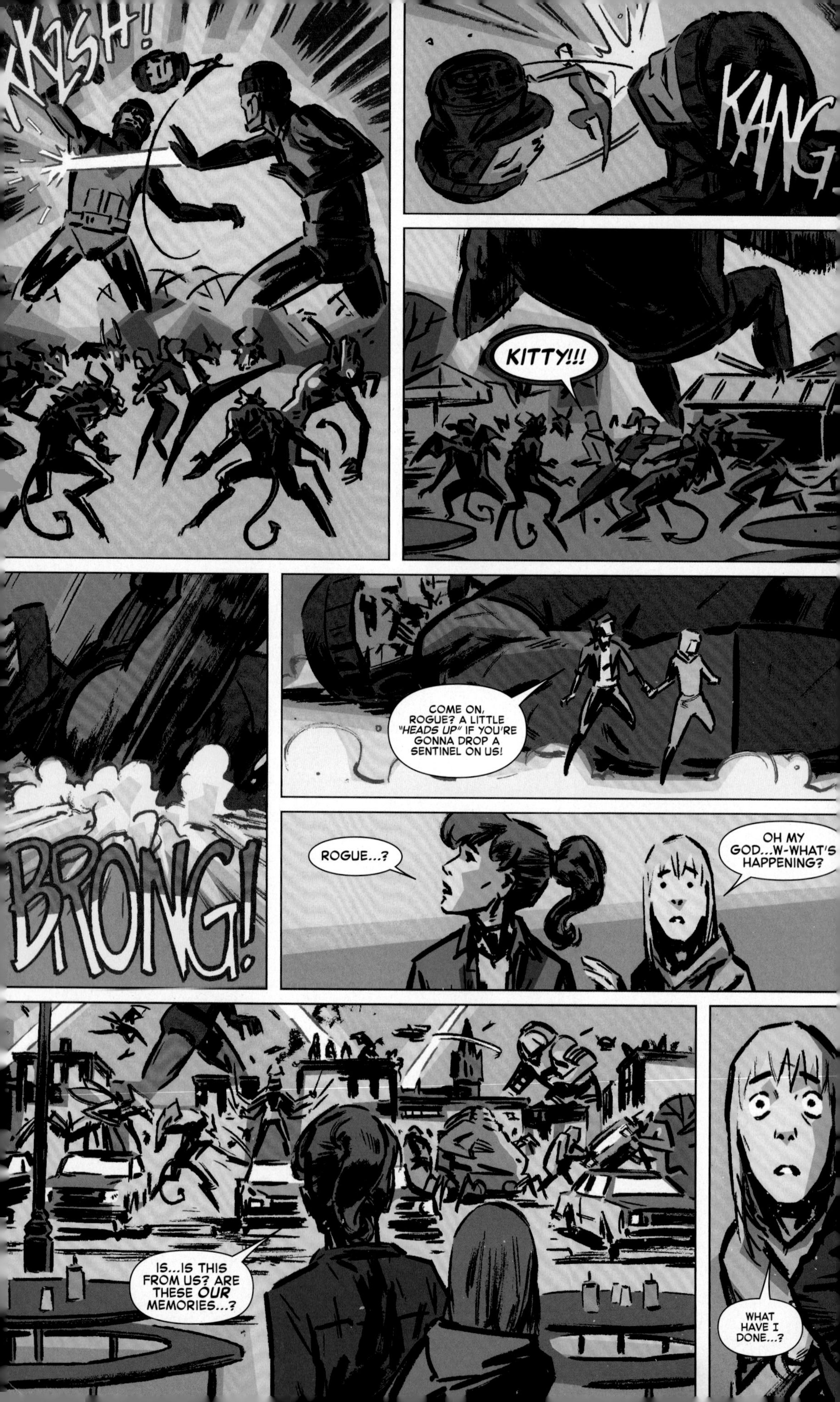
KZSH!
KANG
KITTY!!!
BRONG!
COME ON, ROGUE? A LITTLE "HEADS UP" IF YOU'RE GONNA DROP A SENTINEL ON US!
ROGUE...?
OH MY GOD...W-WHAT'S HAPPENING?
IS...IS THIS FROM US? ARE THESE OUR MEMORIES...?
WHAT HAVE I DONE...?

WE'VE BEEN DOING BUSINESS FOR QUITE SOME TIME NOW, HAVEN'T WE, SHERIFF?

YEAH...COUPLE YEARS AT LEAST...LISTEN, IS THERE A PROBLEM? ANYTHING I DID? CUZ I'M GONNA TAKE CARE OF THEM MUTANTS FOR YOU... I JUST WANTED TO--

NO, NO...WE'VE BEEN VERY HAPPY WITH THIS PARTNERSHIP. YOU'VE PROVIDED US WITH EVERYTHING WE'VE ASKED FOR.

AND I'M NOT WRONG IN ASSUMING THE FEELING'S MUTUAL? I'M SURE YOU'VE NOTICED THE QUALITY OF OUR PRODUCT IMPROVE OVER THE PAST FEW MONTHS.

SO YOU HAVEN'T TRIED IT?

NOT MY THING. MY KIND OF RELAXATION COMES IN A BOTTLE.

I UNDERSTAND. IT'S NOT FOR EVERYBODY.

STILL, IT'S A SHAME...YOU REALLY DON'T KNOW WHAT YOU'RE MISSING.

IT FILLS YOU WITH AN UNEXPLAINABLE LIGHTNESS.

NOT PERSONALLY. BUT YEAH, I'VE NOTICED A CHANGE...PEOPLE WANT IT MORE NOW...THEY'LL PAY MORE...

AN ENERGY THAT FEELS LIKE IT'S AWAKENING EVERY CELL IN YOUR BODY FOR THE FIRST TIME.

YOU FEEL AMPLIFIED...LIKE THE TRUE YOU...THE YOU YOU WERE ALWAYS MEANT TO BE.

BUT THAT IS JUST THE BEGINNING. THEN YOU BEGIN TO SEE.

YOUR EYES OPEN TO THE HIDDEN GEOMETRY THAT LIES BENEATH THIS ARTIFICIAL WORLD. YOU SEE THE INTERCONNECTEDNESS ON ALL THINGS.

YOUR BODY FADES AWAY AND FOR THE FIRST TIME IN YOUR LIFE YOU FEEL WHAT IT TRULY MEANS...

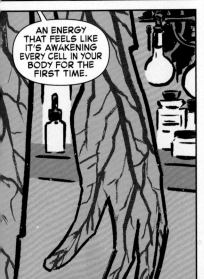

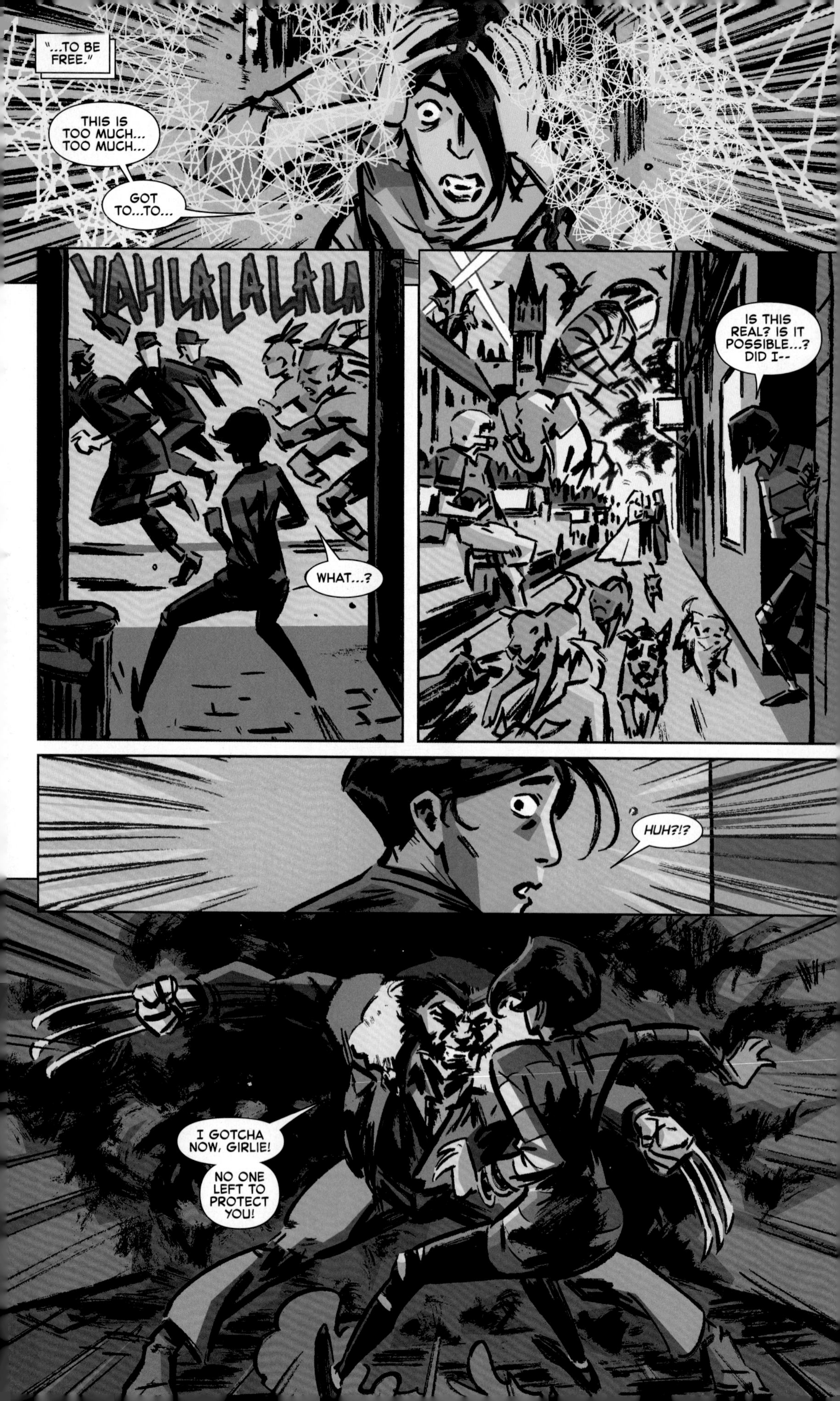

"...TO BE FREE."
THIS IS TOO MUCH... TOO MUCH...
GOT TO...TO...
YAHLALALALA
WHAT...?
IS THIS REAL? IS IT POSSIBLE...? DID I--
HUH?!?
I GOTCHA NOW, GIRLIE!
NO ONE LEFT TO PROTECT YOU!

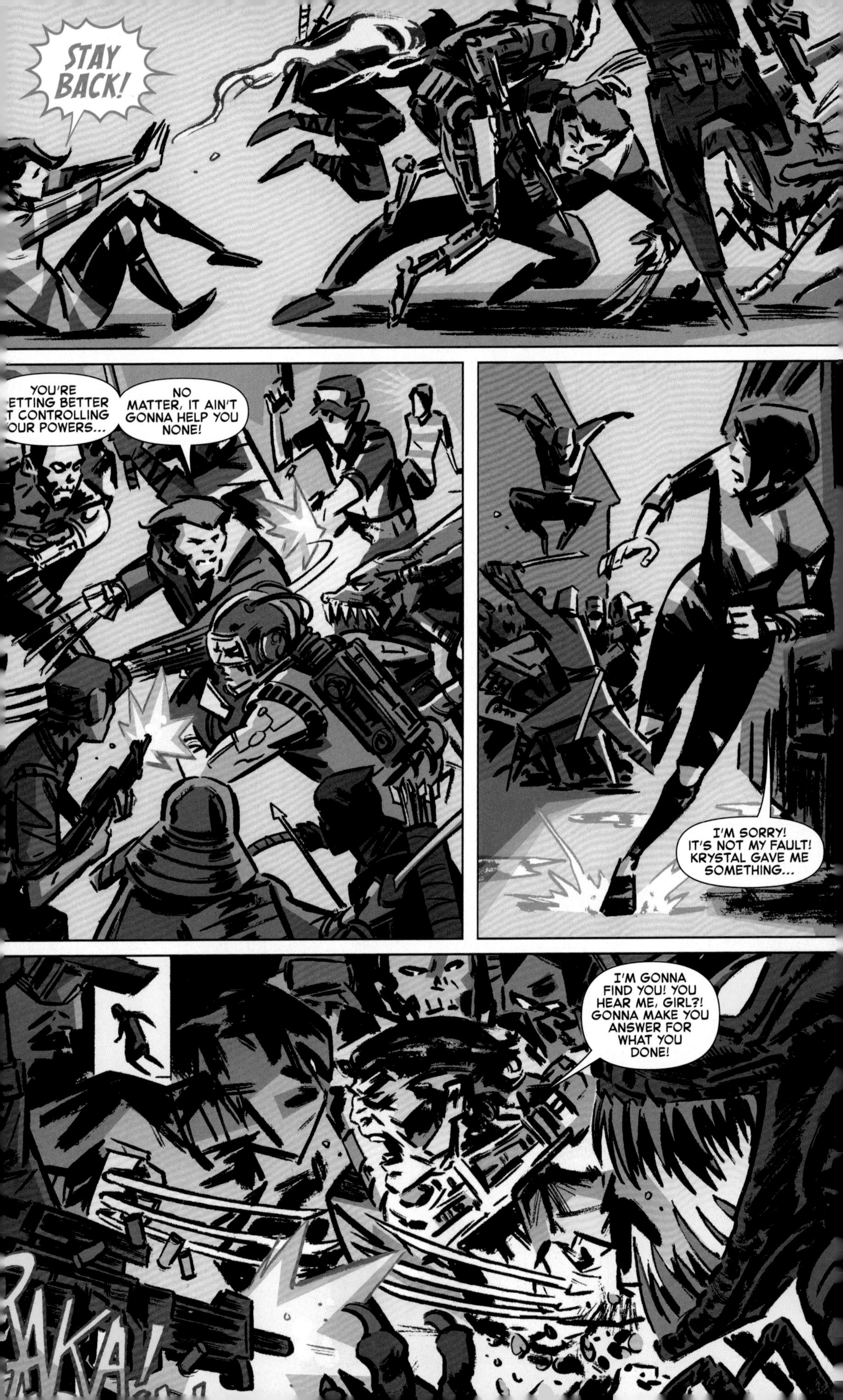
STAY BACK!
YOU'RE ETTING BETTER T CONTROLLING OUR POWERS...
NO MATTER, IT AIN'T GONNA HELP YOU NONE!
I'M SORRY! IT'S NOT MY FAULT! KRYSTAL GAVE ME SOMETHING...
I'M GONNA FIND YOU! YOU HEAR ME, GIRL?! GONNA MAKE YOU ANSWER FOR WHAT YOU DONE!

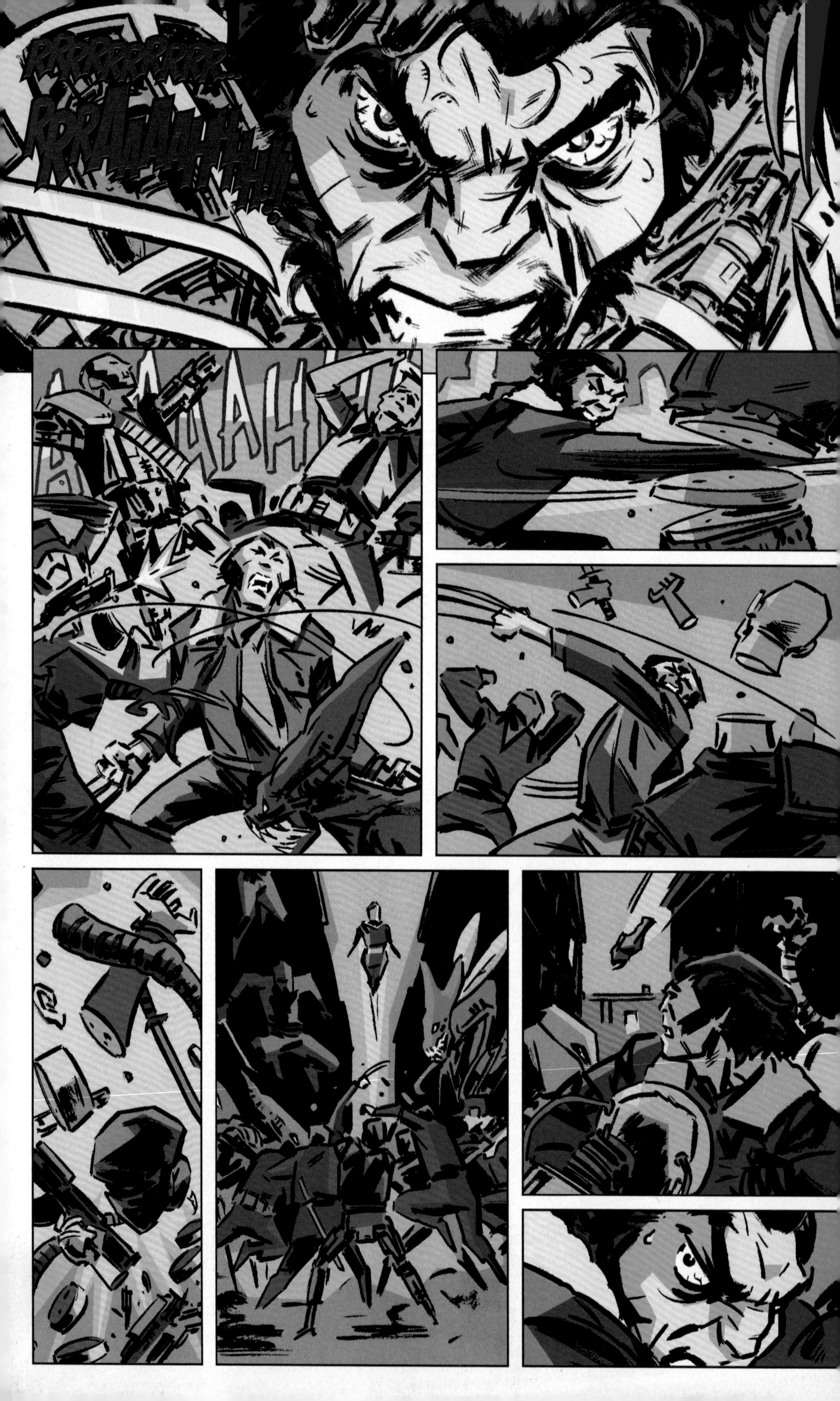
RRRRRRRRRRR...
RRRAAAAAHHHHH!!
AAAAH

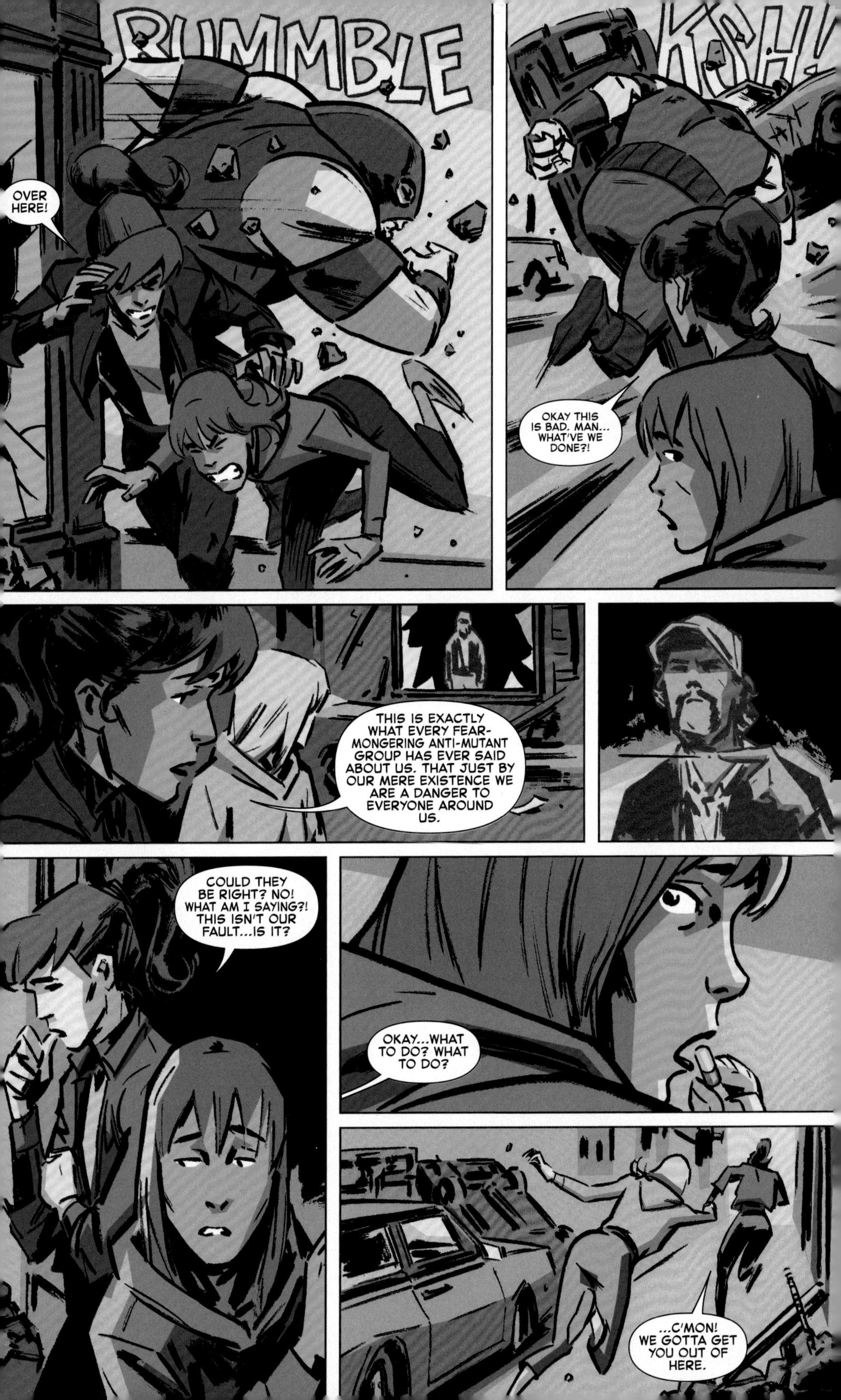
RUMMBLE
OVER HERE!
KSSH!
OKAY THIS IS BAD. MAN... WHAT'VE WE DONE?!
THIS IS EXACTLY WHAT EVERY FEAR-MONGERING ANTI-MUTANT GROUP HAS EVER SAID ABOUT US. THAT JUST BY OUR MERE EXISTENCE WE ARE A DANGER TO EVERYONE AROUND US.
COULD THEY BE RIGHT? NO! WHAT AM I SAYING?! THIS ISN'T OUR FAULT...IS IT?
OKAY...WHAT TO DO? WHAT TO DO?
...C'MON! WE GOTTA GET YOU OUT OF HERE.

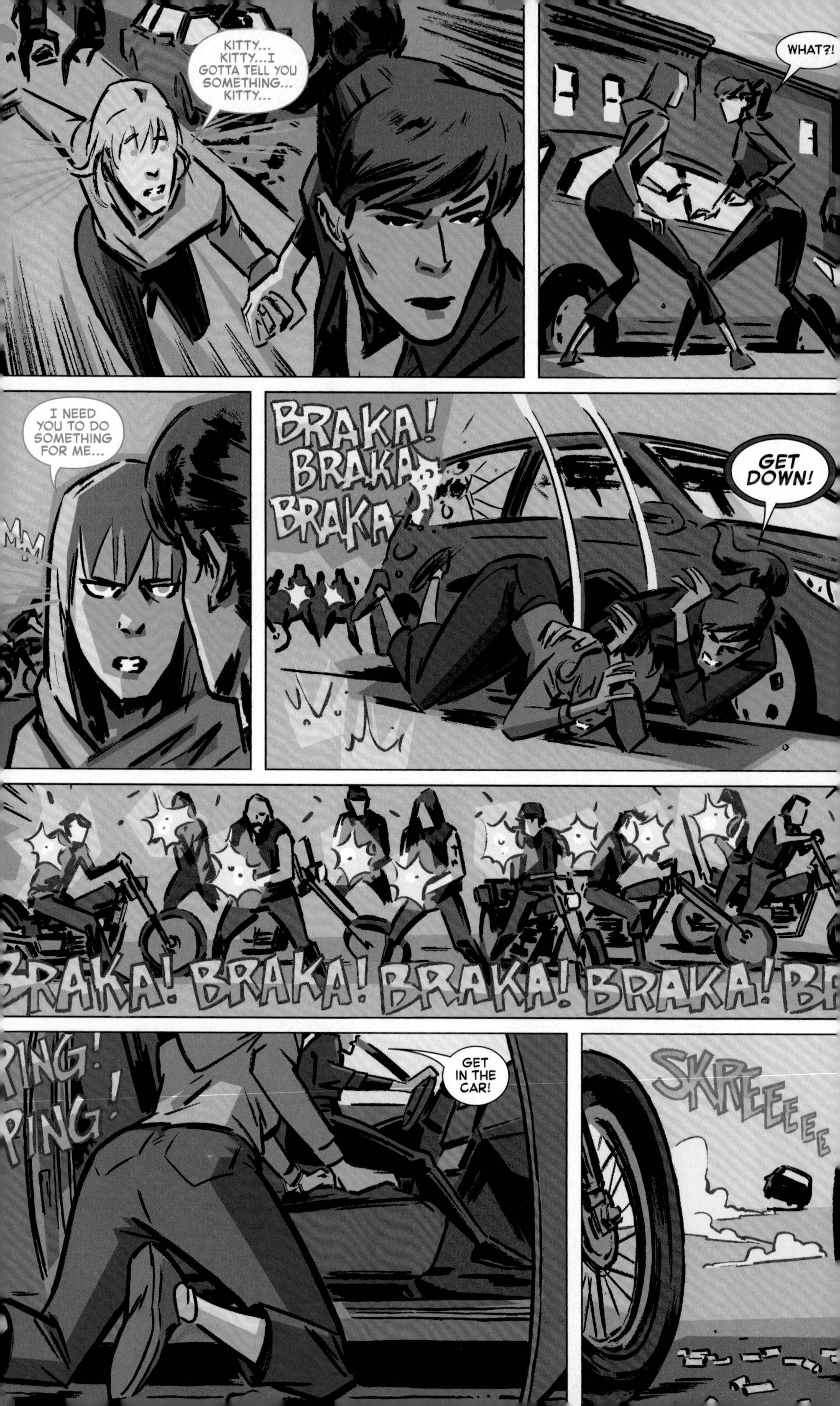

KITTY... KITTY...I GOTTA TELL YOU SOMETHING... KITTY...
WHAT?!
I NEED YOU TO DO SOMETHING FOR ME...
MMM
BRAKA! BRAKA! BRAKA
GET DOWN!
BRAKA! BRAKA! BRAKA! BRAKA!
PING! PING!
GET IN THE CAR!
SKREEEEEE

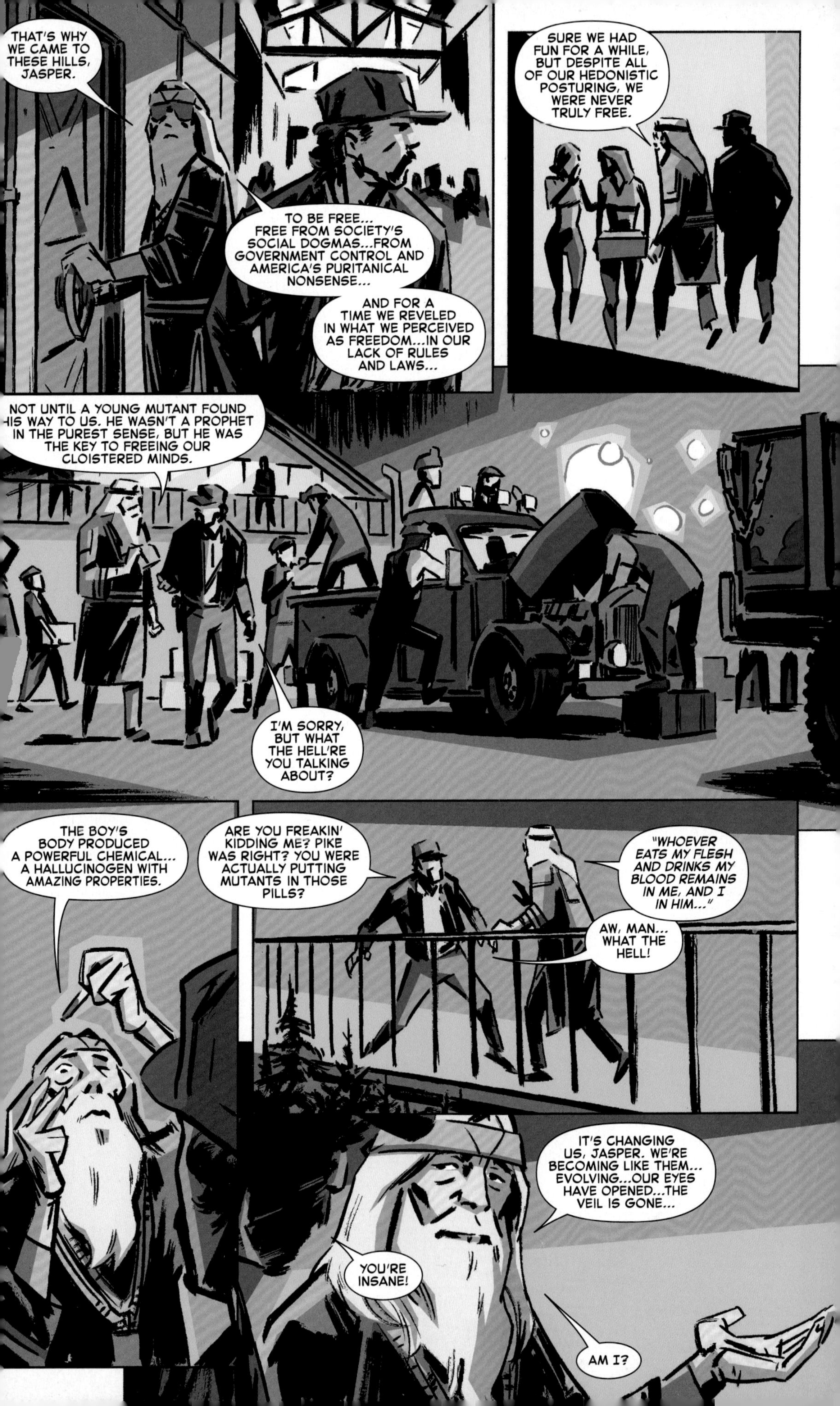
THAT'S WHY WE CAME TO THESE HILLS, JASPER.
TO BE FREE... FREE FROM SOCIETY'S SOCIAL DOGMAS...FROM GOVERNMENT CONTROL AND AMERICA'S PURITANICAL NONSENSE...
AND FOR A TIME WE REVELED IN WHAT WE PERCEIVED AS FREEDOM...IN OUR LACK OF RULES AND LAWS...
SURE WE HAD FUN FOR A WHILE, BUT DESPITE ALL OF OUR HEDONISTIC POSTURING, WE WERE NEVER TRULY FREE.
NOT UNTIL A YOUNG MUTANT FOUND HIS WAY TO US. HE WASN'T A PROPHET IN THE PUREST SENSE, BUT HE WAS THE KEY TO FREEING OUR CLOISTERED MINDS.
I'M SORRY, BUT WHAT THE HELL'RE YOU TALKING ABOUT?
THE BOY'S BODY PRODUCED A POWERFUL CHEMICAL... A HALLUCINOGEN WITH AMAZING PROPERTIES.
ARE YOU FREAKIN' KIDDING ME? PIKE WAS RIGHT? YOU WERE ACTUALLY PUTTING MUTANTS IN THOSE PILLS?
"WHOEVER EATS MY FLESH AND DRINKS MY BLOOD REMAINS IN ME, AND I IN HIM..."
AW, MAN... WHAT THE HELL!
IT'S CHANGING US, JASPER. WE'RE BECOMING LIKE THEM... EVOLVING...OUR EYES HAVE OPENED...THE VEIL IS GONE...
YOU'RE INSANE!
AM I?

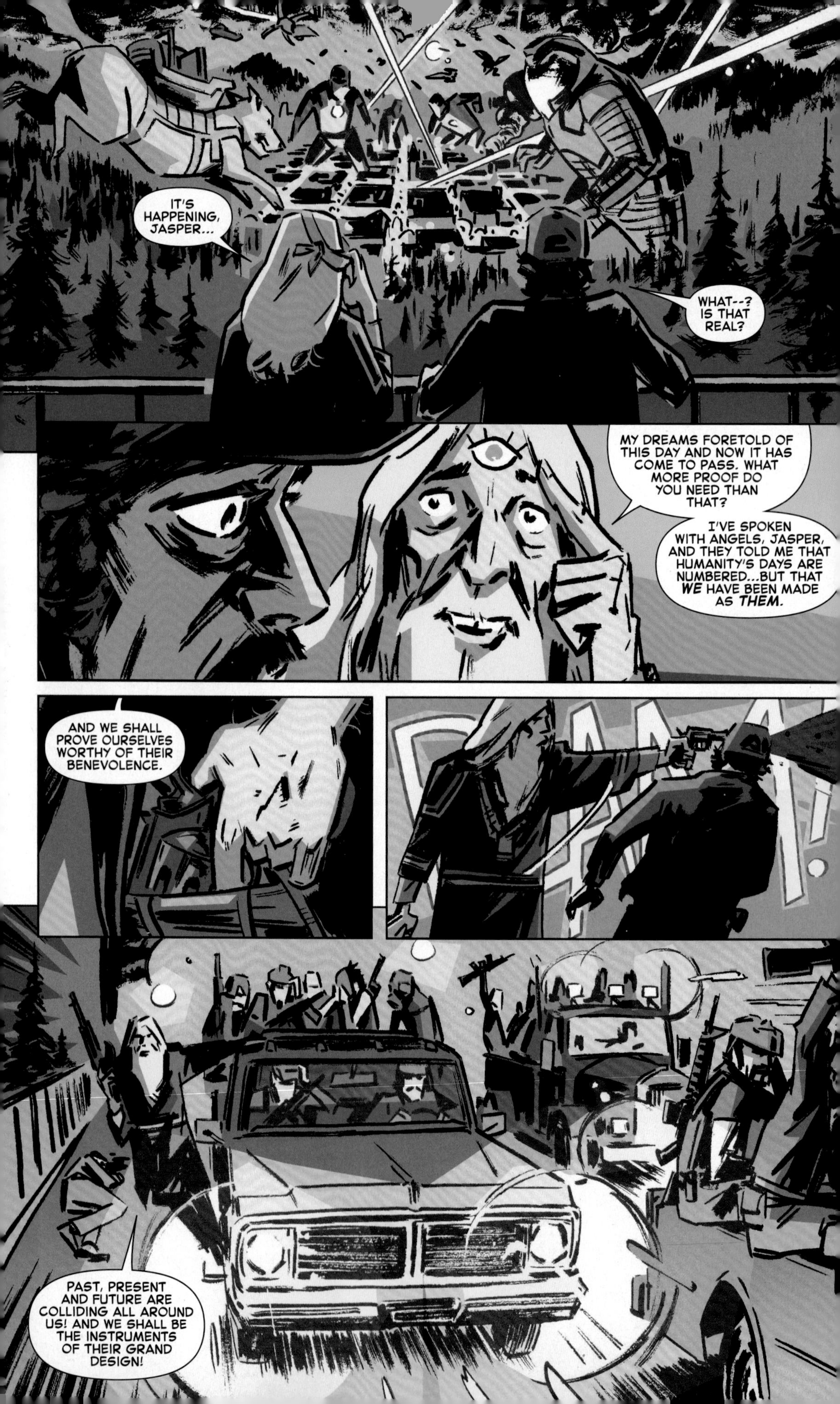
IT'S HAPPENING, JASPER...
WHAT--? IS THAT REAL?
MY DREAMS FORETOLD OF THIS DAY AND NOW IT HAS COME TO PASS. WHAT MORE PROOF DO YOU NEED THAN THAT?
I'VE SPOKEN WITH ANGELS, JASPER, AND THEY TOLD ME THAT HUMANITY'S DAYS ARE NUMBERED...BUT THAT WE HAVE BEEN MADE AS THEM.
AND WE SHALL PROVE OURSELVES WORTHY OF THEIR BENEVOLENCE.
PAST, PRESENT AND FUTURE ARE COLLIDING ALL AROUND US! AND WE SHALL BE THE INSTRUMENTS OF THEIR GRAND DESIGN!

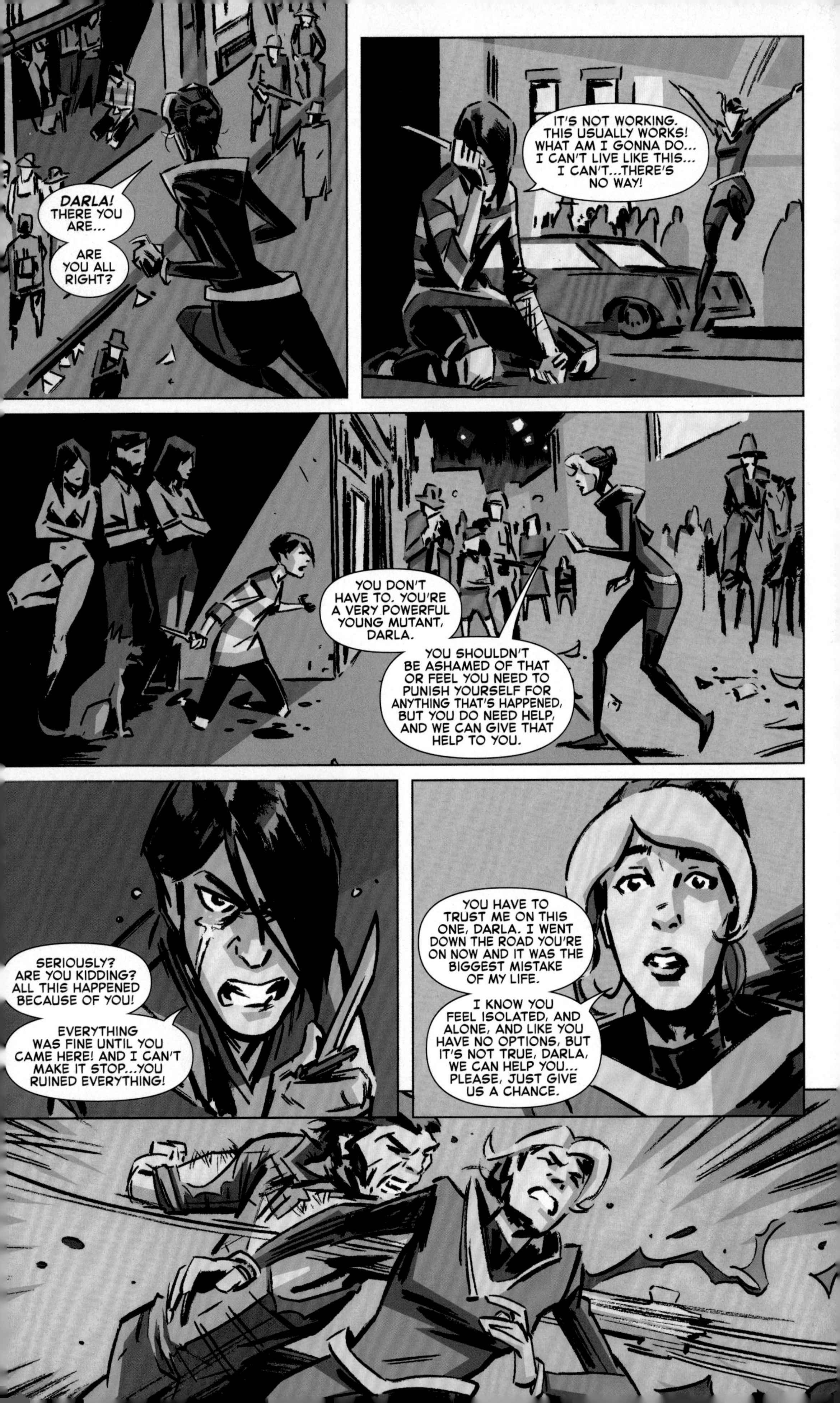
DARLA! THERE YOU ARE...
ARE YOU ALL RIGHT?
IT'S NOT WORKING. THIS USUALLY WORKS! WHAT AM I GONNA DO... I CAN'T LIVE LIKE THIS... I CAN'T...THERE'S NO WAY!
YOU DON'T HAVE TO. YOU'RE A VERY POWERFUL YOUNG MUTANT, DARLA.
YOU SHOULDN'T BE ASHAMED OF THAT OR FEEL YOU NEED TO PUNISH YOURSELF FOR ANYTHING THAT'S HAPPENED, BUT YOU DO NEED HELP, AND WE CAN GIVE THAT HELP TO YOU.
SERIOUSLY? ARE YOU KIDDING? ALL THIS HAPPENED BECAUSE OF YOU!
EVERYTHING WAS FINE UNTIL YOU CAME HERE! AND I CAN'T MAKE IT STOP...YOU RUINED EVERYTHING!
YOU HAVE TO TRUST ME ON THIS ONE, DARLA. I WENT DOWN THE ROAD YOU'RE ON NOW AND IT WAS THE BIGGEST MISTAKE OF MY LIFE.
I KNOW YOU FEEL ISOLATED, AND ALONE, AND LIKE YOU HAVE NO OPTIONS, BUT IT'S NOT TRUE, DARLA, WE CAN HELP YOU... PLEASE, JUST GIVE US A CHANCE.

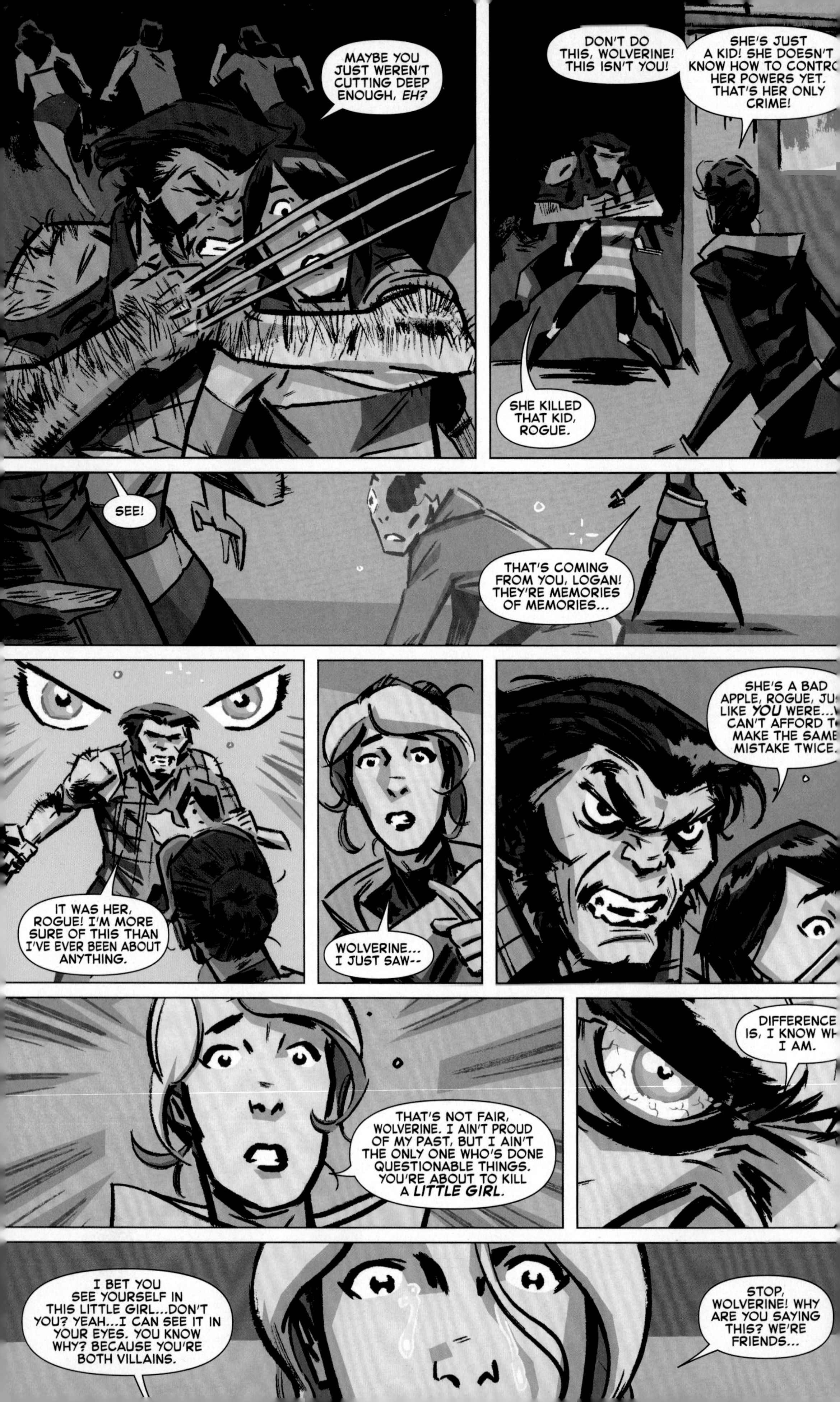

MAYBE YOU JUST WEREN'T CUTTING DEEP ENOUGH, EH?
DON'T DO THIS, WOLVERINE! THIS ISN'T YOU!
SHE'S JUST A KID! SHE DOESN'T KNOW HOW TO CONTRO HER POWERS YET. THAT'S HER ONLY CRIME!
SHE KILLED THAT KID, ROGUE.
SEE!
THAT'S COMING FROM YOU, LOGAN! THEY'RE MEMORIES OF MEMORIES...
IT WAS HER, ROGUE! I'M MORE SURE OF THIS THAN I'VE EVER BEEN ABOUT ANYTHING.
WOLVERINE... I JUST SAW--
SHE'S A BAD APPLE, ROGUE, JU LIKE YOU WERE... CAN'T AFFORD T MAKE THE SAME MISTAKE TWICE.
THAT'S NOT FAIR, WOLVERINE. I AIN'T PROUD OF MY PAST, BUT I AIN'T THE ONLY ONE WHO'S DONE QUESTIONABLE THINGS. YOU'RE ABOUT TO KILL A LITTLE GIRL.
DIFFERENCE IS, I KNOW WH I AM.
I BET YOU SEE YOURSELF IN THIS LITTLE GIRL...DON'T YOU? YEAH...I CAN SEE IT IN YOUR EYES. YOU KNOW WHY? BECAUSE YOU'RE BOTH VILLAINS.
STOP, WOLVERINE! WHY ARE YOU SAYING THIS? WE'RE FRIENDS...

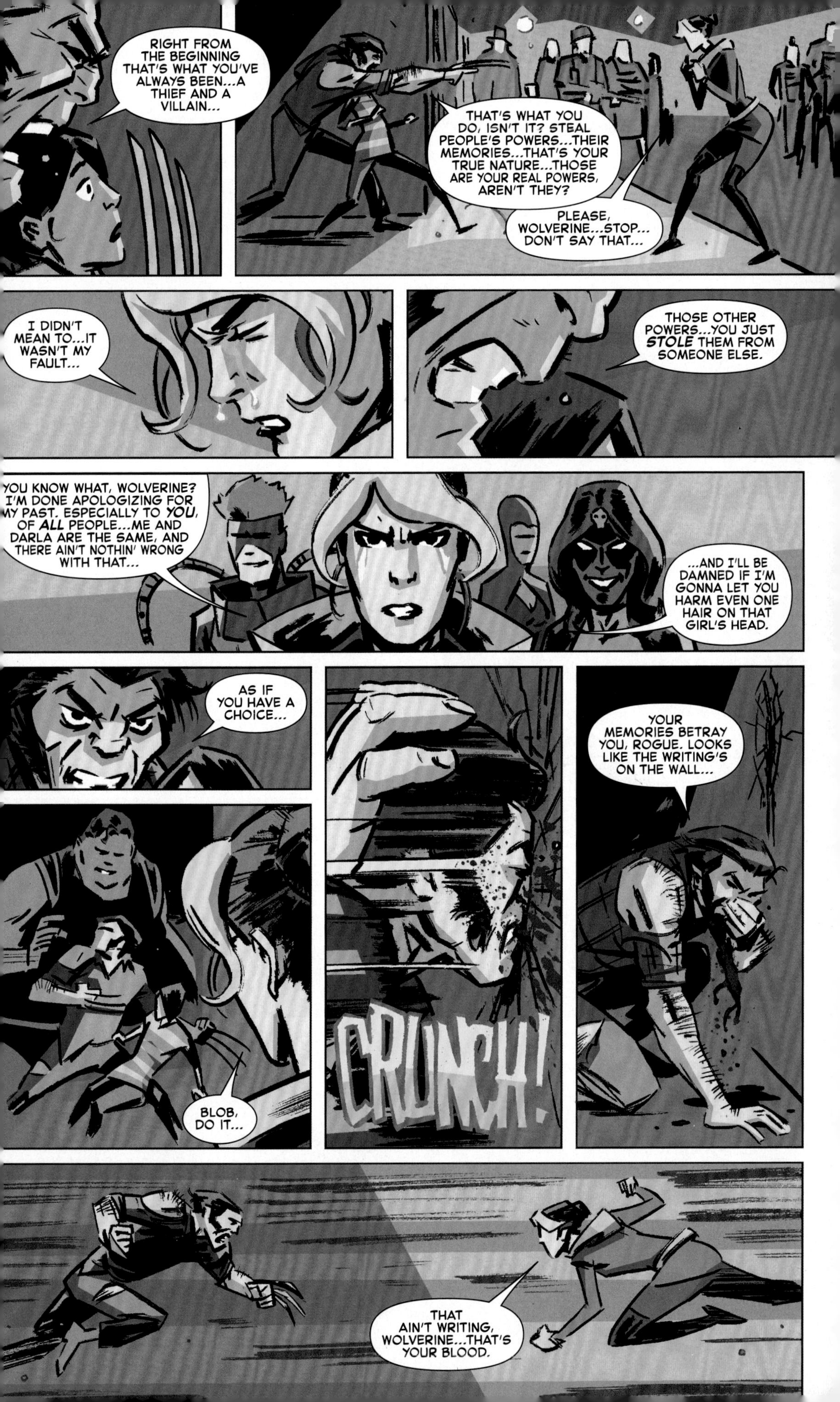
RIGHT FROM THE BEGINNING THAT'S WHAT YOU'VE ALWAYS BEEN...A THIEF AND A VILLAIN...
THAT'S WHAT YOU DO, ISN'T IT? STEAL PEOPLE'S POWERS...THEIR MEMORIES...THAT'S YOUR TRUE NATURE...THOSE ARE YOUR REAL POWERS, AREN'T THEY?
PLEASE, WOLVERINE...STOP... DON'T SAY THAT...
I DIDN'T MEAN TO...IT WASN'T MY FAULT...
THOSE OTHER POWERS...YOU JUST *STOLE* THEM FROM SOMEONE ELSE.
YOU KNOW WHAT, WOLVERINE? I'M DONE APOLOGIZING FOR MY PAST. ESPECIALLY TO *YOU*, OF *ALL* PEOPLE...ME AND DARLA ARE THE SAME, AND THERE AIN'T NOTHIN' WRONG WITH THAT...
...AND I'LL BE DAMNED IF I'M GONNA LET YOU HARM EVEN ONE HAIR ON THAT GIRL'S HEAD.
AS IF YOU HAVE A CHOICE...
BLOB, DO IT...
CRUNCH!
YOUR MEMORIES BETRAY YOU, ROGUE. LOOKS LIKE THE WRITING'S ON THE WALL...
THAT AIN'T WRITING, WOLVERINE...THAT'S YOUR BLOOD.

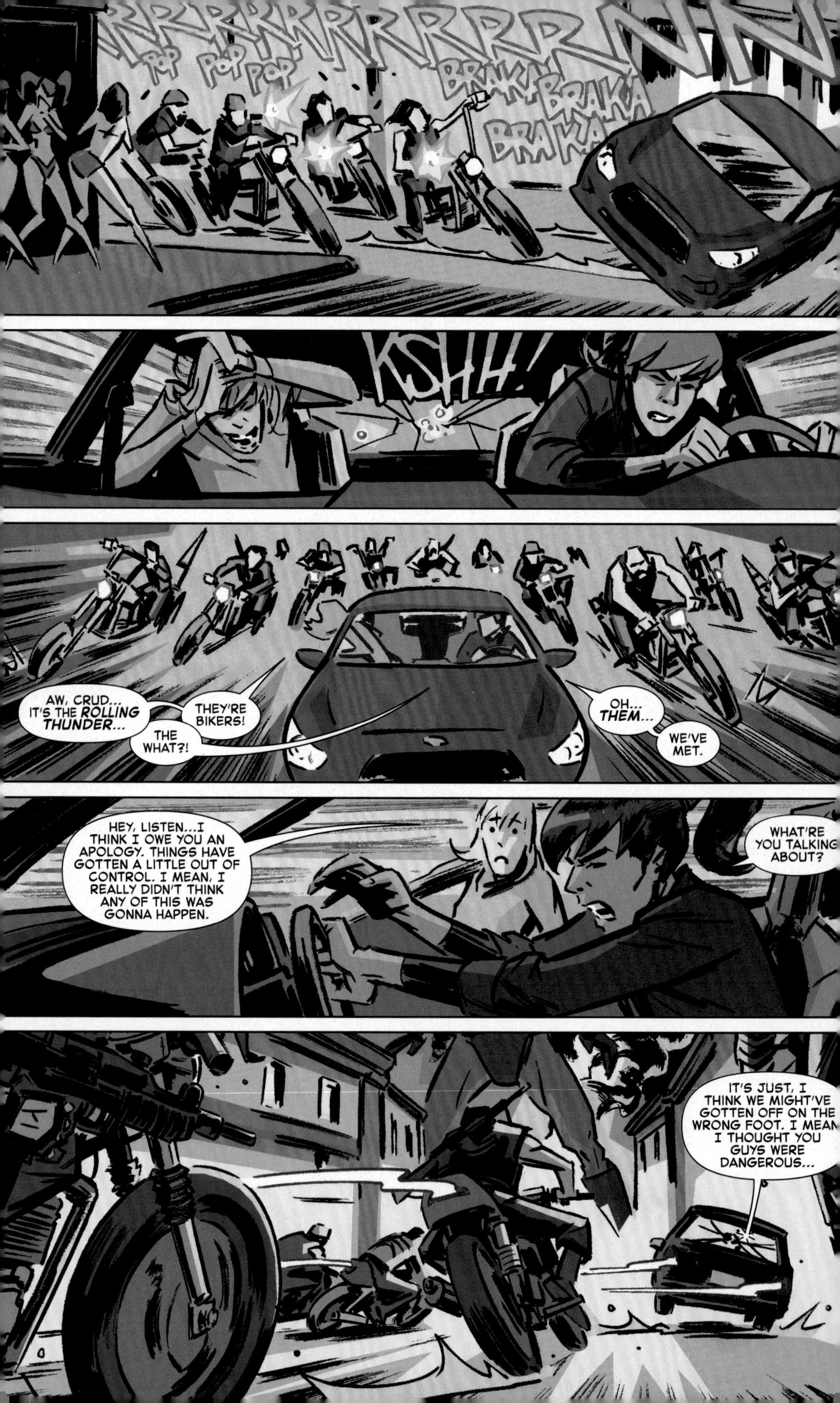
RRRRRRRRRRRNNN
POP POP POP POP
BRAKA BRAKA BRAKA
KSHH!
AW, CRUD... IT'S THE *ROLLING THUNDER*...
THEY'RE BIKERS!
THE WHAT?!
OH... *THEM*...
WE'VE MET.
HEY, LISTEN...I THINK I OWE YOU AN APOLOGY. THINGS HAVE GOTTEN A LITTLE OUT OF CONTROL. I MEAN, I REALLY DIDN'T THINK ANY OF THIS WAS GONNA HAPPEN.
WHAT'RE YOU TALKING ABOUT?
IT'S JUST, I THINK WE MIGHT'VE GOTTEN OFF ON THE WRONG FOOT. I MEAN I THOUGHT YOU GUYS WERE DANGEROUS...

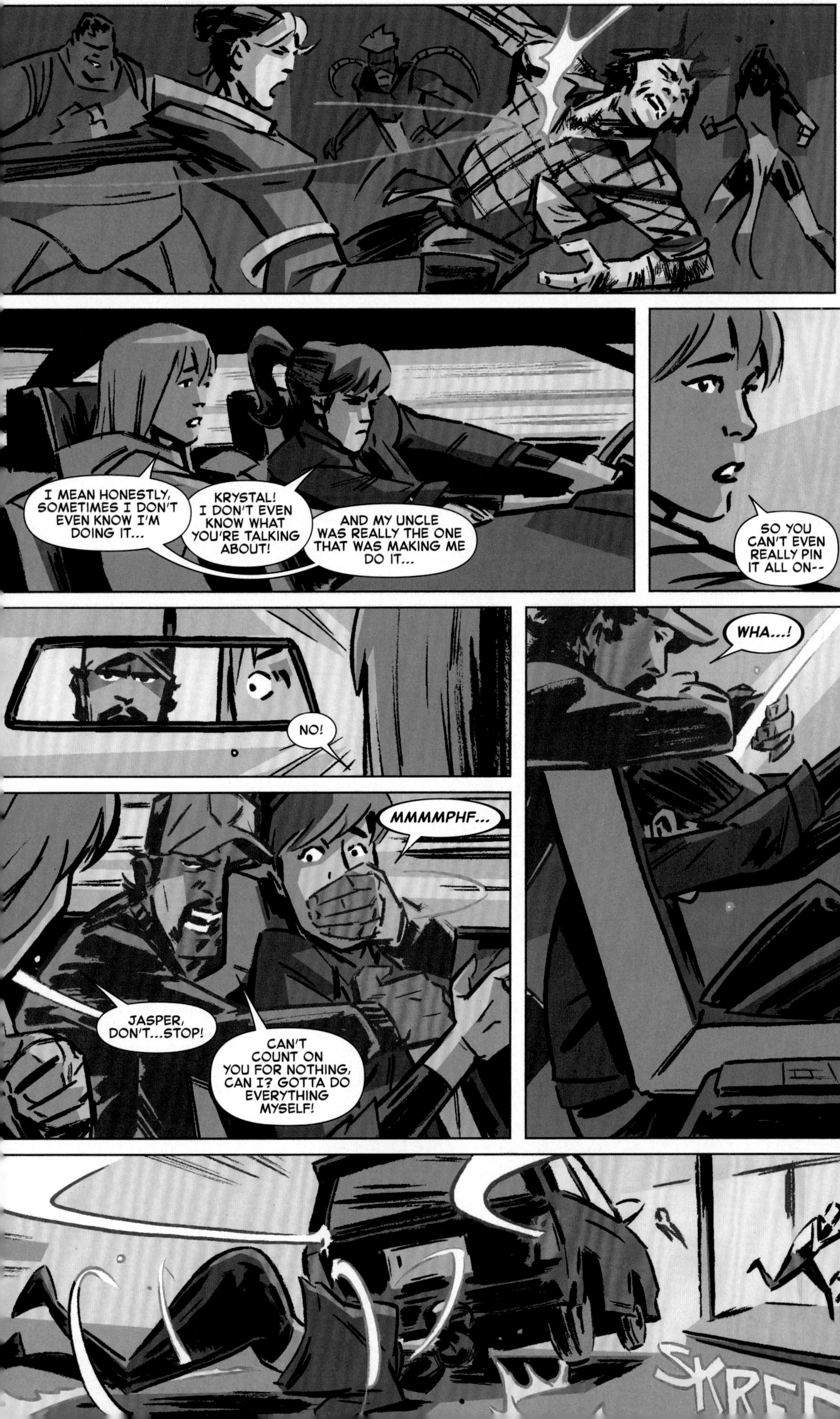
I MEAN HONESTLY, SOMETIMES I DON'T EVEN KNOW I'M DOING IT...
KRYSTAL! I DON'T EVEN KNOW WHAT YOU'RE TALKING ABOUT!
AND MY UNCLE WAS REALLY THE ONE THAT WAS MAKING ME DO IT...
SO YOU CAN'T EVEN REALLY PIN IT ALL ON--
NO!
WHA...!
MMMMPHF...
JASPER, DON'T...STOP!
CAN'T COUNT ON YOU FOR NOTHING, CAN I? GOTTA DO EVERYTHING MYSELF!

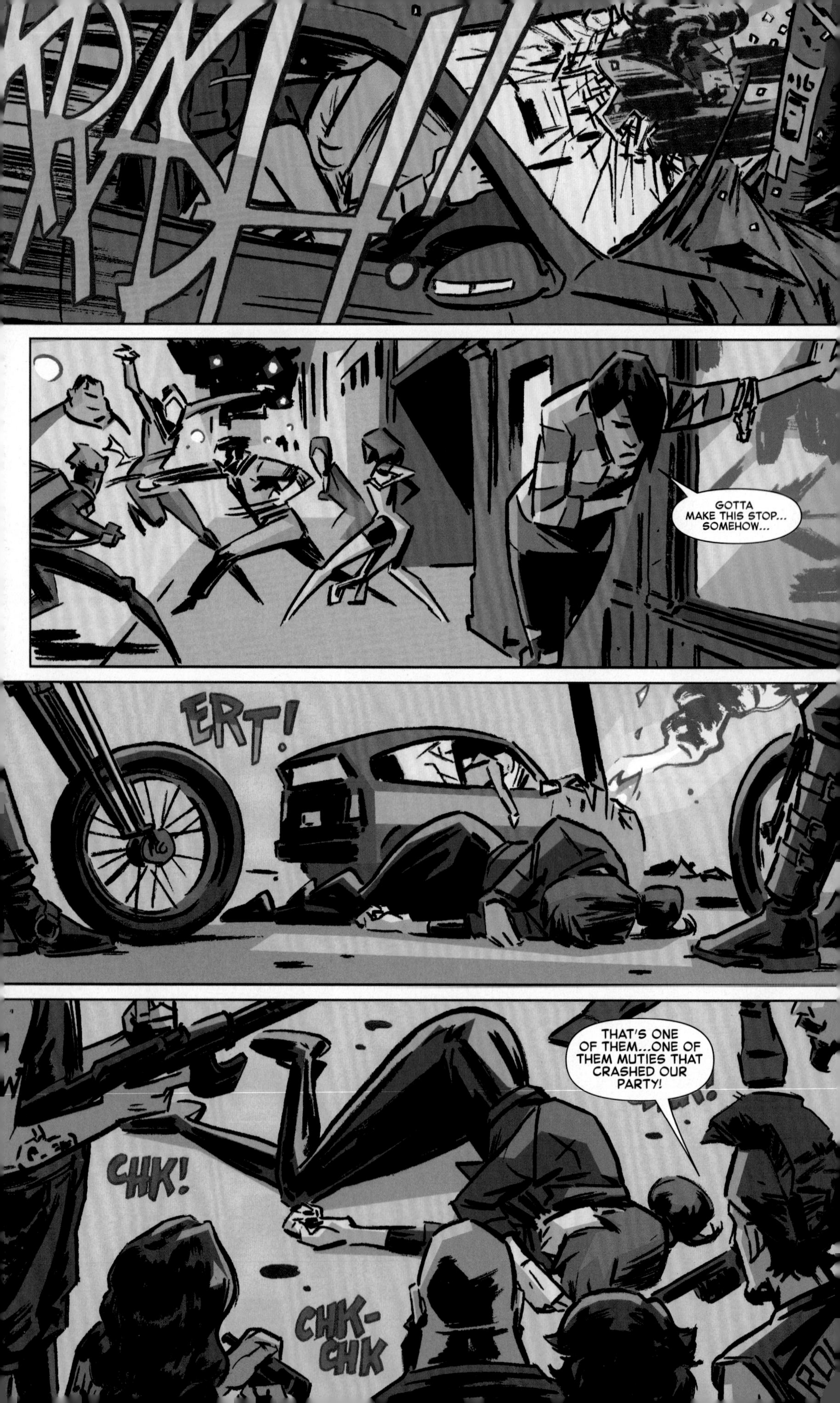

KROOM
GOTTA MAKE THIS STOP... SOMEHOW...
ERT!
THAT'S ONE OF THEM...ONE OF THEM MUTIES THAT CRASHED OUR PARTY!
CHK!
CHK-CHK

4

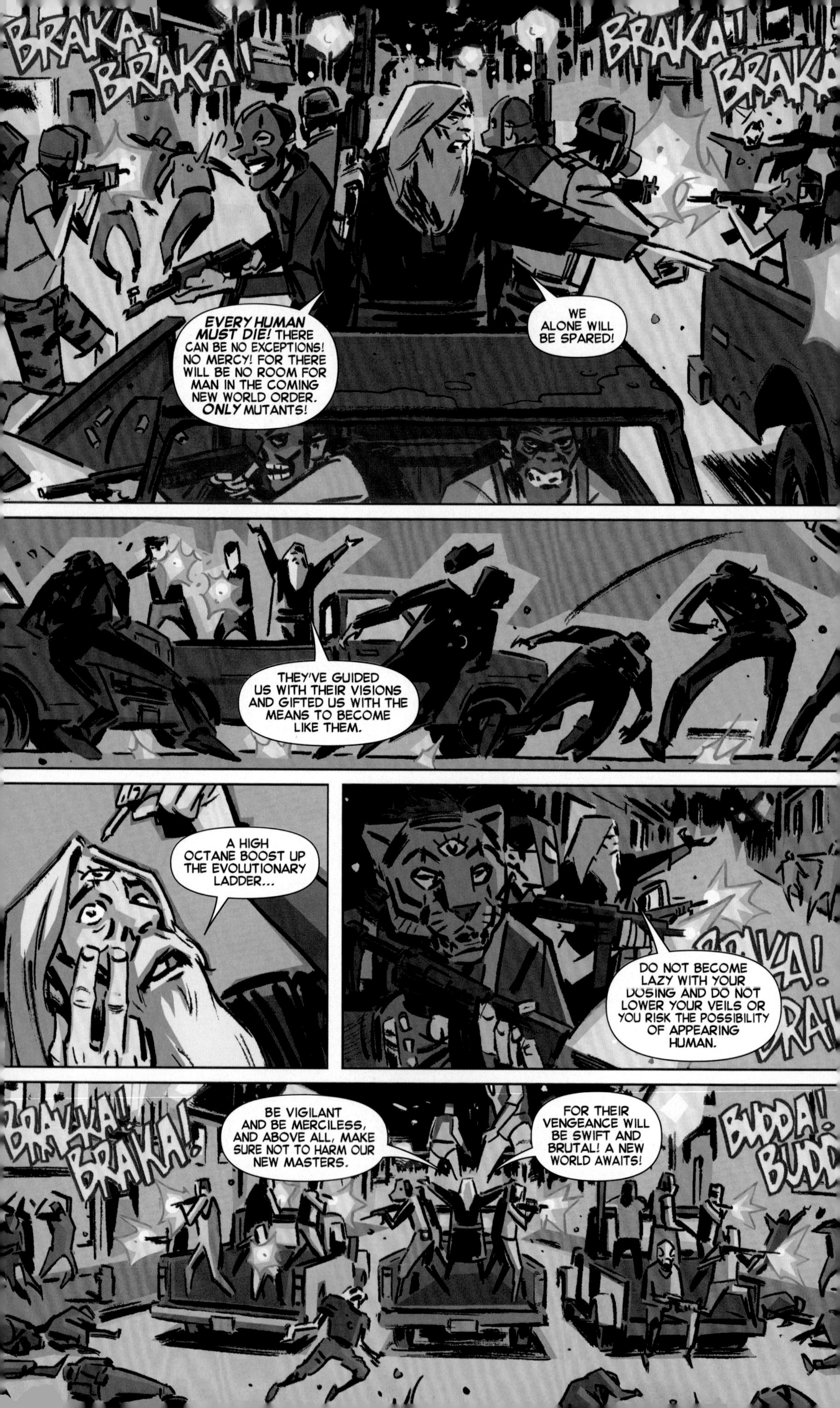

BRAKA! BRAKA!
BRAKA!
EVERY HUMAN MUST DIE! THERE CAN BE NO EXCEPTIONS! NO MERCY! FOR THERE WILL BE NO ROOM FOR MAN IN THE COMING NEW WORLD ORDER. ONLY MUTANTS!
WE ALONE WILL BE SPARED!
THEY'VE GUIDED US WITH THEIR VISIONS AND GIFTED US WITH THE MEANS TO BECOME LIKE THEM.
A HIGH OCTANE BOOST UP THE EVOLUTIONARY LADDER...
DO NOT BECOME LAZY WITH YOUR DOSING AND DO NOT LOWER YOUR VEILS OR YOU RISK THE POSSIBILITY OF APPEARING HUMAN.
BRAKA!
BE VIGILANT AND BE MERCILESS, AND ABOVE ALL, MAKE SURE NOT TO HARM OUR NEW MASTERS.
FOR THEIR VENGEANCE WILL BE SWIFT AND BRUTAL! A NEW WORLD AWAITS!
BUDDA!

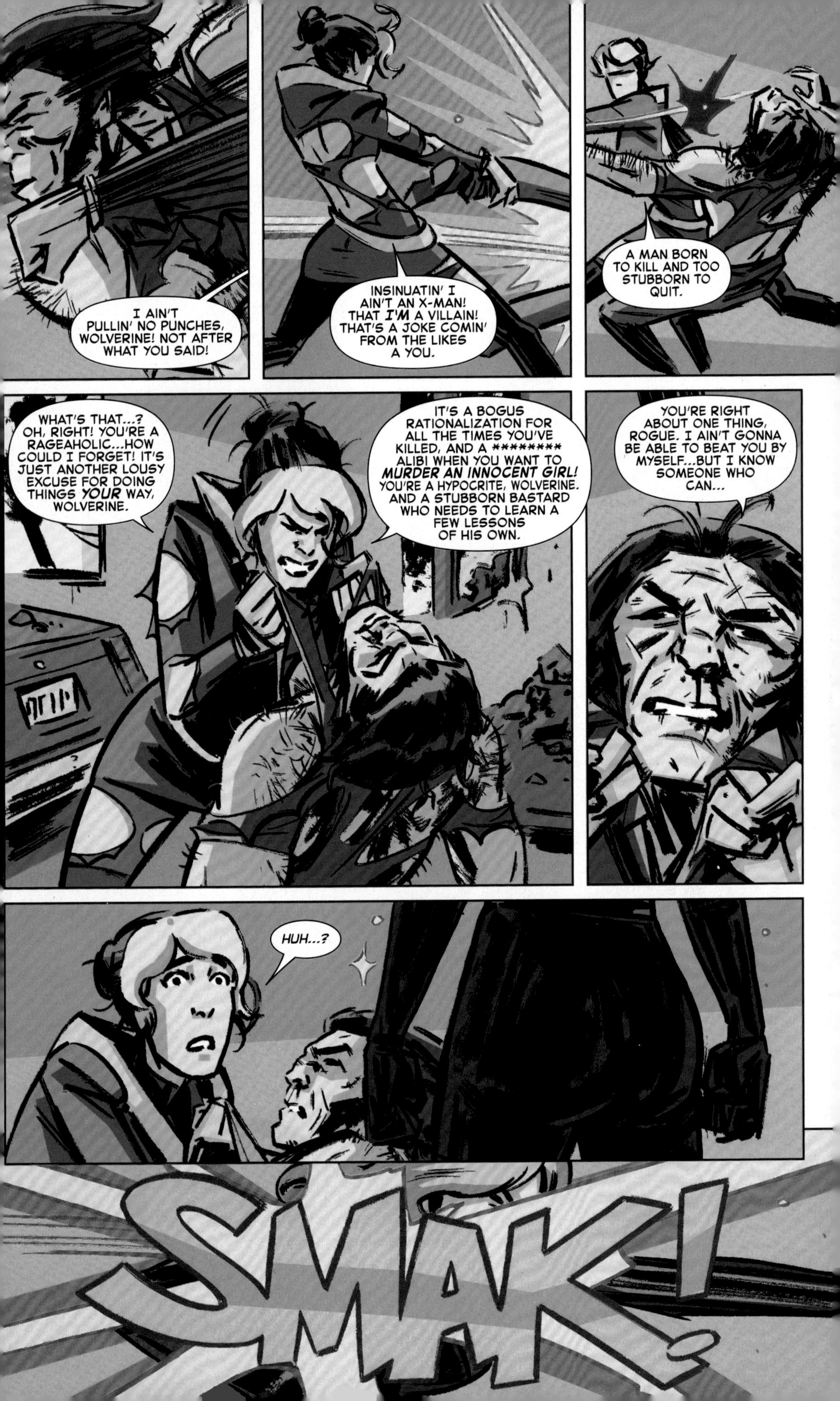
I AIN'T PULLIN' NO PUNCHES, WOLVERINE! NOT AFTER WHAT YOU SAID!
INSINUATIN' I AIN'T AN X-MAN! THAT *I'M* A VILLAIN! THAT'S A JOKE COMIN' FROM THE LIKES A YOU.
A MAN BORN TO KILL AND TOO STUBBORN TO QUIT.
WHAT'S THAT...? OH, RIGHT! YOU'RE A RAGEAHOLIC...HOW COULD I FORGET! IT'S JUST ANOTHER LOUSY EXCUSE FOR DOING THINGS *YOUR* WAY, WOLVERINE.
IT'S A BOGUS RATIONALIZATION FOR ALL THE TIMES YOU'VE KILLED, AND A ******** ALIBI WHEN YOU WANT TO ***MURDER AN INNOCENT GIRL!*** YOU'RE A HYPOCRITE, WOLVERINE. AND A STUBBORN BASTARD WHO NEEDS TO LEARN A FEW LESSONS OF HIS OWN.
YOU'RE RIGHT ABOUT ONE THING, ROGUE. I AIN'T GONNA BE ABLE TO BEAT YOU BY MYSELF...BUT I KNOW SOMEONE WHO CAN...
HUH...?
SMAK!

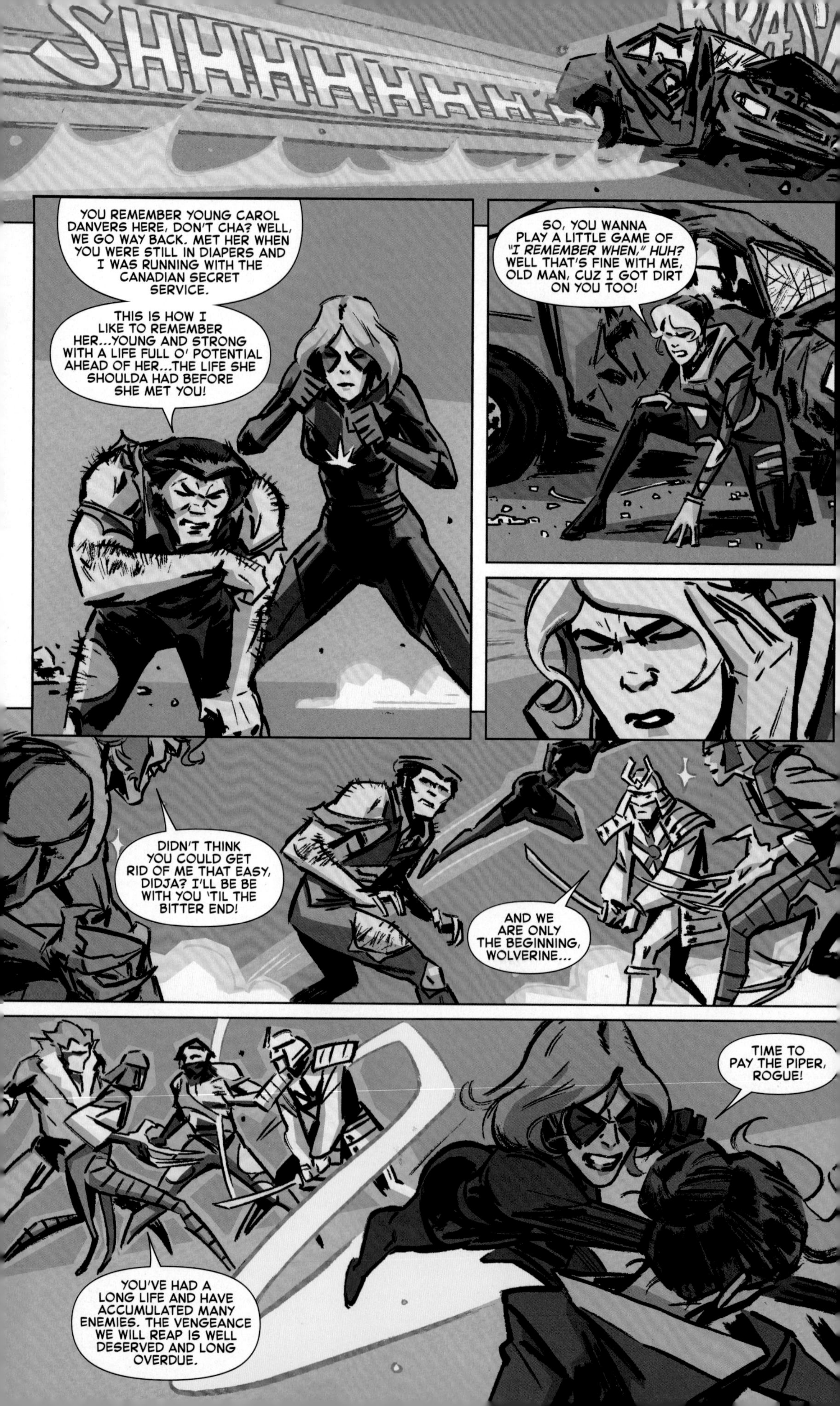
SHHHHHHHH
KRAY
YOU REMEMBER YOUNG CAROL DANVERS HERE, DON'T CHA? WELL, WE GO WAY BACK. MET HER WHEN YOU WERE STILL IN DIAPERS AND I WAS RUNNING WITH THE CANADIAN SECRET SERVICE.
THIS IS HOW I LIKE TO REMEMBER HER...YOUNG AND STRONG WITH A LIFE FULL O' POTENTIAL AHEAD OF HER...THE LIFE SHE SHOULDA HAD BEFORE SHE MET YOU!
SO, YOU WANNA PLAY A LITTLE GAME OF *"I REMEMBER WHEN,"* HUH? WELL THAT'S FINE WITH ME, OLD MAN, CUZ I GOT DIRT ON YOU TOO!
DIDN'T THINK YOU COULD GET RID OF ME THAT EASY, DIDJA? I'LL BE BE WITH YOU 'TIL THE BITTER END!
AND WE ARE ONLY THE BEGINNING, WOLVERINE...
TIME TO PAY THE PIPER, ROGUE!
YOU'VE HAD A LONG LIFE AND HAVE ACCUMULATED MANY ENEMIES. THE VENGEANCE WE WILL REAP IS WELL DESERVED AND LONG OVERDUE.

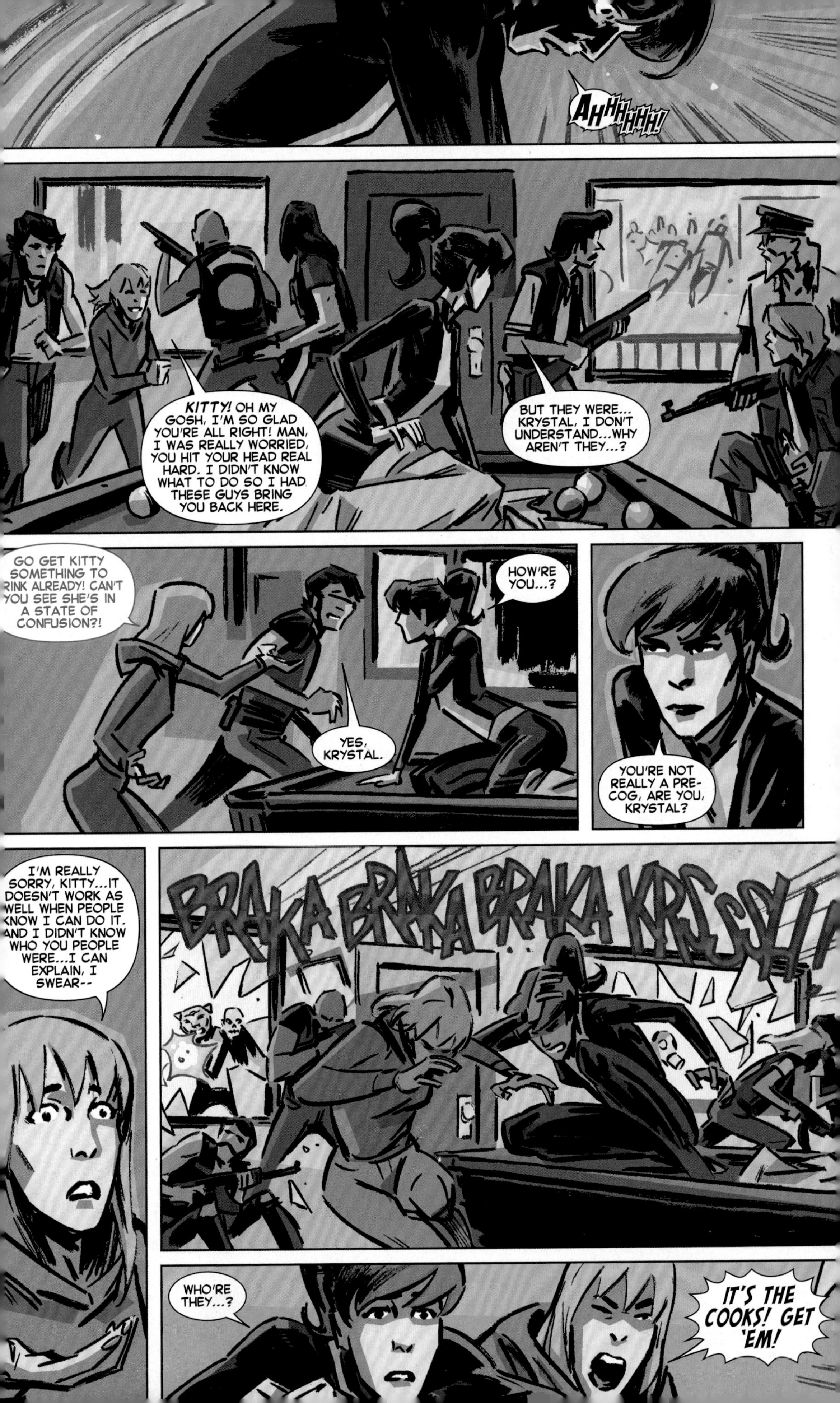
AHHHHHH!
KITTY! OH MY GOSH, I'M SO GLAD YOU'RE ALL RIGHT! MAN, I WAS REALLY WORRIED. YOU HIT YOUR HEAD REAL HARD. I DIDN'T KNOW WHAT TO DO SO I HAD THESE GUYS BRING YOU BACK HERE.
BUT THEY WERE... KRYSTAL, I DON'T UNDERSTAND...WHY AREN'T THEY...?
GO GET KITTY SOMETHING TO RINK ALREADY! CAN'T YOU SEE SHE'S IN A STATE OF CONFUSION?!
HOW'RE YOU...?
YES, KRYSTAL.
YOU'RE NOT REALLY A PRE-COG, ARE YOU, KRYSTAL?
I'M REALLY SORRY, KITTY...IT DOESN'T WORK AS WELL WHEN PEOPLE KNOW I CAN DO IT. AND I DIDN'T KNOW WHO YOU PEOPLE WERE...I CAN EXPLAIN, I SWEAR--
BRAKA BRAKA BRAKA KRSSSH
WHO'RE THEY...?
IT'S THE COOKS! GET 'EM!

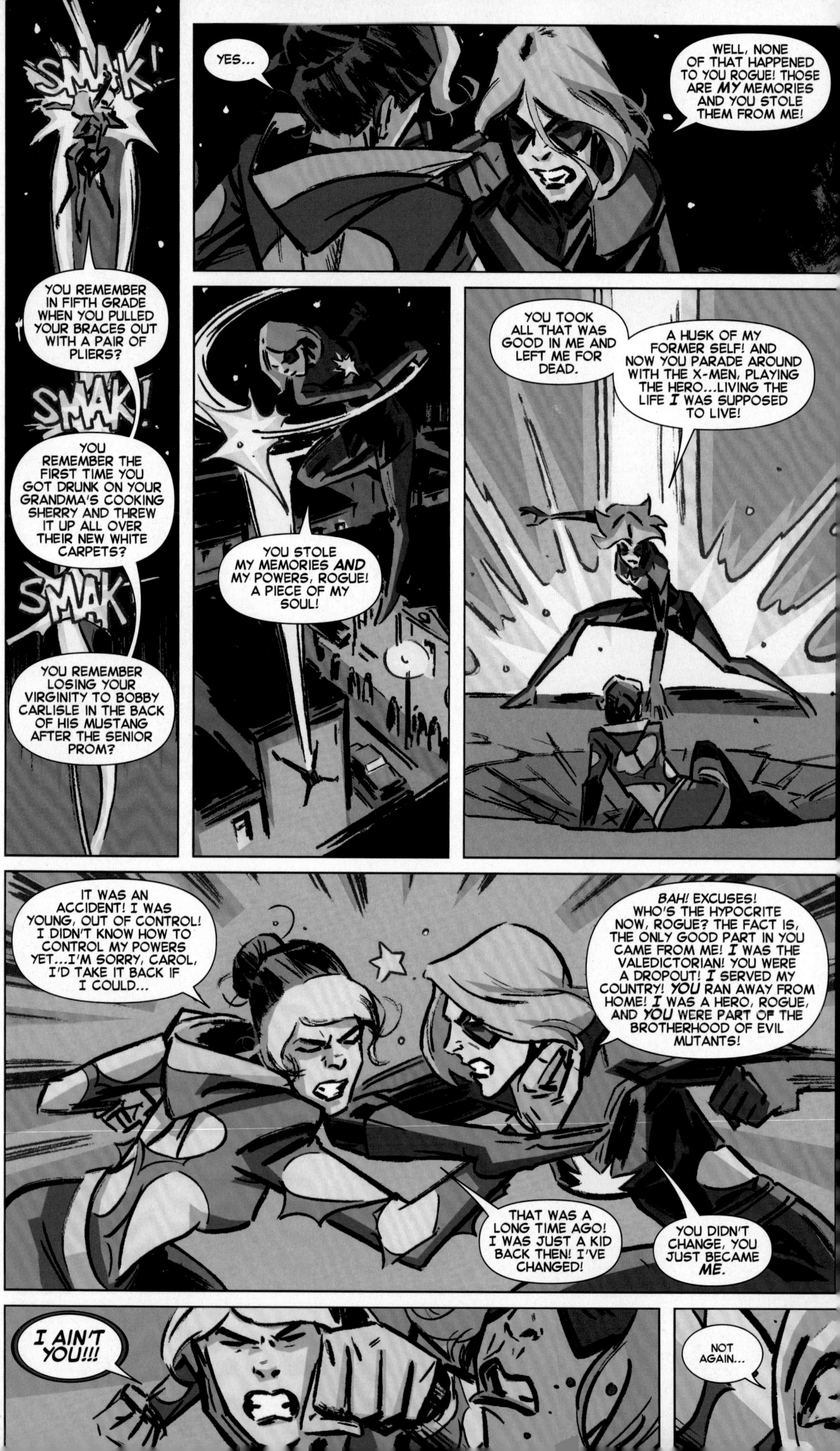
SMAK!
YES...
WELL, NONE OF THAT HAPPENED TO YOU ROGUE! THOSE ARE MY MEMORIES AND YOU STOLE THEM FROM ME!
YOU REMEMBER IN FIFTH GRADE WHEN YOU PULLED YOUR BRACES OUT WITH A PAIR OF PLIERS?
SMAK!
YOU REMEMBER THE FIRST TIME YOU GOT DRUNK ON YOUR GRANDMA'S COOKING SHERRY AND THREW IT UP ALL OVER THEIR NEW WHITE CARPETS?
SMAK
YOU REMEMBER LOSING YOUR VIRGINITY TO BOBBY CARLISLE IN THE BACK OF HIS MUSTANG AFTER THE SENIOR PROM?
YOU STOLE MY MEMORIES AND MY POWERS, ROGUE! A PIECE OF MY SOUL!
YOU TOOK ALL THAT WAS GOOD IN ME AND LEFT ME FOR DEAD.
A HUSK OF MY FORMER SELF! AND NOW YOU PARADE AROUND WITH THE X-MEN, PLAYING THE HERO...LIVING THE LIFE I WAS SUPPOSED TO LIVE!
IT WAS AN ACCIDENT! I WAS YOUNG, OUT OF CONTROL! I DIDN'T KNOW HOW TO CONTROL MY POWERS YET...I'M SORRY, CAROL, I'D TAKE IT BACK IF I COULD...
BAH! EXCUSES! WHO'S THE HYPOCRITE NOW, ROGUE? THE FACT IS, THE ONLY GOOD PART IN YOU CAME FROM ME! I WAS THE VALEDICTORIAN! YOU WERE A DROPOUT! I SERVED MY COUNTRY! YOU RAN AWAY FROM HOME! I WAS A HERO, ROGUE, AND YOU WERE PART OF THE BROTHERHOOD OF EVIL MUTANTS!
THAT WAS A LONG TIME AGO! I WAS JUST A KID BACK THEN! I'VE CHANGED!
YOU DIDN'T CHANGE, YOU JUST BECAME ME.
I AIN'T YOU!!!
NOT AGAIN...

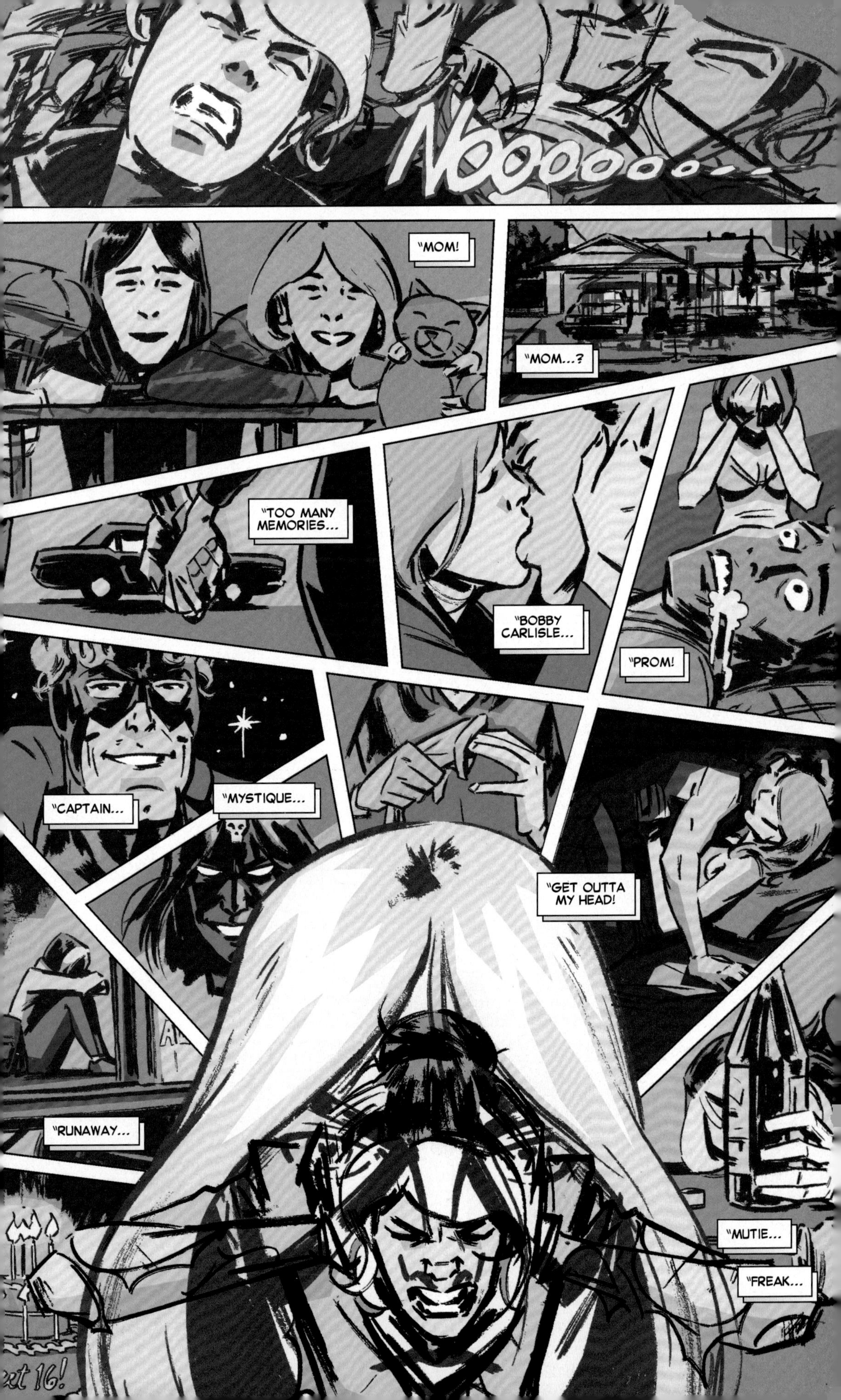
NOOOOOO...
"MOM!
"MOM...?
"TOO MANY MEMORIES...
"BOBBY CARLISLE...
"PROM!
"CAPTAIN...
"MYSTIQUE...
"GET OUTTA MY HEAD!
"RUNAWAY...
"MUTIE...
"FREAK...

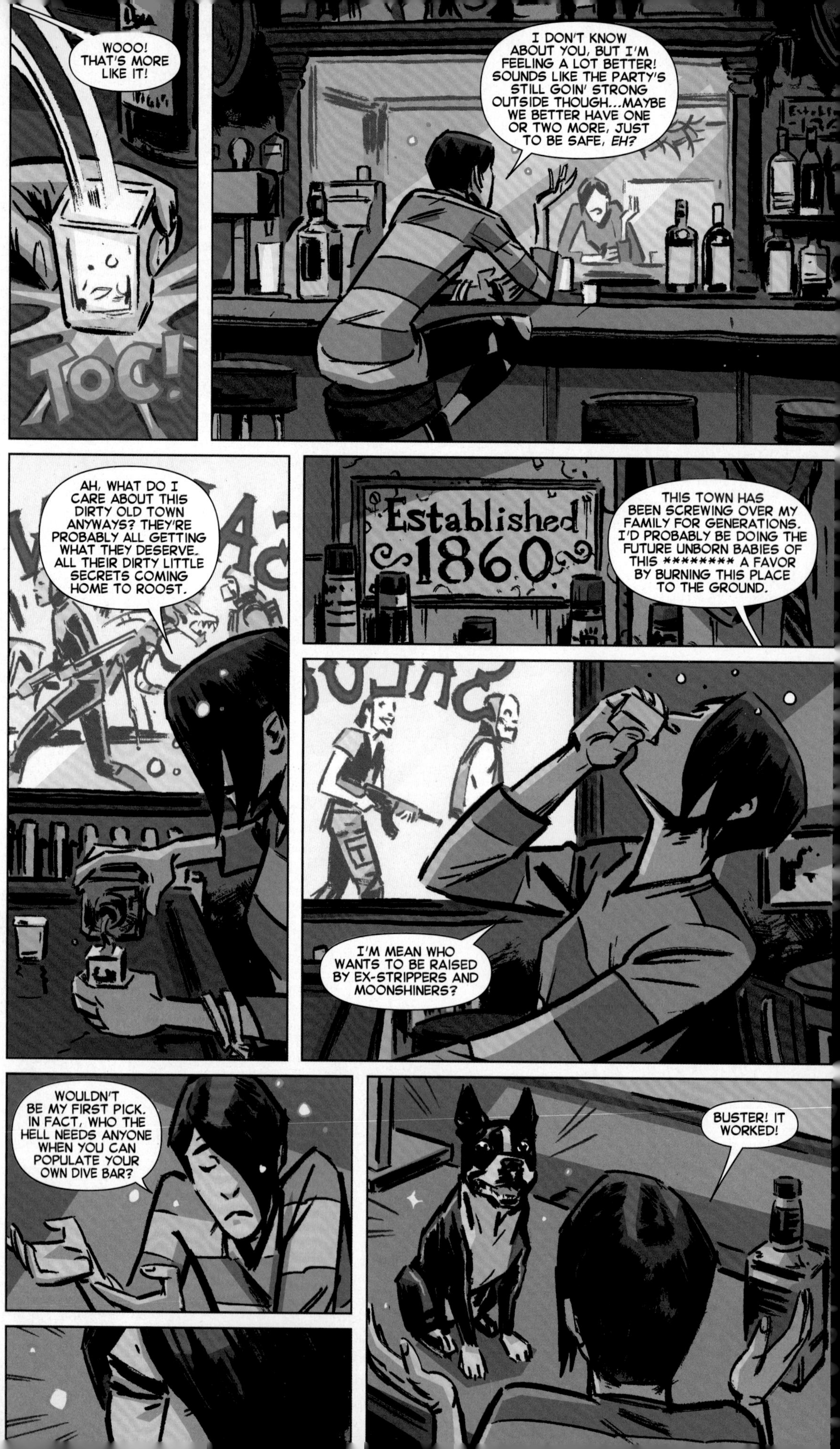
WOOO! THAT'S MORE LIKE IT!
TOC!
I DON'T KNOW ABOUT YOU, BUT I'M FEELING A LOT BETTER! SOUNDS LIKE THE PARTY'S STILL GOIN' STRONG OUTSIDE THOUGH...MAYBE WE BETTER HAVE ONE OR TWO MORE, JUST TO BE SAFE, EH?
AH, WHAT DO I CARE ABOUT THIS DIRTY OLD TOWN ANYWAYS? THEY'RE PROBABLY ALL GETTING WHAT THEY DESERVE. ALL THEIR DIRTY LITTLE SECRETS COMING HOME TO ROOST.
Established 1860
THIS TOWN HAS BEEN SCREWING OVER MY FAMILY FOR GENERATIONS. I'D PROBABLY BE DOING THE FUTURE UNBORN BABIES OF THIS ******** A FAVOR BY BURNING THIS PLACE TO THE GROUND.
I'M MEAN WHO WANTS TO BE RAISED BY EX-STRIPPERS AND MOONSHINERS?
WOULDN'T BE MY FIRST PICK. IN FACT, WHO THE HELL NEEDS ANYONE WHEN YOU CAN POPULATE YOUR OWN DIVE BAR?
BUSTER! IT WORKED!

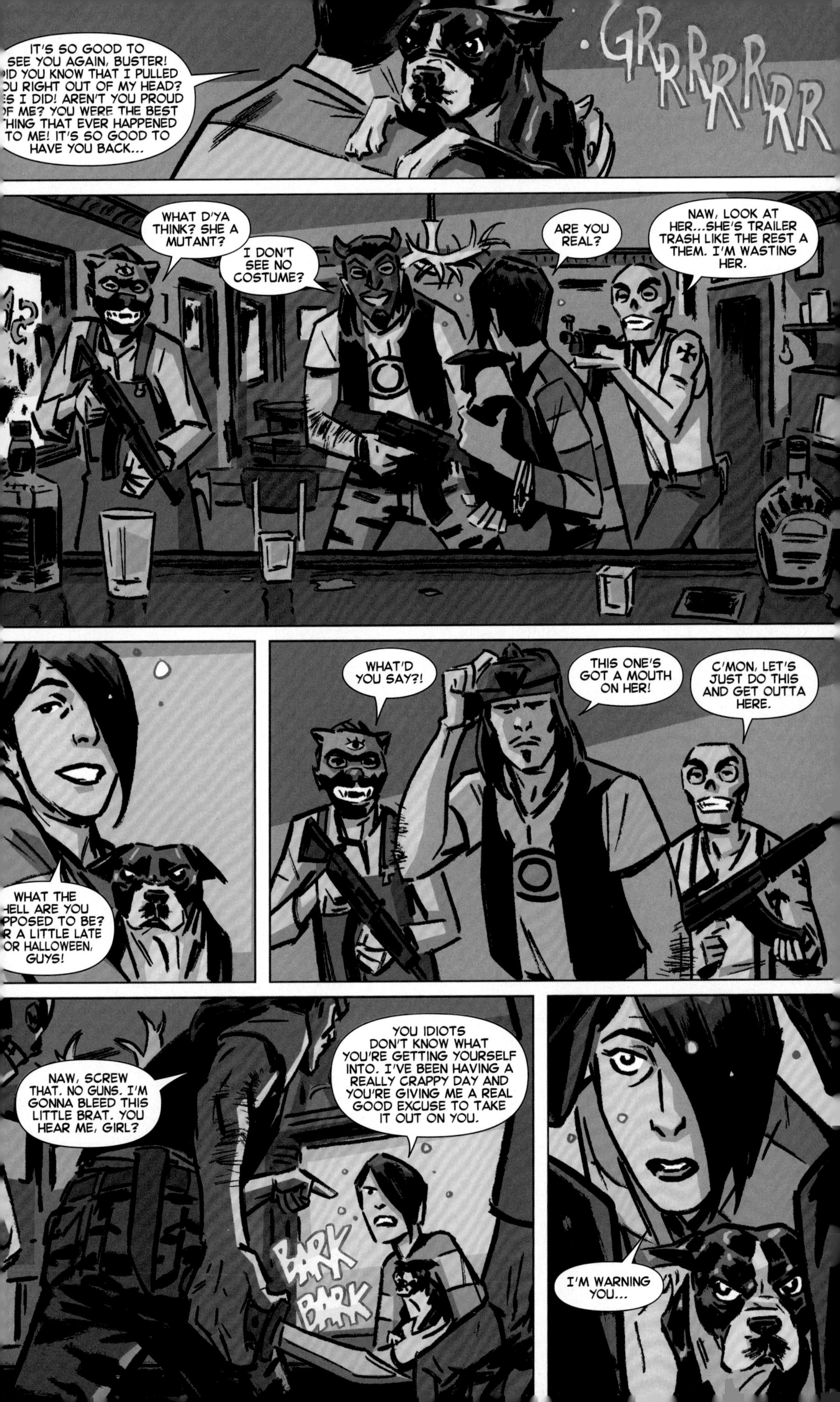

IT'S SO GOOD TO SEE YOU AGAIN, BUSTER! ID YOU KNOW THAT I PULLED OU RIGHT OUT OF MY HEAD? ES I DID! AREN'T YOU PROUD F ME? YOU WERE THE BEST HING THAT EVER HAPPENED TO ME! IT'S SO GOOD TO HAVE YOU BACK...
GRRRRRRRR
WHAT D'YA THINK? SHE A MUTANT?
I DON'T SEE NO COSTUME?
ARE YOU REAL?
NAW, LOOK AT HER...SHE'S TRAILER TRASH LIKE THE REST A THEM. I'M WASTING HER.
WHAT THE HELL ARE YOU PPOSED TO BE? R A LITTLE LATE OR HALLOWEEN, GUYS!
WHAT'D YOU SAY?!
THIS ONE'S GOT A MOUTH ON HER!
C'MON, LET'S JUST DO THIS AND GET OUTTA HERE.
NAW, SCREW THAT. NO GUNS. I'M GONNA BLEED THIS LITTLE BRAT. YOU HEAR ME, GIRL?
YOU IDIOTS DON'T KNOW WHAT YOU'RE GETTING YOURSELF INTO. I'VE BEEN HAVING A REALLY CRAPPY DAY AND YOU'RE GIVING ME A REAL GOOD EXCUSE TO TAKE IT OUT ON YOU.
BARK BARK
I'M WARNING YOU...

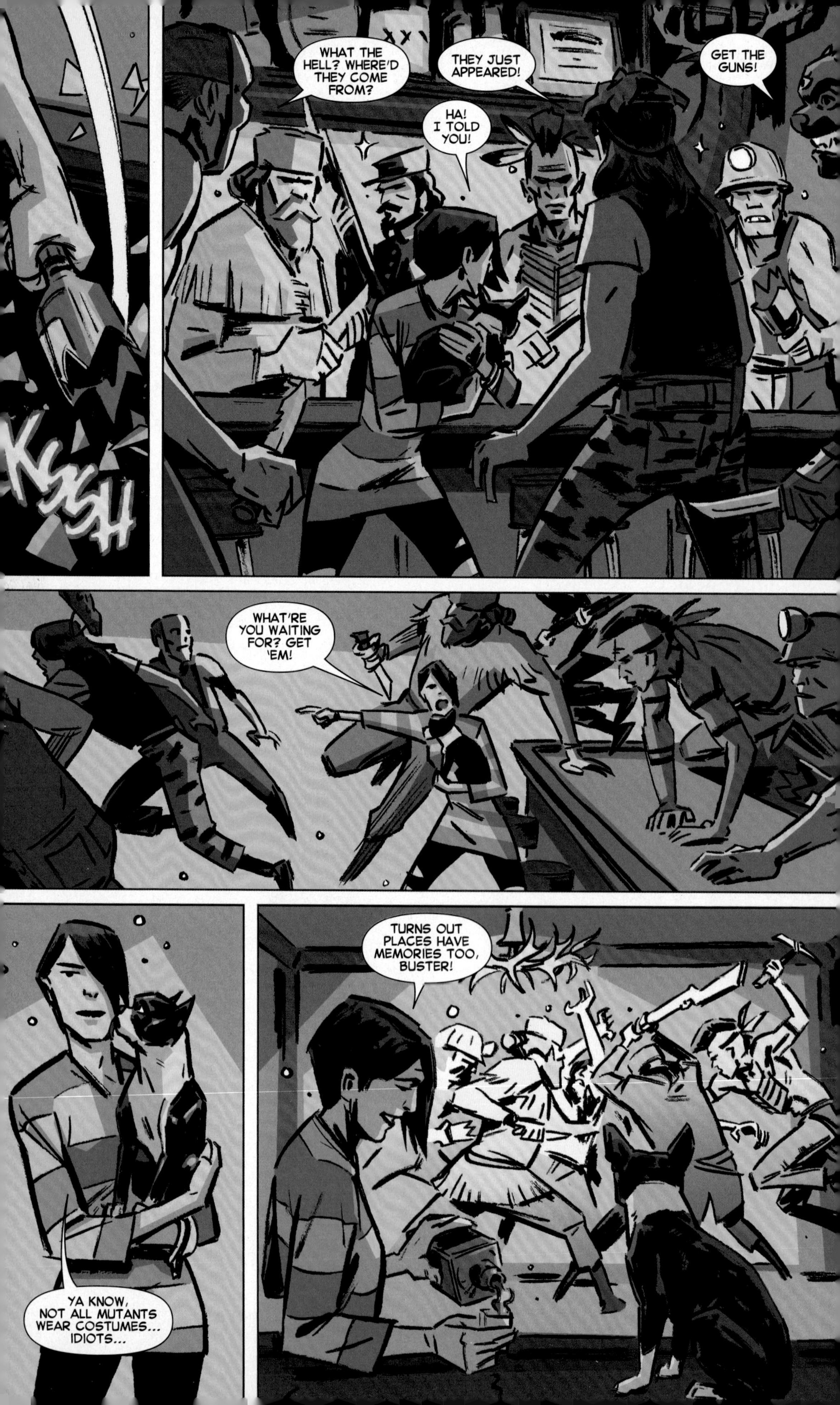
KSSH
WHAT THE HELL? WHERE'D THEY COME FROM?
THEY JUST APPEARED!
HA! I TOLD YOU!
GET THE GUNS!
WHAT'RE YOU WAITING FOR? GET 'EM!
YA KNOW, NOT ALL MUTANTS WEAR COSTUMES... IDIOTS...
TURNS OUT PLACES HAVE MEMORIES TOO, BUSTER!

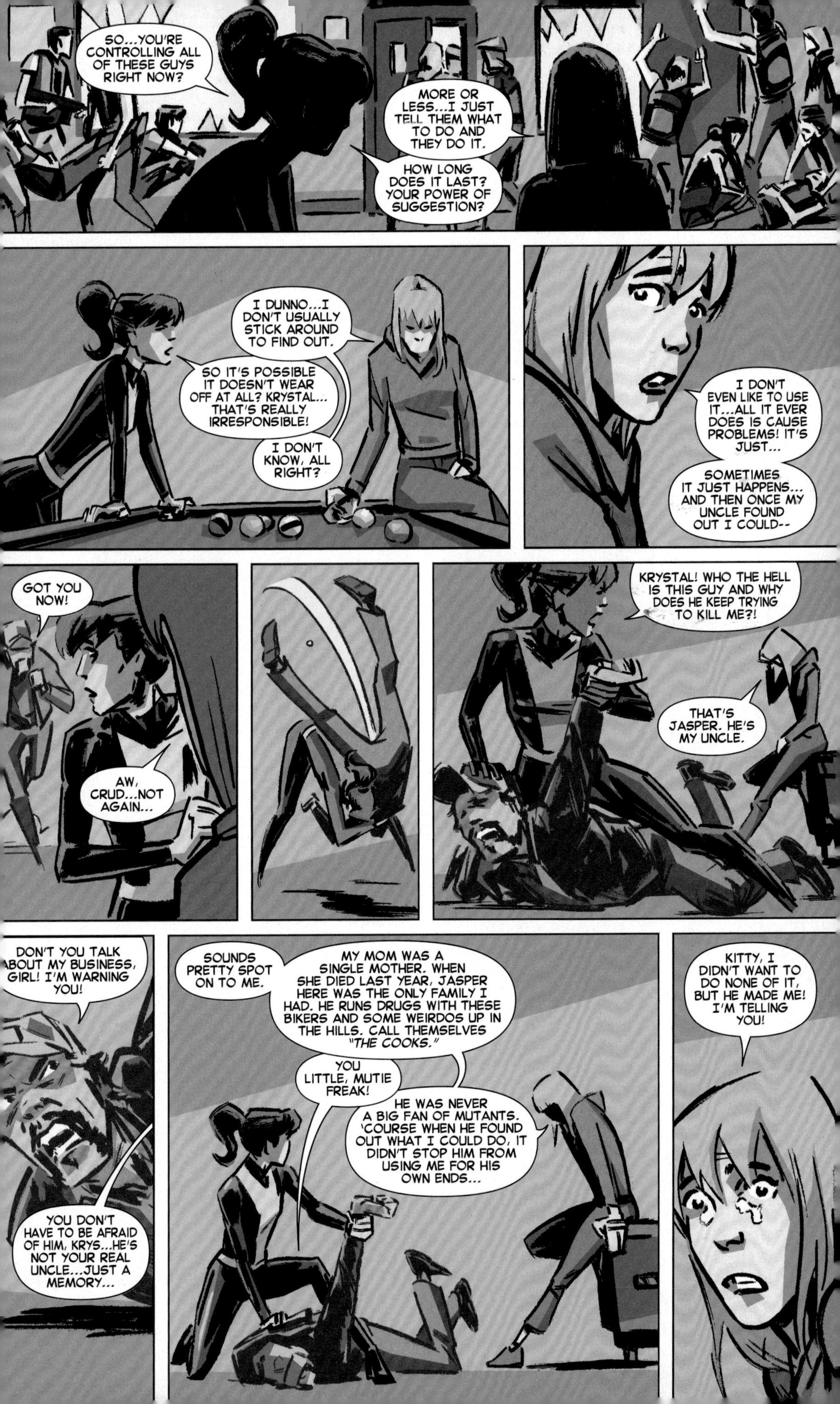

SO...YOU'RE CONTROLLING ALL OF THESE GUYS RIGHT NOW?
MORE OR LESS...I JUST TELL THEM WHAT TO DO AND THEY DO IT.
HOW LONG DOES IT LAST? YOUR POWER OF SUGGESTION?
I DUNNO...I DON'T USUALLY STICK AROUND TO FIND OUT.
SO IT'S POSSIBLE IT DOESN'T WEAR OFF AT ALL? KRYSTAL... THAT'S REALLY IRRESPONSIBLE!
I DON'T KNOW, ALL RIGHT?
I DON'T EVEN LIKE TO USE IT...ALL IT EVER DOES IS CAUSE PROBLEMS! IT'S JUST...
SOMETIMES IT JUST HAPPENS... AND THEN ONCE MY UNCLE FOUND OUT I COULD--
GOT YOU NOW!
AW, CRUD...NOT AGAIN...
KRYSTAL! WHO THE HELL IS THIS GUY AND WHY DOES HE KEEP TRYING TO KILL ME?!
THAT'S JASPER. HE'S MY UNCLE.
DON'T YOU TALK ABOUT MY BUSINESS, GIRL! I'M WARNING YOU!
YOU DON'T HAVE TO BE AFRAID OF HIM, KRYS...HE'S NOT YOUR REAL UNCLE...JUST A MEMORY...
SOUNDS PRETTY SPOT ON TO ME.
MY MOM WAS A SINGLE MOTHER. WHEN SHE DIED LAST YEAR, JASPER HERE WAS THE ONLY FAMILY I HAD. HE RUNS DRUGS WITH THESE BIKERS AND SOME WEIRDOS UP IN THE HILLS. CALL THEMSELVES "THE COOKS."
YOU LITTLE, MUTIE FREAK!
HE WAS NEVER A BIG FAN OF MUTANTS. 'COURSE WHEN HE FOUND OUT WHAT I COULD DO, IT DIDN'T STOP HIM FROM USING ME FOR HIS OWN ENDS...
KITTY, I DIDN'T WANT TO DO NONE OF IT, BUT HE MADE ME! I'M TELLING YOU!

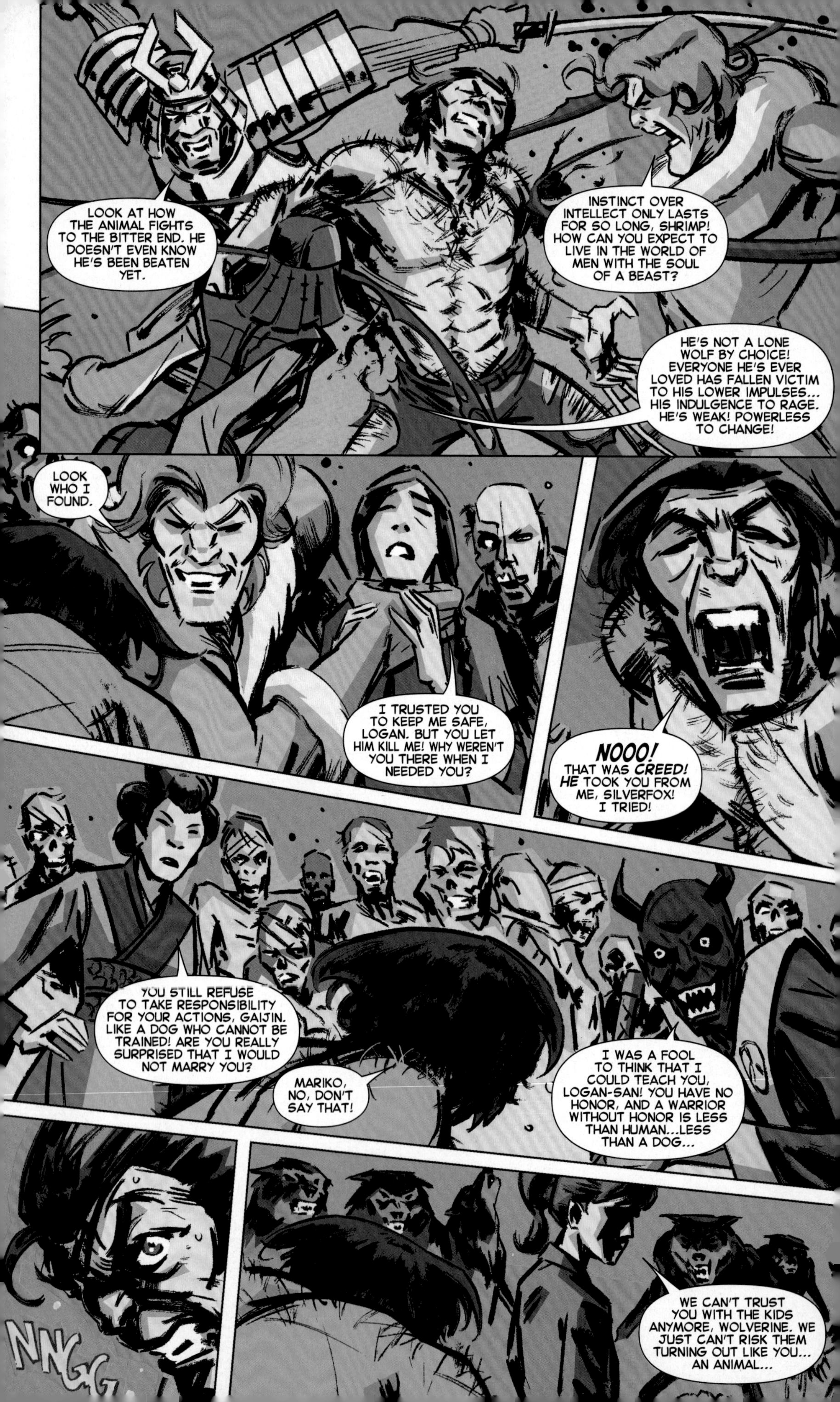

LOOK AT HOW THE ANIMAL FIGHTS TO THE BITTER END. HE DOESN'T EVEN KNOW HE'S BEEN BEATEN YET.
INSTINCT OVER INTELLECT ONLY LASTS FOR SO LONG, SHRIMP! HOW CAN YOU EXPECT TO LIVE IN THE WORLD OF MEN WITH THE SOUL OF A BEAST?
HE'S NOT A LONE WOLF BY CHOICE! EVERYONE HE'S EVER LOVED HAS FALLEN VICTIM TO HIS LOWER IMPULSES... HIS INDULGENCE TO RAGE. HE'S WEAK! POWERLESS TO CHANGE!
LOOK WHO I FOUND.
I TRUSTED YOU TO KEEP ME SAFE, LOGAN. BUT YOU LET HIM KILL ME! WHY WEREN'T YOU THERE WHEN I NEEDED YOU?
NOOO! THAT WAS CREED! HE TOOK YOU FROM ME, SILVERFOX! I TRIED!
YOU STILL REFUSE TO TAKE RESPONSIBILITY FOR YOUR ACTIONS, GAIJIN. LIKE A DOG WHO CANNOT BE TRAINED! ARE YOU REALLY SURPRISED THAT I WOULD NOT MARRY YOU?
MARIKO, NO, DON'T SAY THAT!
I WAS A FOOL TO THINK THAT I COULD TEACH YOU, LOGAN-SAN! YOU HAVE NO HONOR, AND A WARRIOR WITHOUT HONOR IS LESS THAN HUMAN...LESS THAN A DOG...
NNGG
WE CAN'T TRUST YOU WITH THE KIDS ANYMORE, WOLVERINE. WE JUST CAN'T RISK THEM TURNING OUT LIKE YOU... AN ANIMAL...

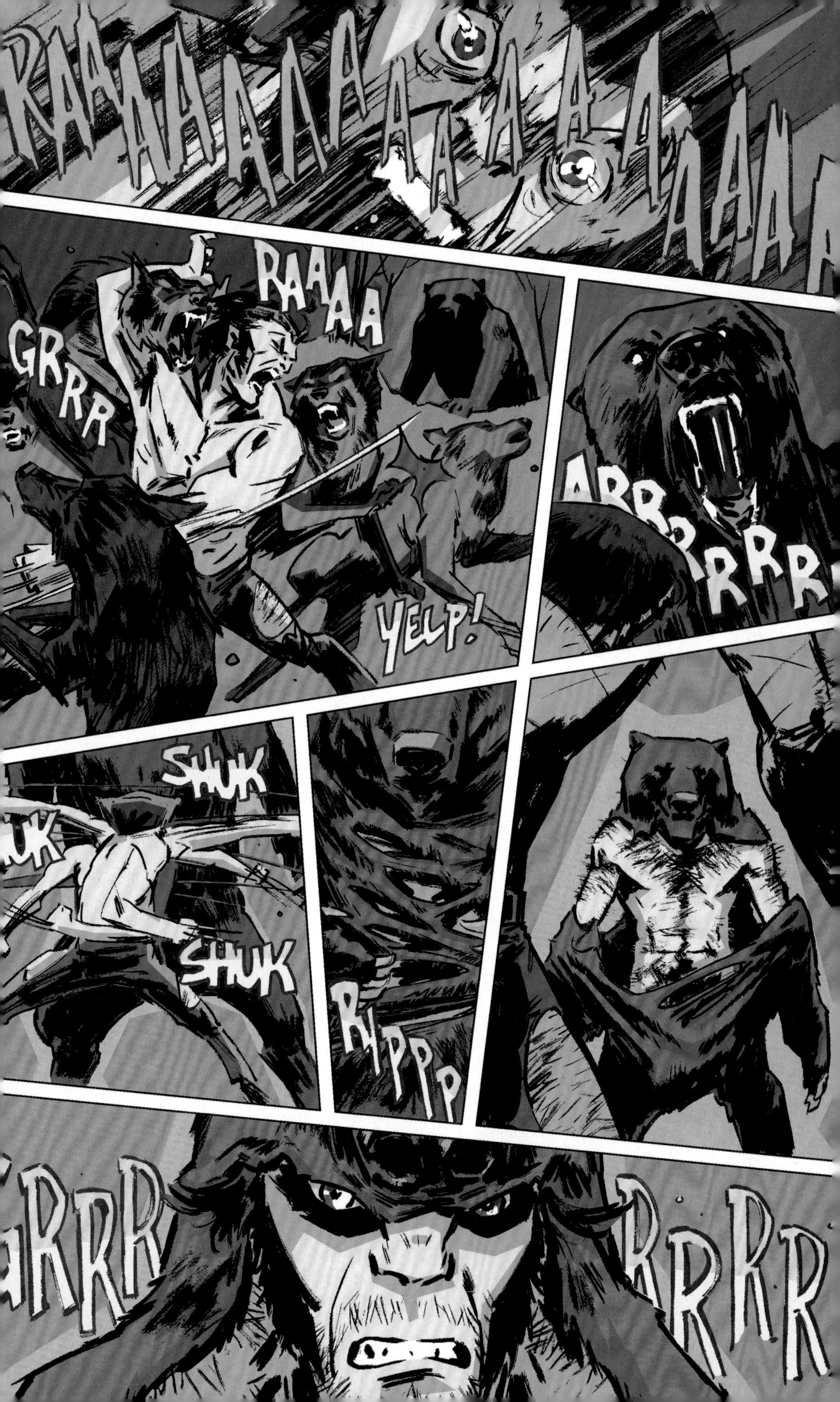
RAAAAAAAAAAAAAAA
GRRRR
RAAAAA
YELP!
ARRRRRRR
SHUK
HUK
SHUK
RIPPPP
RRRR
RRRRR

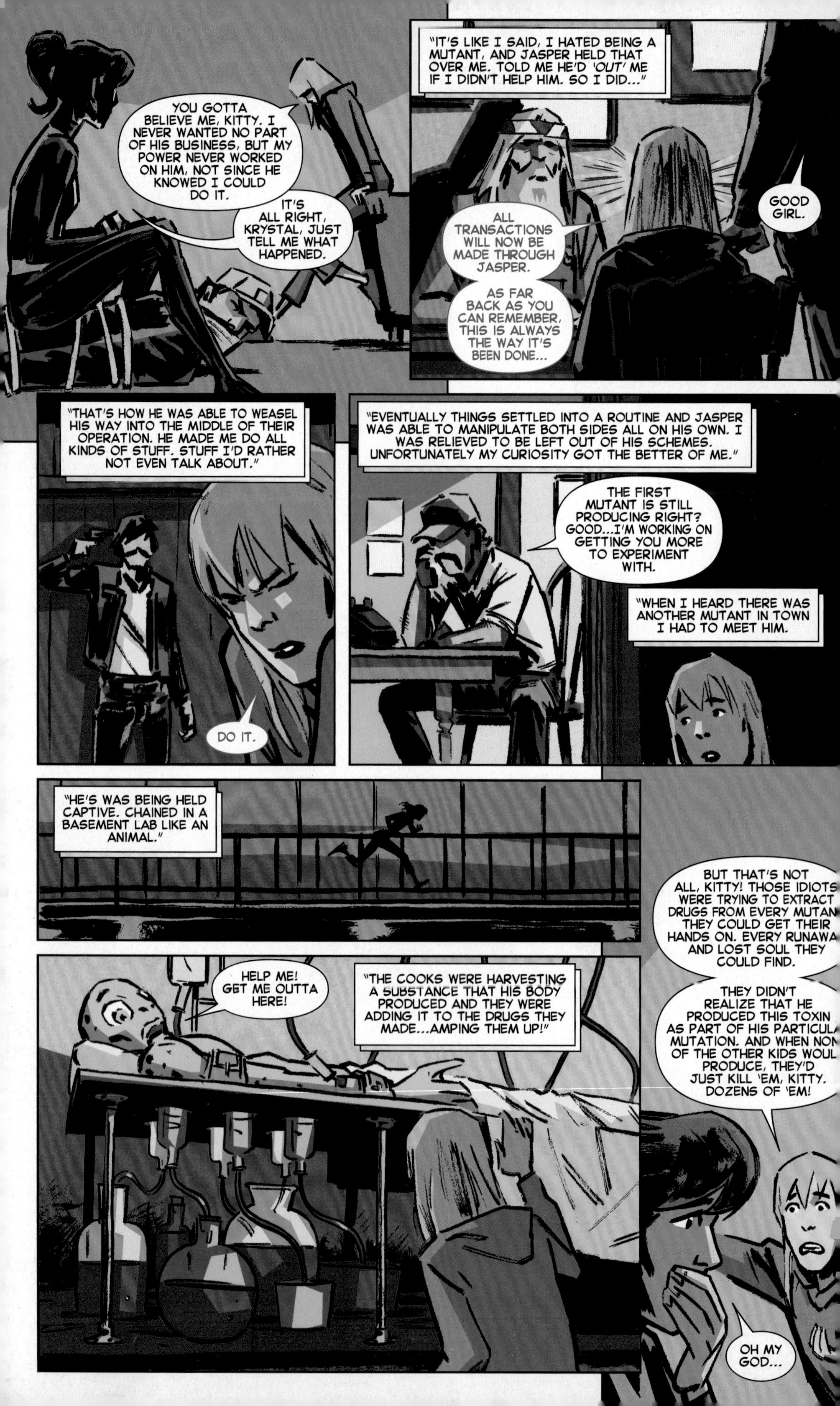
YOU GOTTA BELIEVE ME, KITTY. I NEVER WANTED NO PART OF HIS BUSINESS, BUT MY POWER NEVER WORKED ON HIM, NOT SINCE HE KNOWED I COULD DO IT.
IT'S ALL RIGHT, KRYSTAL, JUST TELL ME WHAT HAPPENED.
"IT'S LIKE I SAID, I HATED BEING A MUTANT, AND JASPER HELD THAT OVER ME. TOLD ME HE'D 'OUT' ME IF I DIDN'T HELP HIM. SO I DID..."
ALL TRANSACTIONS WILL NOW BE MADE THROUGH JASPER.
AS FAR BACK AS YOU CAN REMEMBER, THIS IS ALWAYS THE WAY IT'S BEEN DONE...
GOOD GIRL.
"THAT'S HOW HE WAS ABLE TO WEASEL HIS WAY INTO THE MIDDLE OF THEIR OPERATION. HE MADE ME DO ALL KINDS OF STUFF. STUFF I'D RATHER NOT EVEN TALK ABOUT."
DO IT.
"EVENTUALLY THINGS SETTLED INTO A ROUTINE AND JASPER WAS ABLE TO MANIPULATE BOTH SIDES ALL ON HIS OWN. I WAS RELIEVED TO BE LEFT OUT OF HIS SCHEMES. UNFORTUNATELY MY CURIOSITY GOT THE BETTER OF ME."
THE FIRST MUTANT IS STILL PRODUCING RIGHT? GOOD...I'M WORKING ON GETTING YOU MORE TO EXPERIMENT WITH.
"WHEN I HEARD THERE WAS ANOTHER MUTANT IN TOWN I HAD TO MEET HIM.
"HE'S WAS BEING HELD CAPTIVE. CHAINED IN A BASEMENT LAB LIKE AN ANIMAL."
HELP ME! GET ME OUTTA HERE!
"THE COOKS WERE HARVESTING A SUBSTANCE THAT HIS BODY PRODUCED AND THEY WERE ADDING IT TO THE DRUGS THEY MADE...AMPING THEM UP!"
BUT THAT'S NOT ALL, KITTY! THOSE IDIOTS WERE TRYING TO EXTRACT DRUGS FROM EVERY MUTAN THEY COULD GET THEIR HANDS ON. EVERY RUNAWA AND LOST SOUL THEY COULD FIND.
THEY DIDN'T REALIZE THAT HE PRODUCED THIS TOXIN AS PART OF HIS PARTICUL MUTATION. AND WHEN NON OF THE OTHER KIDS WOUL PRODUCE, THEY'D JUST KILL 'EM, KITTY. DOZENS OF 'EM!
OH MY GOD...

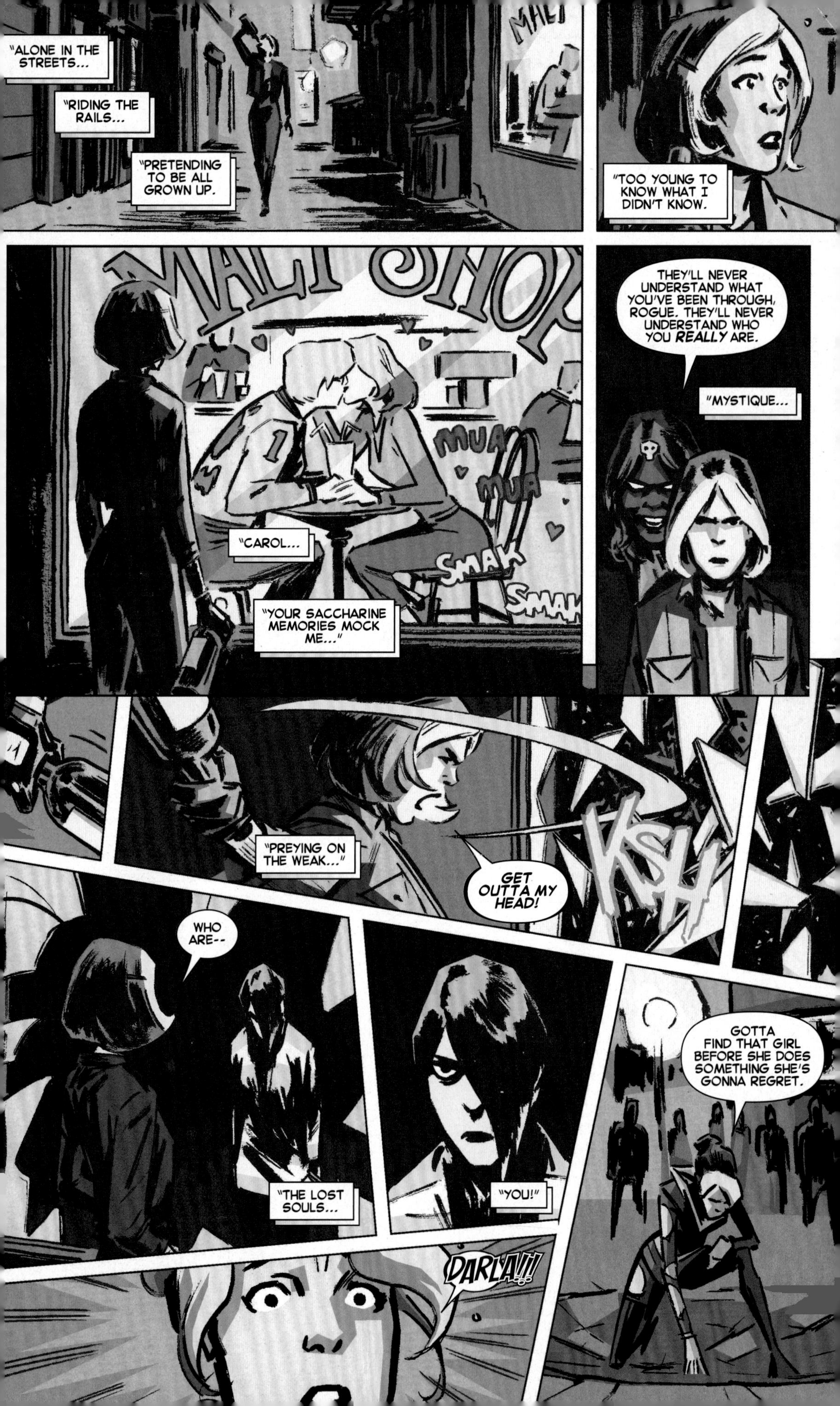

"ALONE IN THE STREETS...
"RIDING THE RAILS...
"PRETENDING TO BE ALL GROWN UP.
"TOO YOUNG TO KNOW WHAT I DIDN'T KNOW.
MALT SHOP
MUA
MUA
"CAROL...
SMAK
SMAK
"YOUR SACCHARINE MEMORIES MOCK ME..."
THEY'LL NEVER UNDERSTAND WHAT YOU'VE BEEN THROUGH, ROGUE. THEY'LL NEVER UNDERSTAND WHO YOU *REALLY* ARE.
"MYSTIQUE...
"PREYING ON THE WEAK..."
GET OUTTA MY HEAD!
KSH
WHO ARE--
"THE LOST SOULS...
"YOU!"
GOTTA FIND THAT GIRL BEFORE SHE DOES SOMETHING SHE'S GONNA REGRET.
DARLA!!!

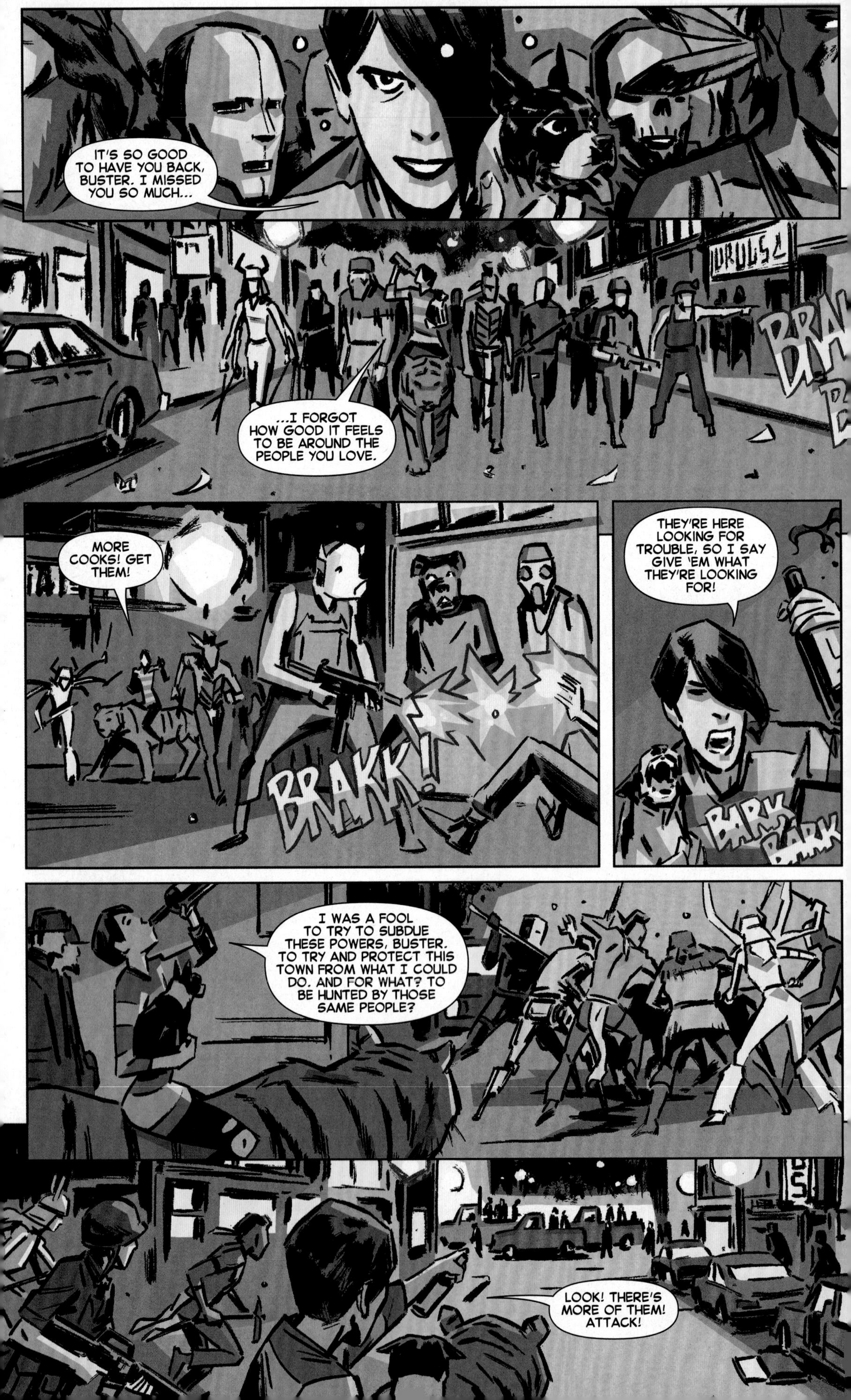
IT'S SO GOOD TO HAVE YOU BACK, BUSTER. I MISSED YOU SO MUCH...
...I FORGOT HOW GOOD IT FEELS TO BE AROUND THE PEOPLE YOU LOVE.
MORE COOKS! GET THEM!
BRAKK!
THEY'RE HERE LOOKING FOR TROUBLE, SO I SAY GIVE 'EM WHAT THEY'RE LOOKING FOR!
BARK BARK
I WAS A FOOL TO TRY TO SUBDUE THESE POWERS, BUSTER. TO TRY AND PROTECT THIS TOWN FROM WHAT I COULD DO. AND FOR WHAT? TO BE HUNTED BY THOSE SAME PEOPLE?
LOOK! THERE'S MORE OF THEM! ATTACK!

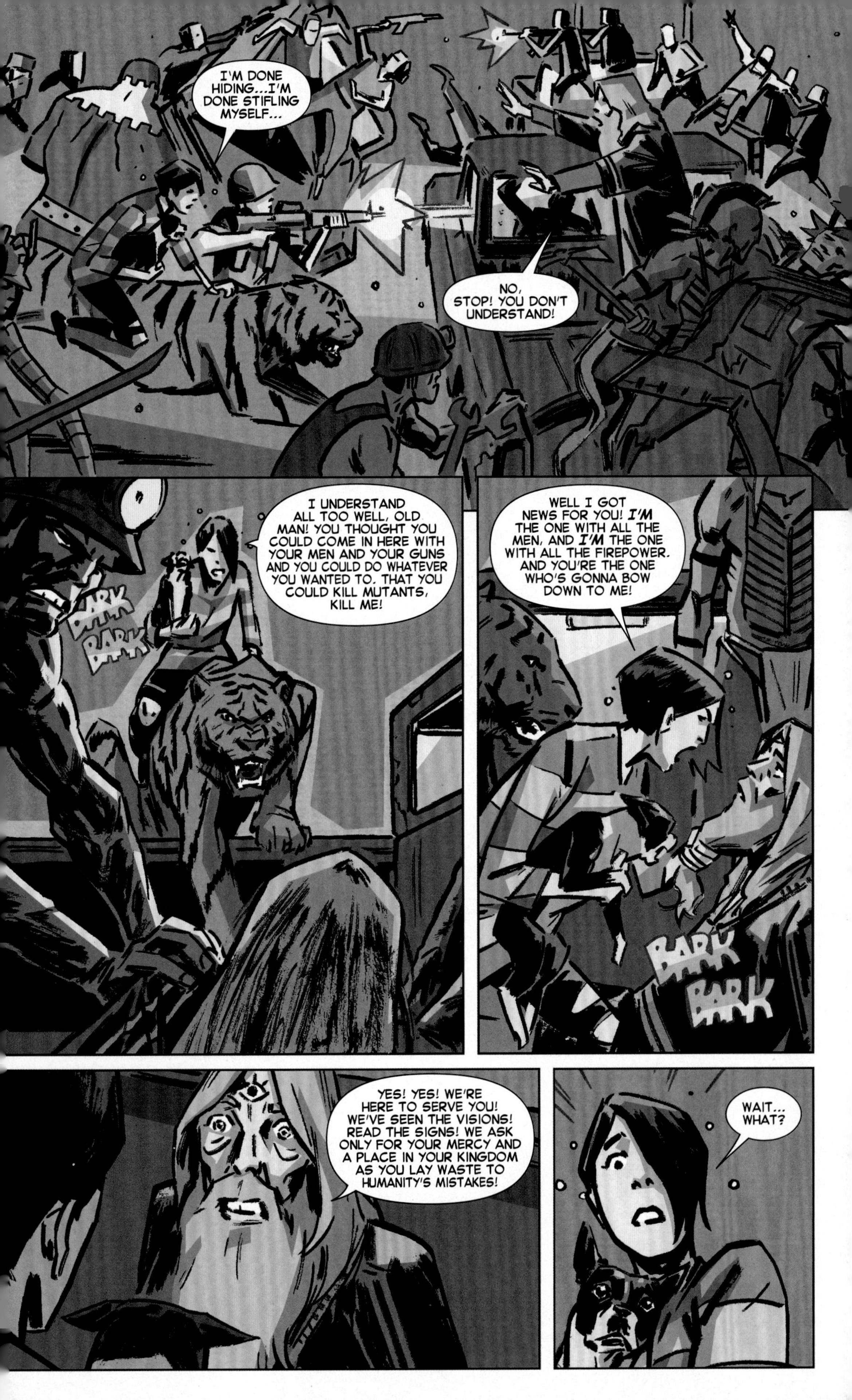

I'M DONE HIDING...I'M DONE STIFLING MYSELF...
NO, STOP! YOU DON'T UNDERSTAND!
I UNDERSTAND ALL TOO WELL, OLD MAN! YOU THOUGHT YOU COULD COME IN HERE WITH YOUR MEN AND YOUR GUNS AND YOU COULD DO WHATEVER YOU WANTED TO. THAT YOU COULD KILL MUTANTS, KILL ME!
BARK BARK BARK
WELL I GOT NEWS FOR YOU! I'M THE ONE WITH ALL THE MEN, AND I'M THE ONE WITH ALL THE FIREPOWER. AND YOU'RE THE ONE WHO'S GONNA BOW DOWN TO ME!
BARK BARK
YES! YES! WE'RE HERE TO SERVE YOU! WE'VE SEEN THE VISIONS! READ THE SIGNS! WE ASK ONLY FOR YOUR MERCY AND A PLACE IN YOUR KINGDOM AS YOU LAY WASTE TO HUMANITY'S MISTAKES!
WAIT... WHAT?

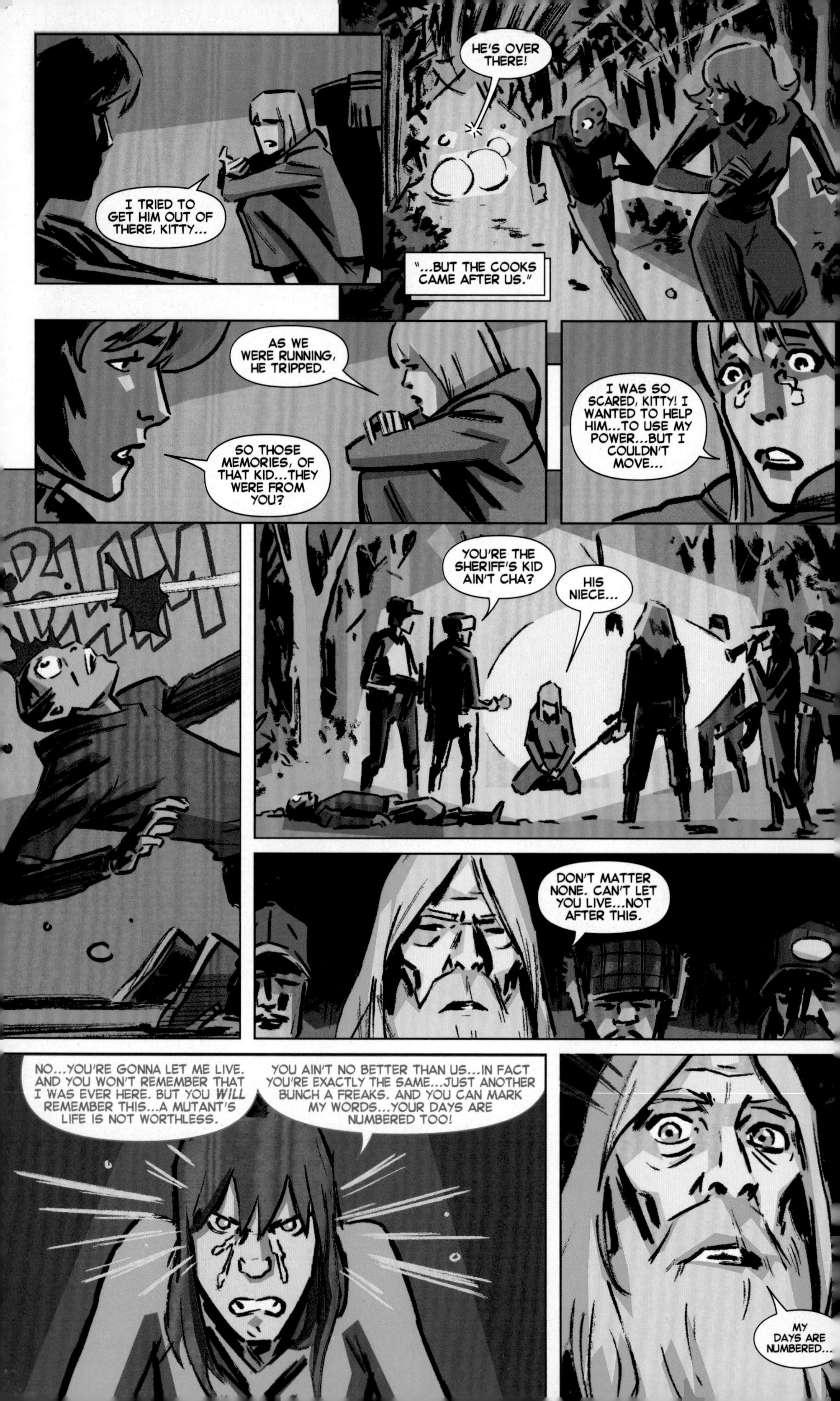
I TRIED TO GET HIM OUT OF THERE, KITTY...
HE'S OVER THERE!
"...BUT THE COOKS CAME AFTER US."
AS WE WERE RUNNING, HE TRIPPED.
SO THOSE MEMORIES, OF THAT KID...THEY WERE FROM YOU?
I WAS SO SCARED, KITTY! I WANTED TO HELP HIM...TO USE MY POWER...BUT I COULDN'T MOVE...
BLAM
YOU'RE THE SHERIFF'S KID AIN'T CHA?
HIS NIECE...
DON'T MATTER NONE. CAN'T LET YOU LIVE...NOT AFTER THIS.
NO...YOU'RE GONNA LET ME LIVE. AND YOU WON'T REMEMBER THAT I WAS EVER HERE. BUT YOU WILL REMEMBER THIS...A MUTANT'S LIFE IS NOT WORTHLESS.
YOU AIN'T NO BETTER THAN US...IN FACT YOU'RE EXACTLY THE SAME...JUST ANOTHER BUNCH A FREAKS. AND YOU CAN MARK MY WORDS...YOUR DAYS ARE NUMBERED TOO!
MY DAYS ARE NUMBERED...

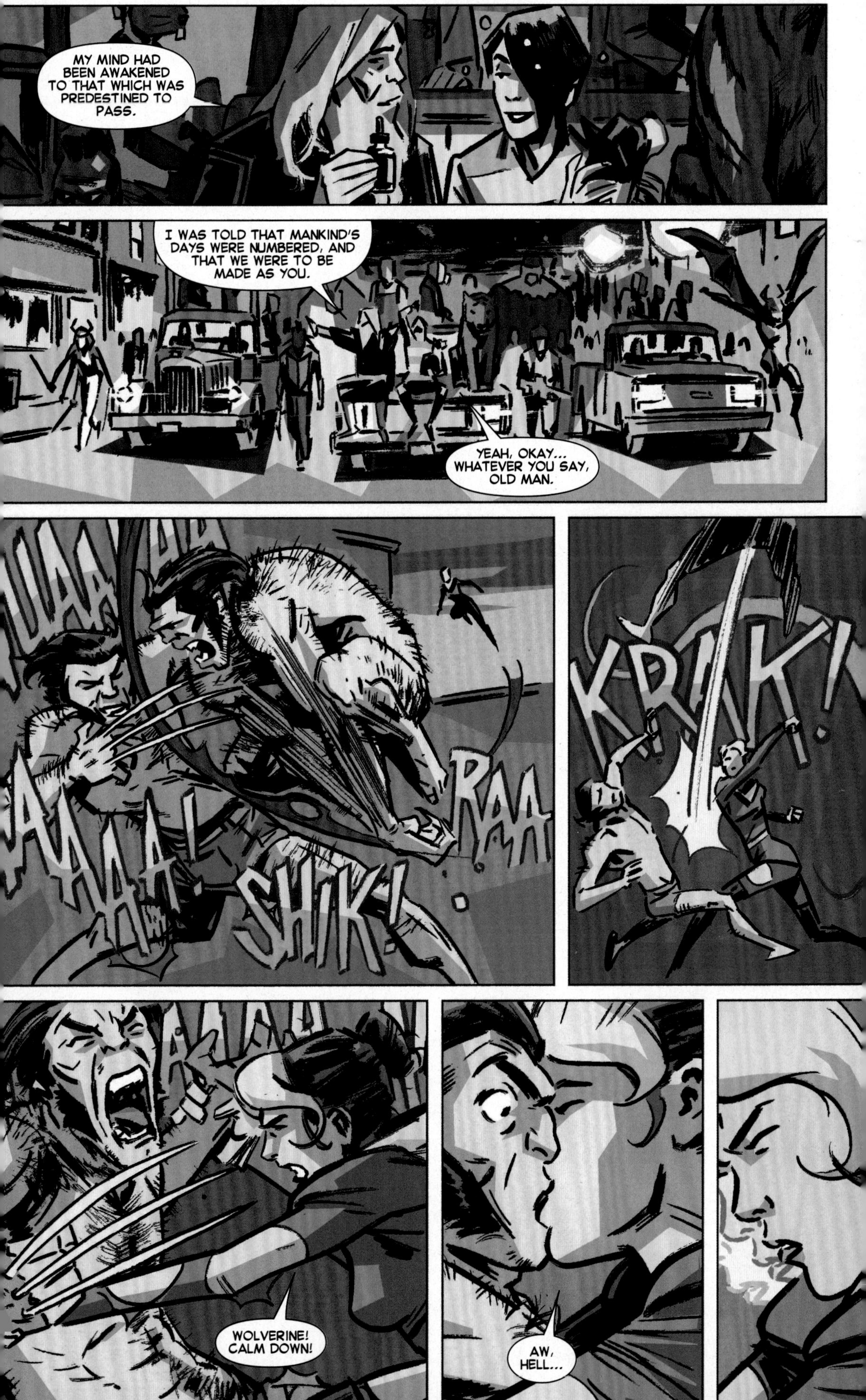
MY MIND HAD BEEN AWAKENED TO THAT WHICH WAS PREDESTINED TO PASS.
I WAS TOLD THAT MANKIND'S DAYS WERE NUMBERED, AND THAT WE WERE TO BE MADE AS YOU.
YEAH, OKAY... WHATEVER YOU SAY, OLD MAN.
RAA
SHIK!
KRAK!
WOLVERINE! CALM DOWN!
AW, HELL...

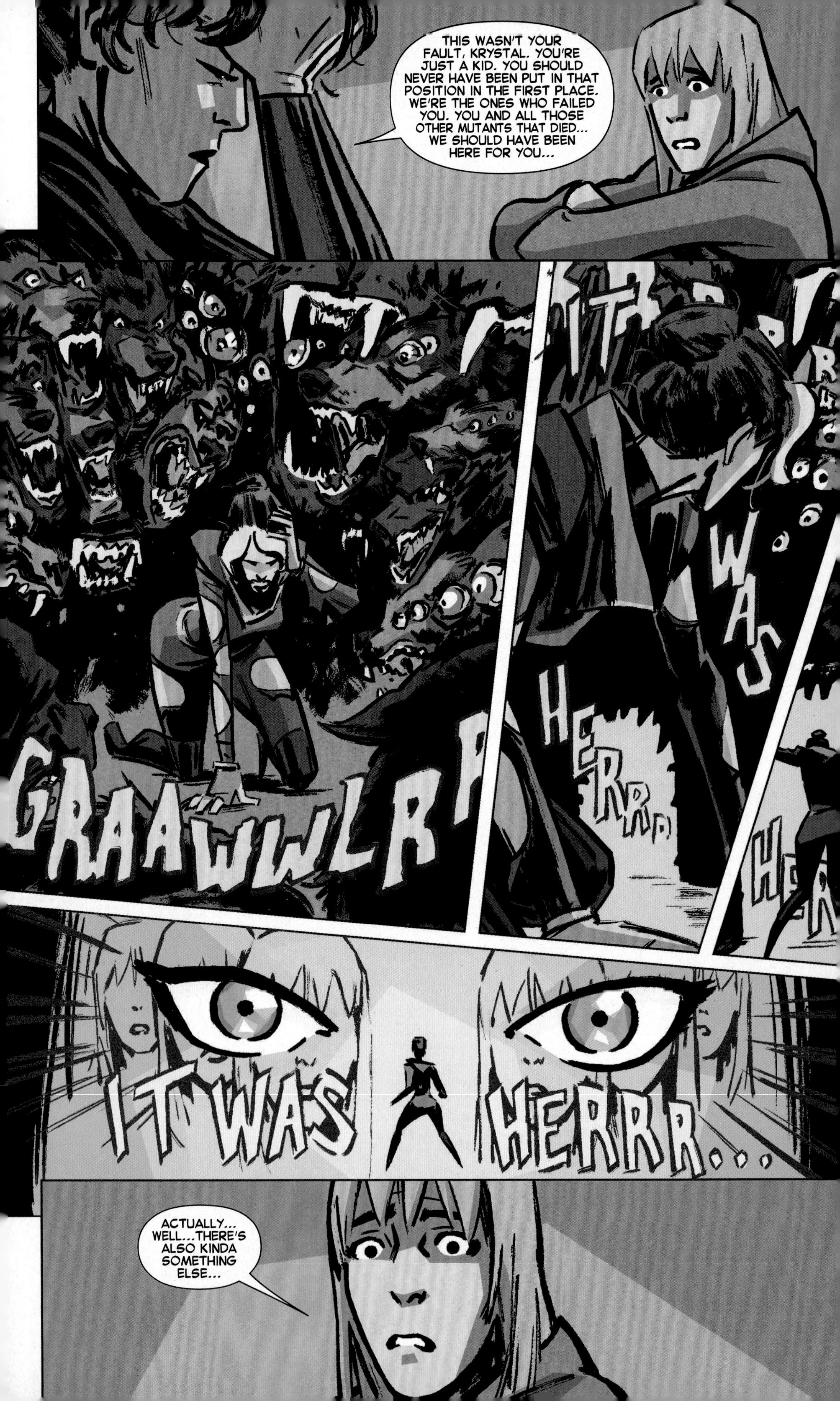

THIS WASN'T YOUR FAULT, KRYSTAL. YOU'RE JUST A KID. YOU SHOULD NEVER HAVE BEEN PUT IN THAT POSITION IN THE FIRST PLACE. WE'RE THE ONES WHO FAILED YOU. YOU AND ALL THOSE OTHER MUTANTS THAT DIED... WE SHOULD HAVE BEEN HERE FOR YOU...
GRAAWWLRR
WAS
HERRR
IT WAS HERRR...
ACTUALLY... WELL...THERE'S ALSO KINDA SOMETHING ELSE...

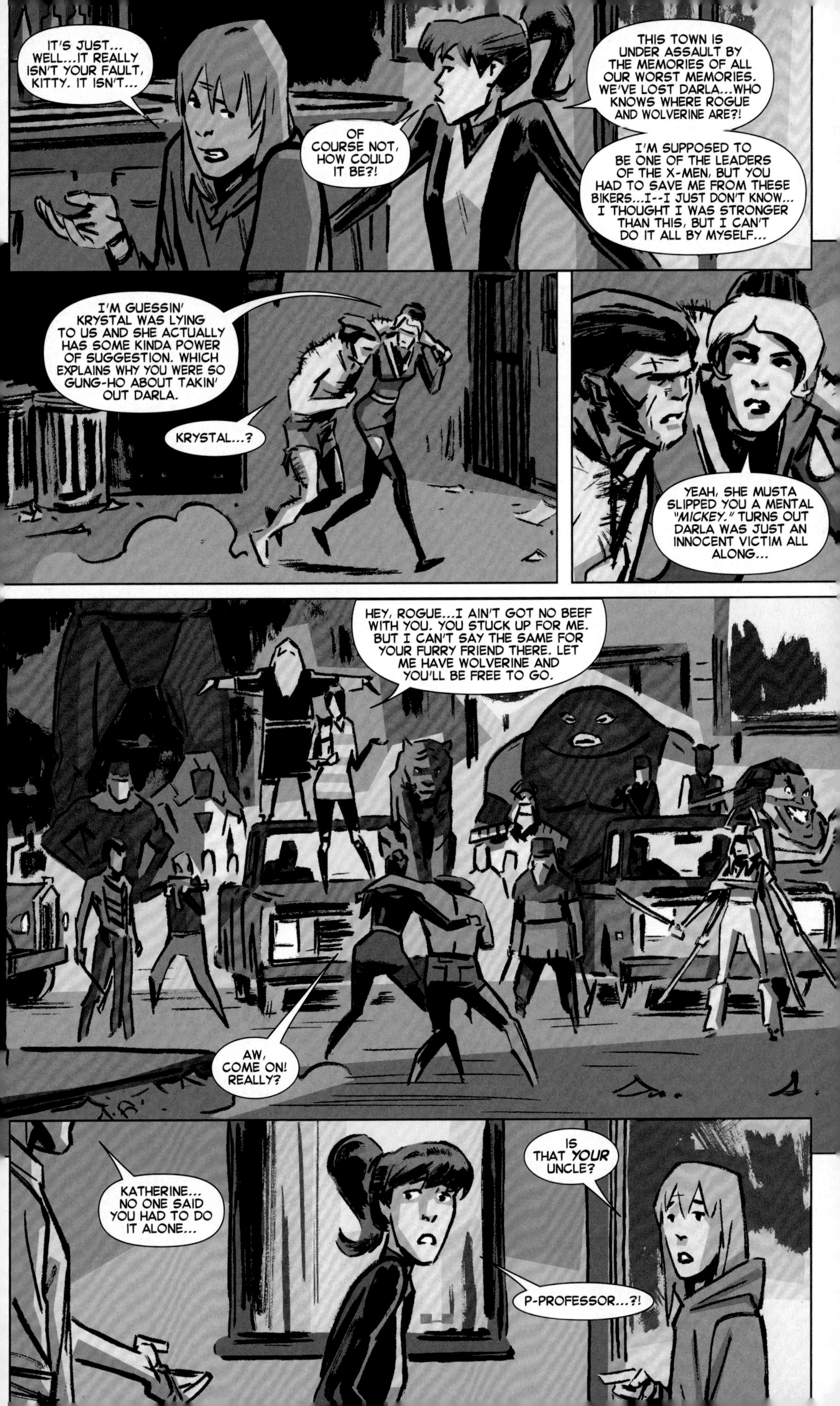

IT'S JUST... WELL...IT REALLY ISN'T YOUR FAULT, KITTY. IT ISN'T...
OF COURSE NOT, HOW COULD IT BE?!
THIS TOWN IS UNDER ASSAULT BY THE MEMORIES OF ALL OUR WORST MEMORIES. WE'VE LOST DARLA...WHO KNOWS WHERE ROGUE AND WOLVERINE ARE?!
I'M SUPPOSED TO BE ONE OF THE LEADERS OF THE X-MEN, BUT YOU HAD TO SAVE ME FROM THESE BIKERS...I--I JUST DON'T KNOW... I THOUGHT I WAS STRONGER THAN THIS, BUT I CAN'T DO IT ALL BY MYSELF...
I'M GUESSIN' KRYSTAL WAS LYING TO US AND SHE ACTUALLY HAS SOME KINDA POWER OF SUGGESTION. WHICH EXPLAINS WHY YOU WERE SO GUNG-HO ABOUT TAKIN' OUT DARLA.
KRYSTAL...?
YEAH, SHE MUSTA SLIPPED YOU A MENTAL "MICKEY." TURNS OUT DARLA WAS JUST AN INNOCENT VICTIM ALL ALONG...
HEY, ROGUE...I AIN'T GOT NO BEEF WITH YOU. YOU STUCK UP FOR ME. BUT I CAN'T SAY THE SAME FOR YOUR FURRY FRIEND THERE. LET ME HAVE WOLVERINE AND YOU'LL BE FREE TO GO.
AW, COME ON! REALLY?
KATHERINE... NO ONE SAID YOU HAD TO DO IT ALONE...
IS THAT YOUR UNCLE?
P-PROFESSOR...?!

5

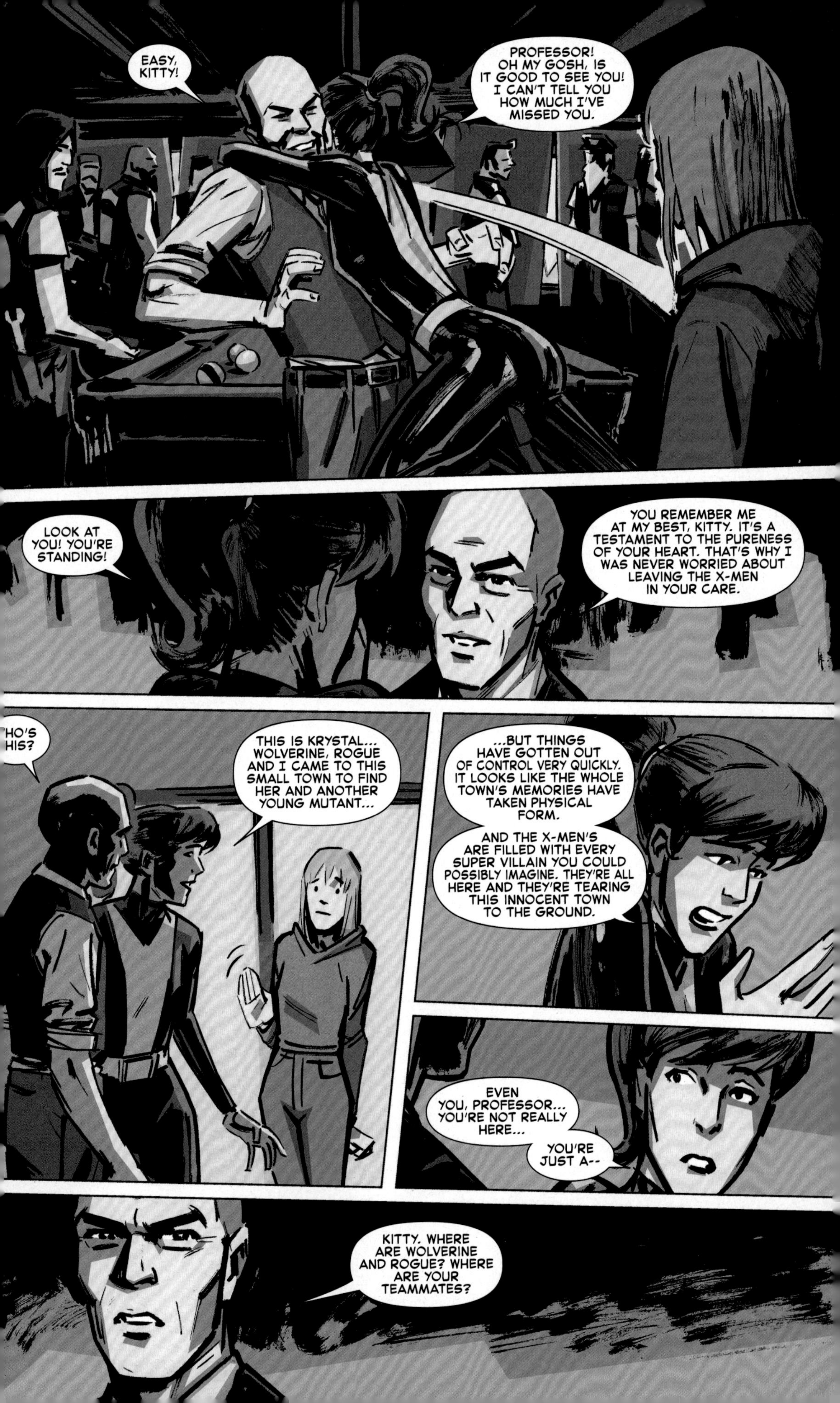
EASY, KITTY!
PROFESSOR! OH MY GOSH, IS IT GOOD TO SEE YOU! I CAN'T TELL YOU HOW MUCH I'VE MISSED YOU.
LOOK AT YOU! YOU'RE STANDING!
YOU REMEMBER ME AT MY BEST, KITTY. IT'S A TESTAMENT TO THE PURENESS OF YOUR HEART. THAT'S WHY I WAS NEVER WORRIED ABOUT LEAVING THE X-MEN IN YOUR CARE.
HO'S HIS?
THIS IS KRYSTAL... WOLVERINE, ROGUE AND I CAME TO THIS SMALL TOWN TO FIND HER AND ANOTHER YOUNG MUTANT...
...BUT THINGS HAVE GOTTEN OUT OF CONTROL VERY QUICKLY. IT LOOKS LIKE THE WHOLE TOWN'S MEMORIES HAVE TAKEN PHYSICAL FORM.
AND THE X-MEN'S ARE FILLED WITH EVERY SUPER VILLAIN YOU COULD POSSIBLY IMAGINE. THEY'RE ALL HERE AND THEY'RE TEARING THIS INNOCENT TOWN TO THE GROUND.
EVEN YOU, PROFESSOR... YOU'RE NOT REALLY HERE...
YOU'RE JUST A--
KITTY. WHERE ARE WOLVERINE AND ROGUE? WHERE ARE YOUR TEAMMATES?

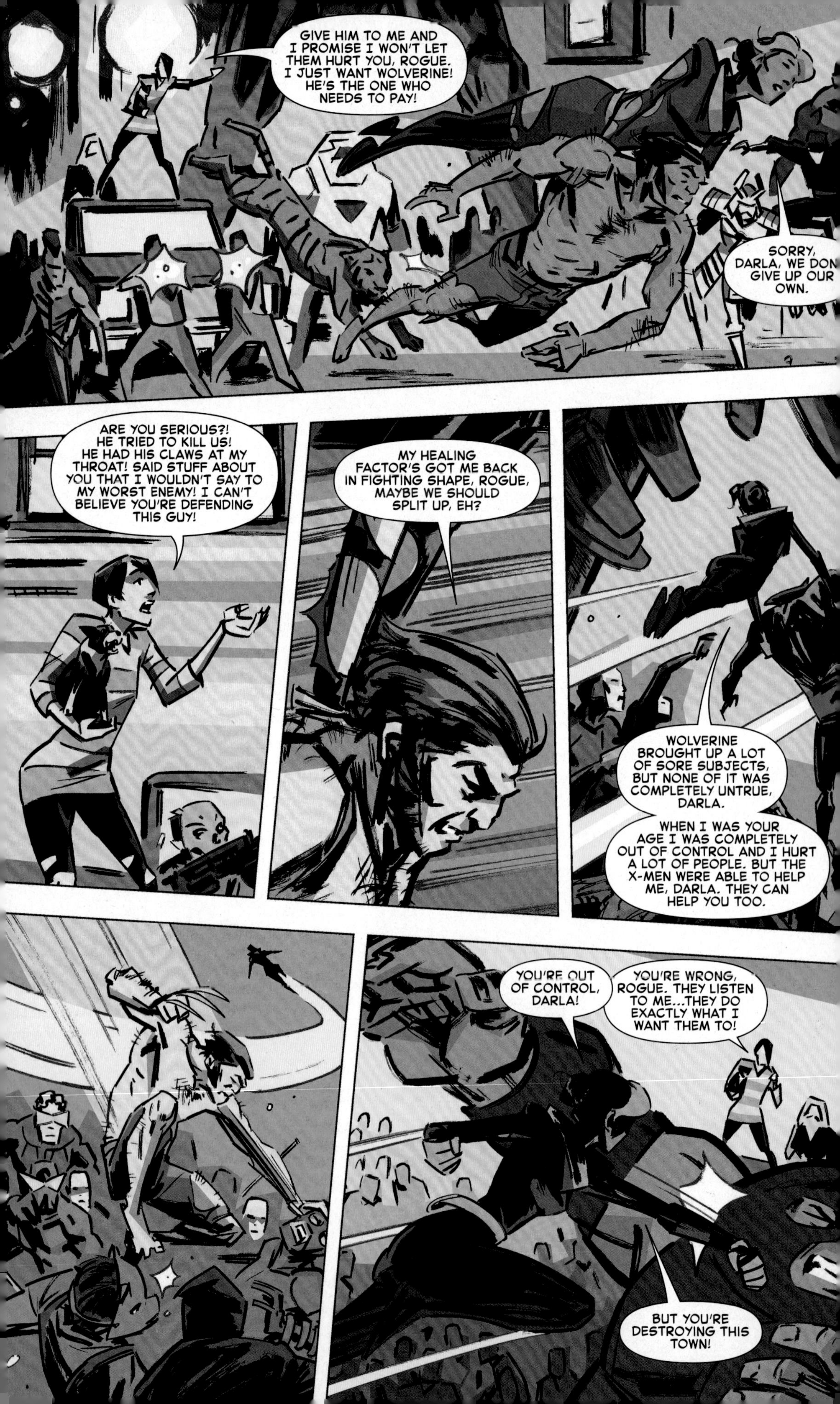
GIVE HIM TO ME AND I PROMISE I WON'T LET THEM HURT YOU, ROGUE. I JUST WANT WOLVERINE! HE'S THE ONE WHO NEEDS TO PAY!
SORRY, DARLA, WE DON GIVE UP OUR OWN.
ARE YOU SERIOUS?! HE TRIED TO KILL US! HE HAD HIS CLAWS AT MY THROAT! SAID STUFF ABOUT YOU THAT I WOULDN'T SAY TO MY WORST ENEMY! I CAN'T BELIEVE YOU'RE DEFENDING THIS GUY!
MY HEALING FACTOR'S GOT ME BACK IN FIGHTING SHAPE, ROGUE, MAYBE WE SHOULD SPLIT UP, EH?
WOLVERINE BROUGHT UP A LOT OF SORE SUBJECTS, BUT NONE OF IT WAS COMPLETELY UNTRUE, DARLA.
WHEN I WAS YOUR AGE I WAS COMPLETELY OUT OF CONTROL AND I HURT A LOT OF PEOPLE. BUT THE X-MEN WERE ABLE TO HELP ME, DARLA. THEY CAN HELP YOU TOO.
YOU'RE OUT OF CONTROL, DARLA!
YOU'RE WRONG, ROGUE. THEY LISTEN TO ME...THEY DO EXACTLY WHAT I WANT THEM TO!
BUT YOU'RE DESTROYING THIS TOWN!

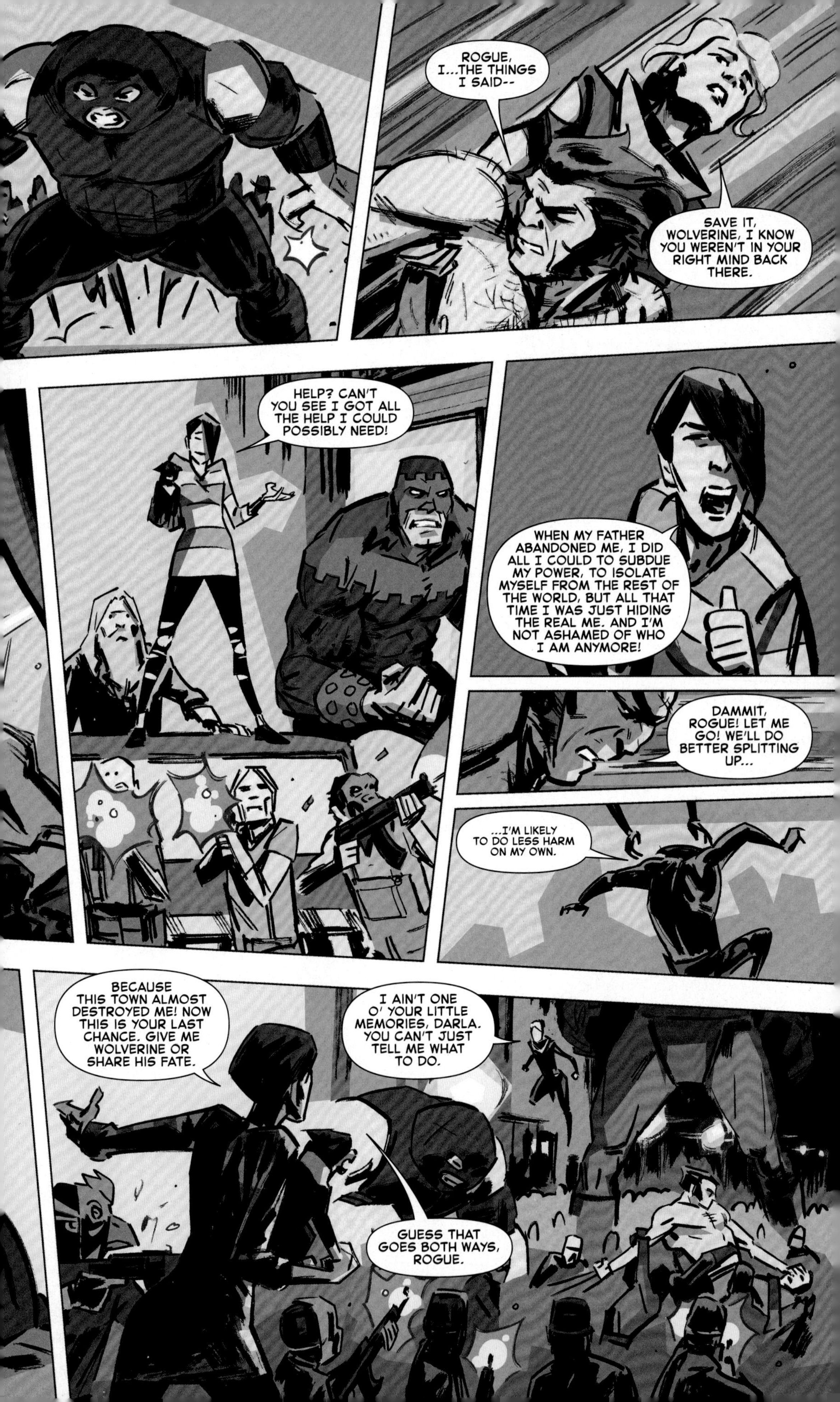
ROGUE, I...THE THINGS I SAID--
SAVE IT, WOLVERINE, I KNOW YOU WEREN'T IN YOUR RIGHT MIND BACK THERE.
HELP? CAN'T YOU SEE I GOT ALL THE HELP I COULD POSSIBLY NEED!
WHEN MY FATHER ABANDONED ME, I DID ALL I COULD TO SUBDUE MY POWER, TO ISOLATE MYSELF FROM THE REST OF THE WORLD, BUT ALL THAT TIME I WAS JUST HIDING THE REAL ME. AND I'M NOT ASHAMED OF WHO I AM ANYMORE!
DAMMIT, ROGUE! LET ME GO! WE'LL DO BETTER SPLITTING UP...
...I'M LIKELY TO DO LESS HARM ON MY OWN.
BECAUSE THIS TOWN ALMOST DESTROYED ME! NOW THIS IS YOUR LAST CHANCE. GIVE ME WOLVERINE OR SHARE HIS FATE.
I AIN'T ONE O' YOUR LITTLE MEMORIES, DARLA. YOU CAN'T JUST TELL ME WHAT TO DO.
GUESS THAT GOES BOTH WAYS, ROGUE.

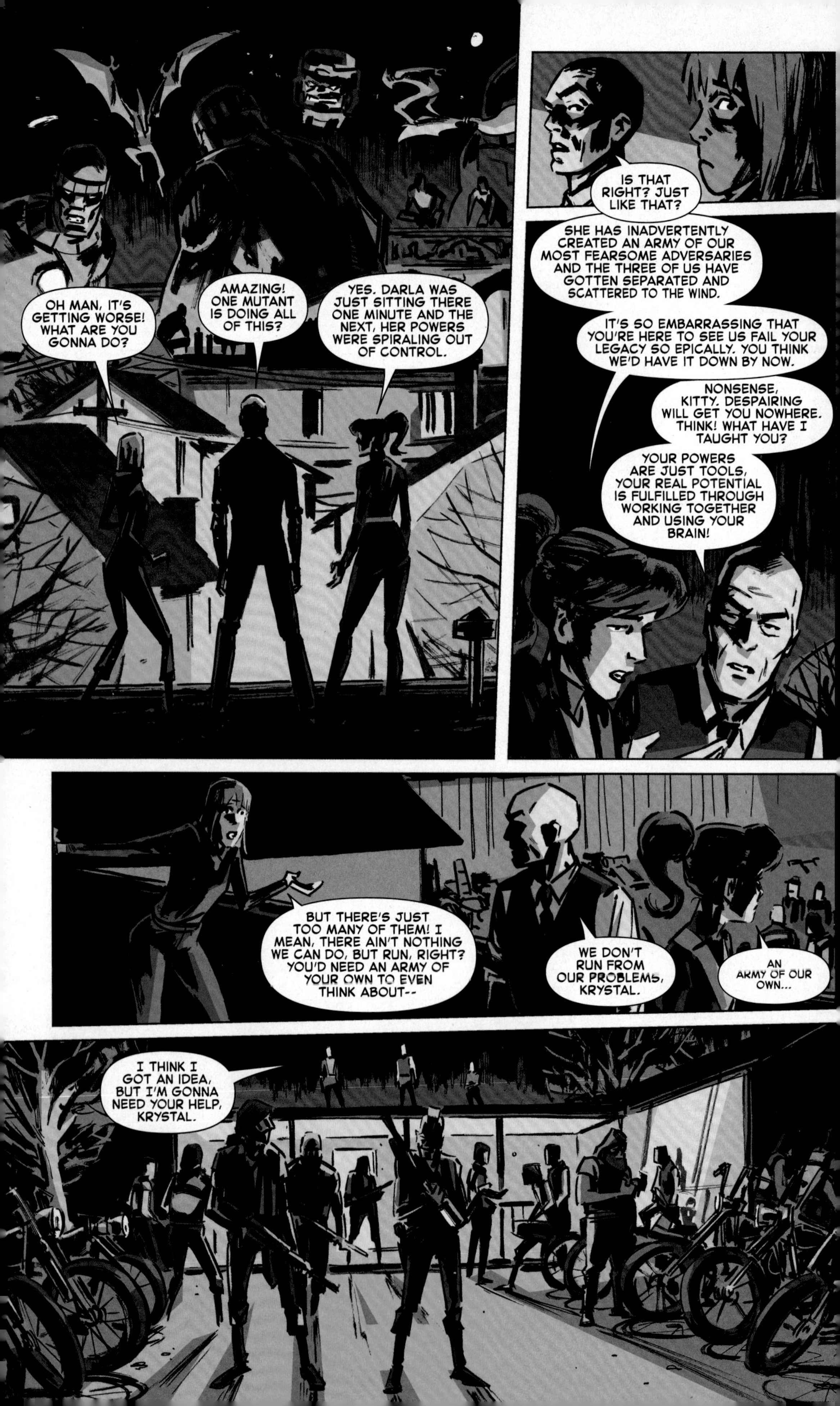
OH MAN, IT'S GETTING WORSE! WHAT ARE YOU GONNA DO?
AMAZING! ONE MUTANT IS DOING ALL OF THIS?
YES. DARLA WAS JUST SITTING THERE ONE MINUTE AND THE NEXT, HER POWERS WERE SPIRALING OUT OF CONTROL.
IS THAT RIGHT? JUST LIKE THAT?
SHE HAS INADVERTENTLY CREATED AN ARMY OF OUR MOST FEARSOME ADVERSARIES AND THE THREE OF US HAVE GOTTEN SEPARATED AND SCATTERED TO THE WIND.
IT'S SO EMBARRASSING THAT YOU'RE HERE TO SEE US FAIL YOUR LEGACY SO EPICALLY. YOU THINK WE'D HAVE IT DOWN BY NOW.
NONSENSE, KITTY. DESPAIRING WILL GET YOU NOWHERE. THINK! WHAT HAVE I TAUGHT YOU?
YOUR POWERS ARE JUST TOOLS, YOUR REAL POTENTIAL IS FULFILLED THROUGH WORKING TOGETHER AND USING YOUR BRAIN!
BUT THERE'S JUST TOO MANY OF THEM! I MEAN, THERE AIN'T NOTHING WE CAN DO, BUT RUN, RIGHT? YOU'D NEED AN ARMY OF YOUR OWN TO EVEN THINK ABOUT--
WE DON'T RUN FROM OUR PROBLEMS, KRYSTAL.
AN ARMY OF OUR OWN...
I THINK I GOT AN IDEA, BUT I'M GONNA NEED YOUR HELP, KRYSTAL.

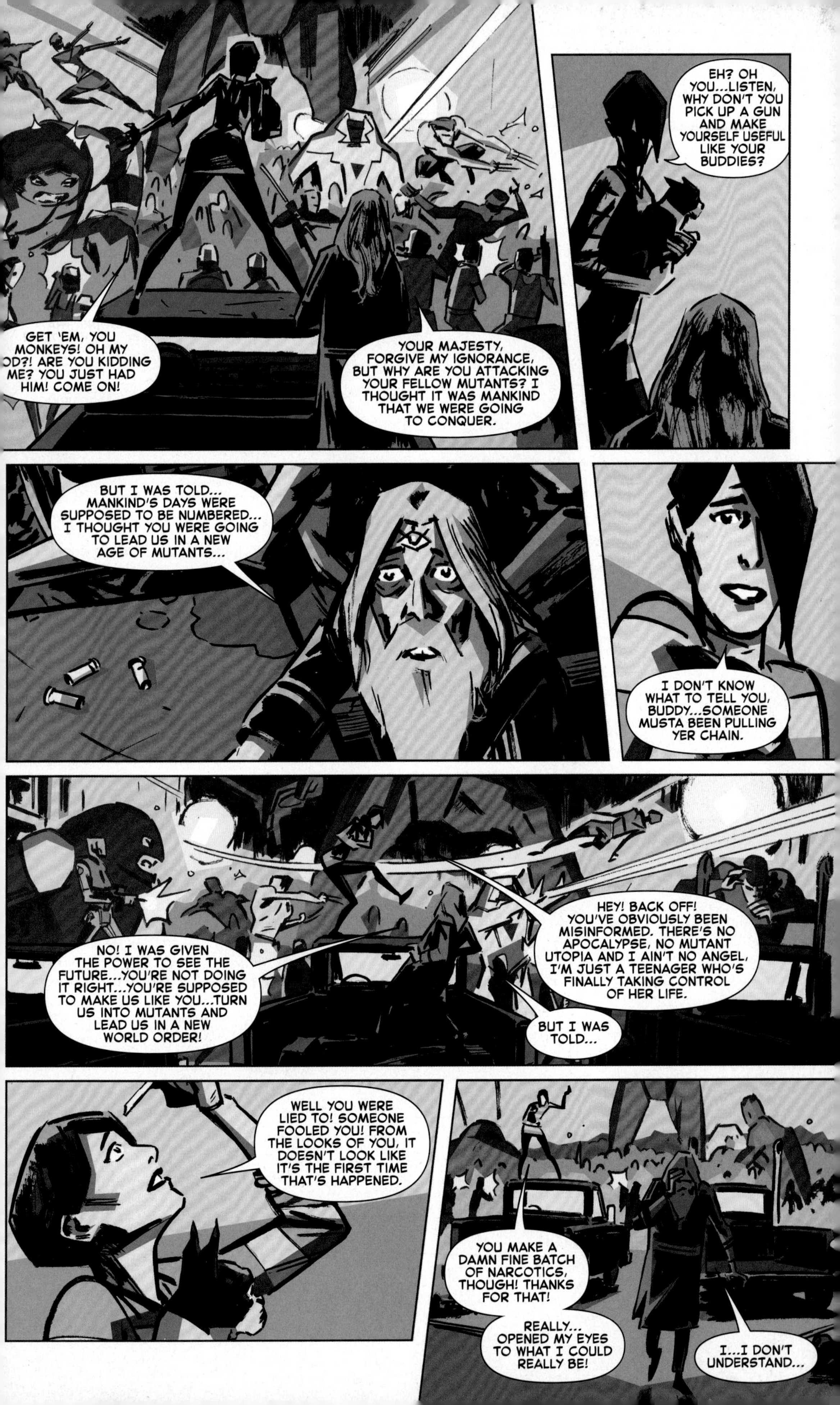
GET 'EM, YOU MONKEYS! OH MY OD?! ARE YOU KIDDING ME? YOU JUST HAD HIM! COME ON!
YOUR MAJESTY, FORGIVE MY IGNORANCE, BUT WHY ARE YOU ATTACKING YOUR FELLOW MUTANTS? I THOUGHT IT WAS MANKIND THAT WE WERE GOING TO CONQUER.
EH? OH YOU...LISTEN, WHY DON'T YOU PICK UP A GUN AND MAKE YOURSELF USEFUL LIKE YOUR BUDDIES?
BUT I WAS TOLD... MANKIND'S DAYS WERE SUPPOSED TO BE NUMBERED... I THOUGHT YOU WERE GOING TO LEAD US IN A NEW AGE OF MUTANTS...
I DON'T KNOW WHAT TO TELL YOU, BUDDY...SOMEONE MUSTA BEEN PULLING YER CHAIN.
NO! I WAS GIVEN THE POWER TO SEE THE FUTURE...YOU'RE NOT DOING IT RIGHT...YOU'RE SUPPOSED TO MAKE US LIKE YOU...TURN US INTO MUTANTS AND LEAD US IN A NEW WORLD ORDER!
HEY! BACK OFF! YOU'VE OBVIOUSLY BEEN MISINFORMED. THERE'S NO APOCALYPSE, NO MUTANT UTOPIA AND I AIN'T NO ANGEL, I'M JUST A TEENAGER WHO'S FINALLY TAKING CONTROL OF HER LIFE.
BUT I WAS TOLD...
WELL YOU WERE LIED TO! SOMEONE FOOLED YOU! FROM THE LOOKS OF YOU, IT DOESN'T LOOK LIKE IT'S THE FIRST TIME THAT'S HAPPENED.
YOU MAKE A DAMN FINE BATCH OF NARCOTICS, THOUGH! THANKS FOR THAT!
REALLY... OPENED MY EYES TO WHAT I COULD REALLY BE!
I...I DON'T UNDERSTAND...

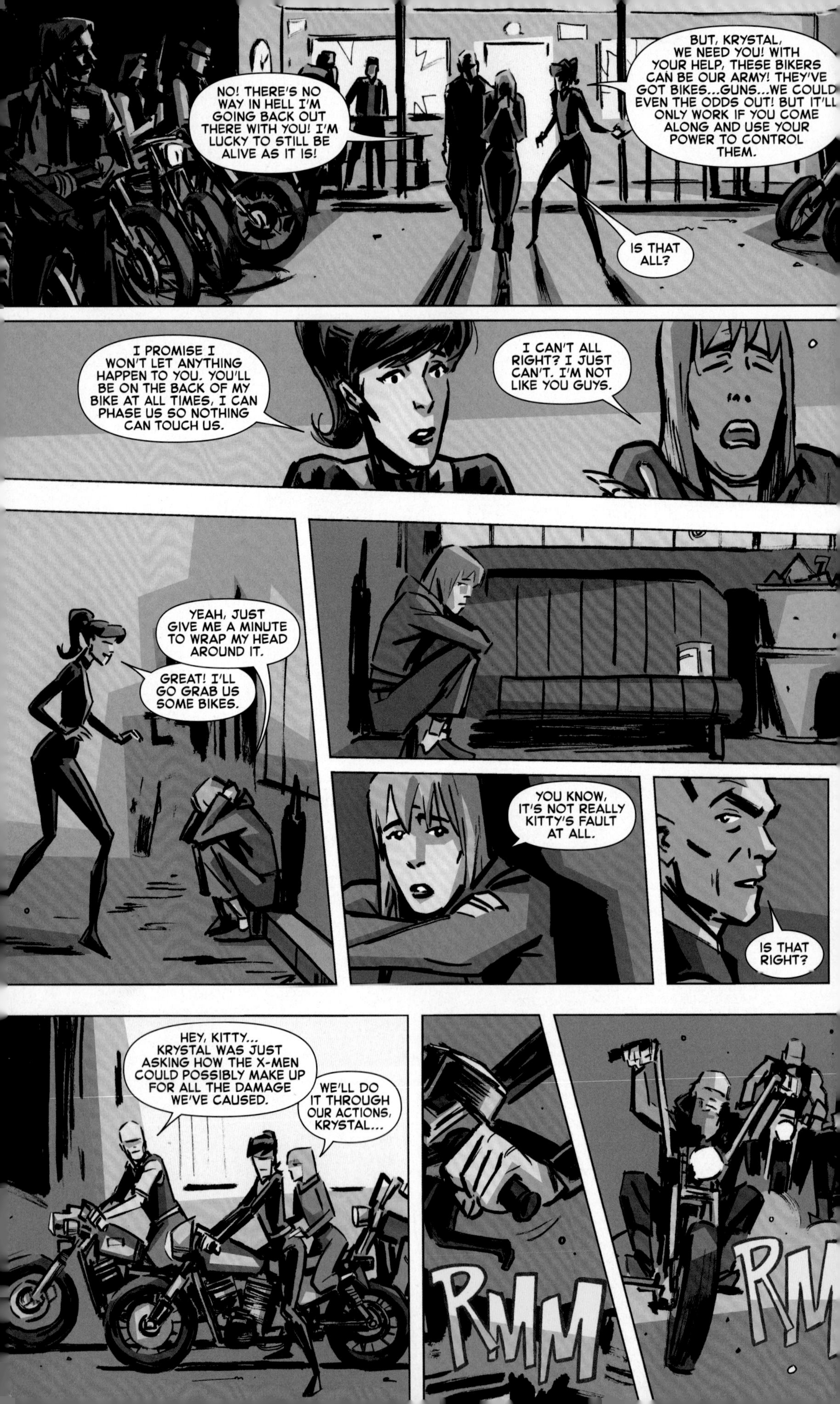
NO! THERE'S NO WAY IN HELL I'M GOING BACK OUT THERE WITH YOU! I'M LUCKY TO STILL BE ALIVE AS IT IS!
BUT, KRYSTAL, WE NEED YOU! WITH YOUR HELP, THESE BIKERS CAN BE OUR ARMY! THEY'VE GOT BIKES...GUNS...WE COULD EVEN THE ODDS OUT! BUT IT'LL ONLY WORK IF YOU COME ALONG AND USE YOUR POWER TO CONTROL THEM.
IS THAT ALL?
I PROMISE I WON'T LET ANYTHING HAPPEN TO YOU. YOU'LL BE ON THE BACK OF MY BIKE AT ALL TIMES, I CAN PHASE US SO NOTHING CAN TOUCH US.
I CAN'T ALL RIGHT? I JUST CAN'T. I'M NOT LIKE YOU GUYS.
YEAH, JUST GIVE ME A MINUTE TO WRAP MY HEAD AROUND IT.
GREAT! I'LL GO GRAB US SOME BIKES.
YOU KNOW, IT'S NOT REALLY KITTY'S FAULT AT ALL.
IS THAT RIGHT?
HEY, KITTY... KRYSTAL WAS JUST ASKING HOW THE X-MEN COULD POSSIBLY MAKE UP FOR ALL THE DAMAGE WE'VE CAUSED.
WE'LL DO IT THROUGH OUR ACTIONS, KRYSTAL...
RMM
RM

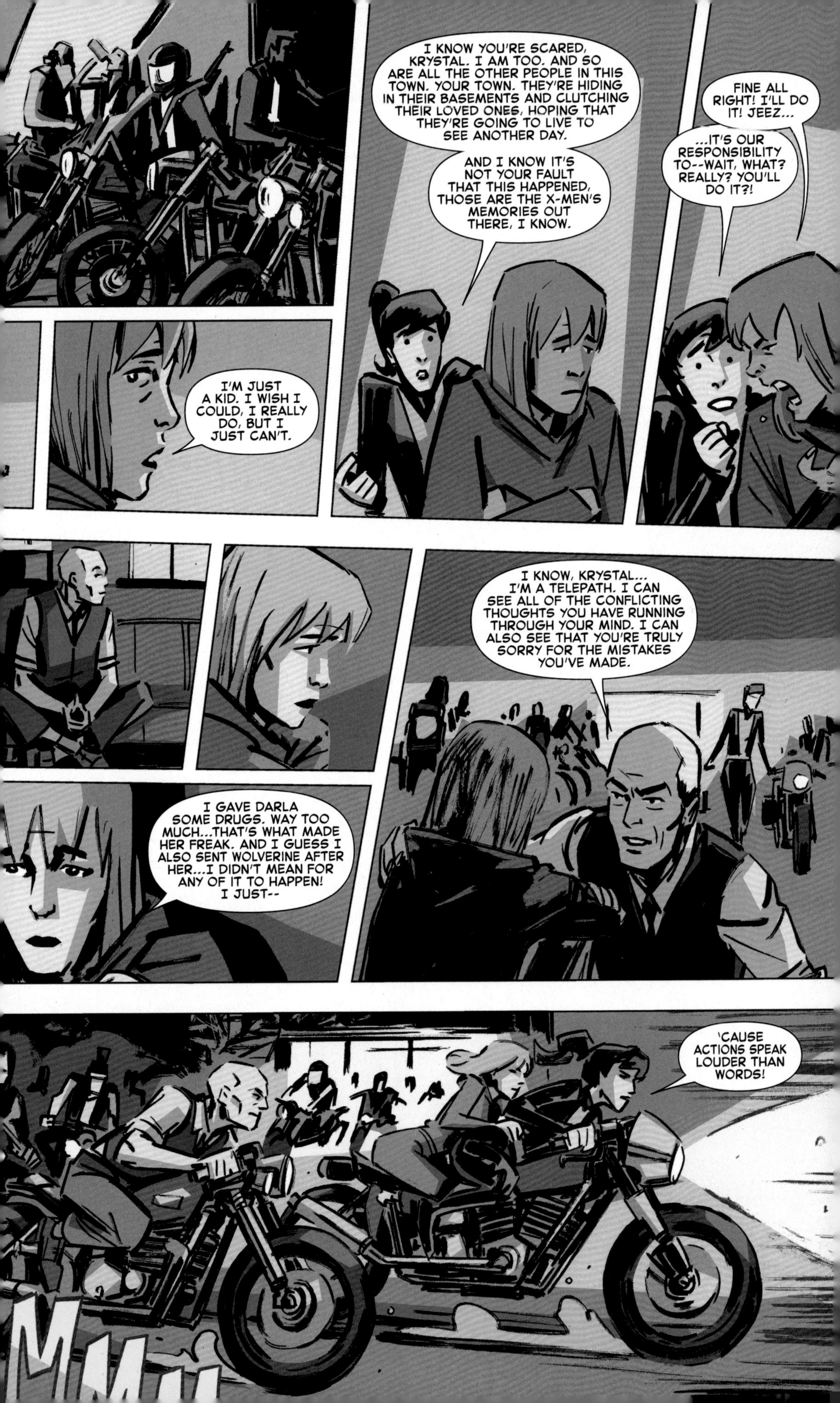
I KNOW YOU'RE SCARED, KRYSTAL. I AM TOO. AND SO ARE ALL THE OTHER PEOPLE IN THIS TOWN. YOUR TOWN. THEY'RE HIDING IN THEIR BASEMENTS AND CLUTCHING THEIR LOVED ONES, HOPING THAT THEY'RE GOING TO LIVE TO SEE ANOTHER DAY.
AND I KNOW IT'S NOT YOUR FAULT THAT THIS HAPPENED, THOSE ARE THE X-MEN'S MEMORIES OUT THERE, I KNOW.
FINE ALL RIGHT! I'LL DO IT! JEEZ...
...IT'S OUR RESPONSIBILITY TO--WAIT, WHAT? REALLY? YOU'LL DO IT?!
I'M JUST A KID. I WISH I COULD, I REALLY DO, BUT I JUST CAN'T.
I KNOW, KRYSTAL... I'M A TELEPATH. I CAN SEE ALL OF THE CONFLICTING THOUGHTS YOU HAVE RUNNING THROUGH YOUR MIND. I CAN ALSO SEE THAT YOU'RE TRULY SORRY FOR THE MISTAKES YOU'VE MADE.
I GAVE DARLA SOME DRUGS. WAY TOO MUCH...THAT'S WHAT MADE HER FREAK. AND I GUESS I ALSO SENT WOLVERINE AFTER HER...I DIDN'T MEAN FOR ANY OF IT TO HAPPEN! I JUST--
'CAUSE ACTIONS SPEAK LOUDER THAN WORDS!
MMM

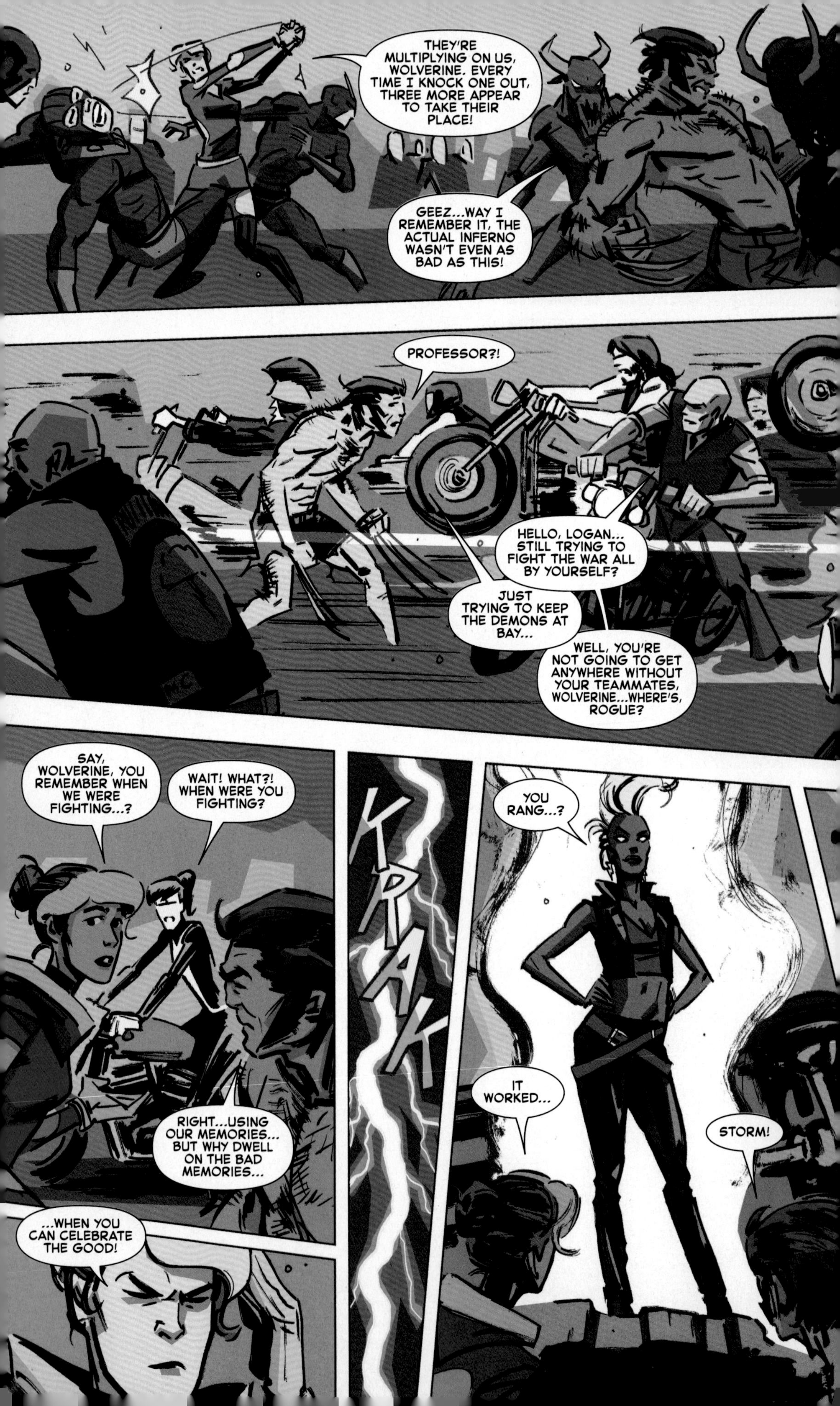
THEY'RE MULTIPLYING ON US, WOLVERINE. EVERY TIME I KNOCK ONE OUT, THREE MORE APPEAR TO TAKE THEIR PLACE!
GEEZ...WAY I REMEMBER IT, THE ACTUAL INFERNO WASN'T EVEN AS BAD AS THIS!
PROFESSOR?!
HELLO, LOGAN... STILL TRYING TO FIGHT THE WAR ALL BY YOURSELF?
JUST TRYING TO KEEP THE DEMONS AT BAY...
WELL, YOU'RE NOT GOING TO GET ANYWHERE WITHOUT YOUR TEAMMATES, WOLVERINE...WHERE'S, ROGUE?
SAY, WOLVERINE, YOU REMEMBER WHEN WE WERE FIGHTING...?
WAIT! WHAT?! WHEN WERE YOU FIGHTING?
RIGHT...USING OUR MEMORIES... BUT WHY DWELL ON THE BAD MEMORIES...
...WHEN YOU CAN CELEBRATE THE GOOD!
KRAK
YOU RANG...?
IT WORKED...
STORM!

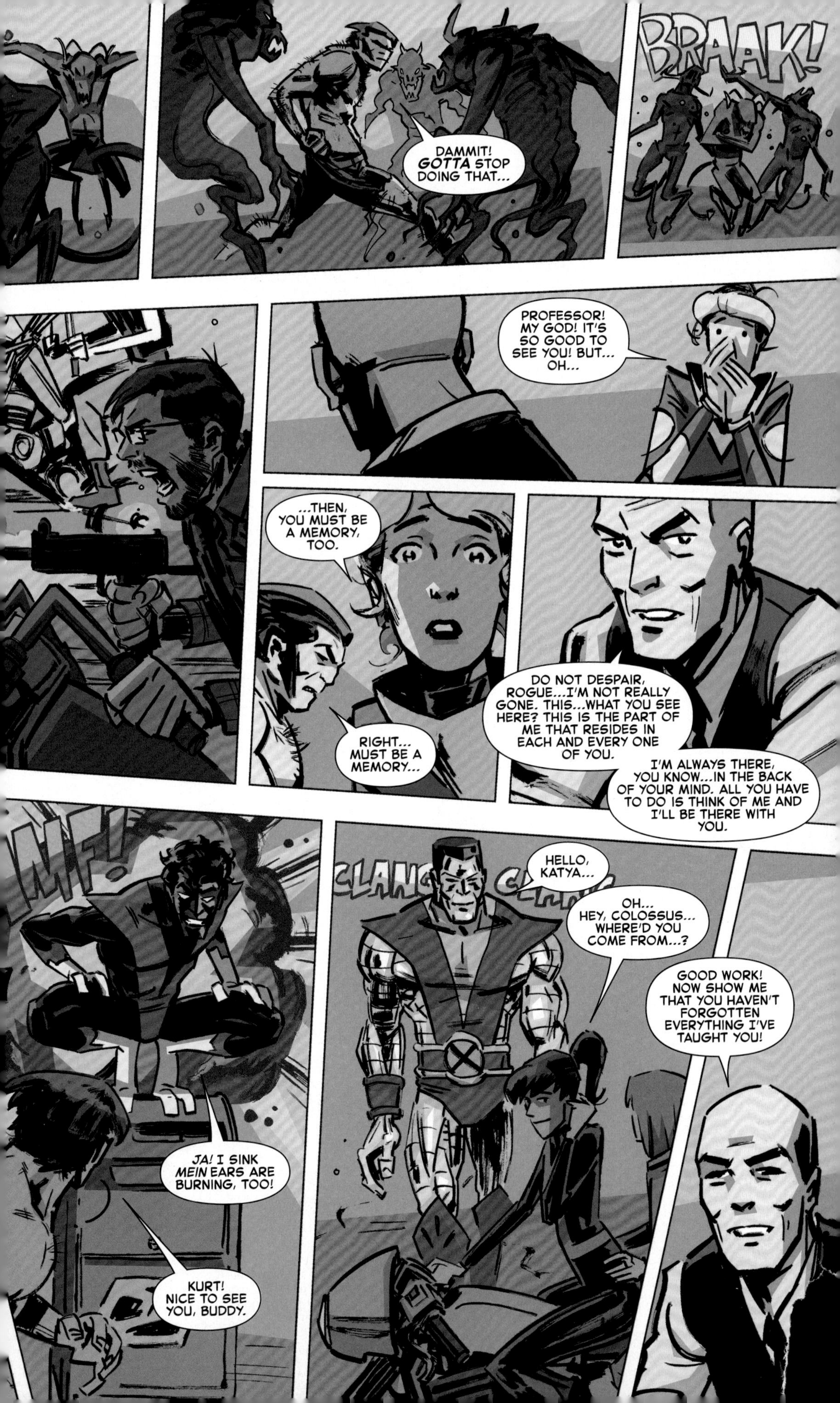
DAMMIT! GOTTA STOP DOING THAT...
BRAAK!
PROFESSOR! MY GOD! IT'S SO GOOD TO SEE YOU! BUT... OH...
...THEN, YOU MUST BE A MEMORY, TOO.
RIGHT... MUST BE A MEMORY...
DO NOT DESPAIR, ROGUE...I'M NOT REALLY GONE. THIS...WHAT YOU SEE HERE? THIS IS THE PART OF ME THAT RESIDES IN EACH AND EVERY ONE OF YOU.
I'M ALWAYS THERE, YOU KNOW...IN THE BACK OF YOUR MIND. ALL YOU HAVE TO DO IS THINK OF ME AND I'LL BE THERE WITH YOU.
JA! I SINK MEIN EARS ARE BURNING, TOO!
KURT! NICE TO SEE YOU, BUDDY.
HELLO, KATYA...
OH... HEY, COLOSSUS... WHERE'D YOU COME FROM...?
GOOD WORK! NOW SHOW ME THAT YOU HAVEN'T FORGOTTEN EVERYTHING I'VE TAUGHT YOU!

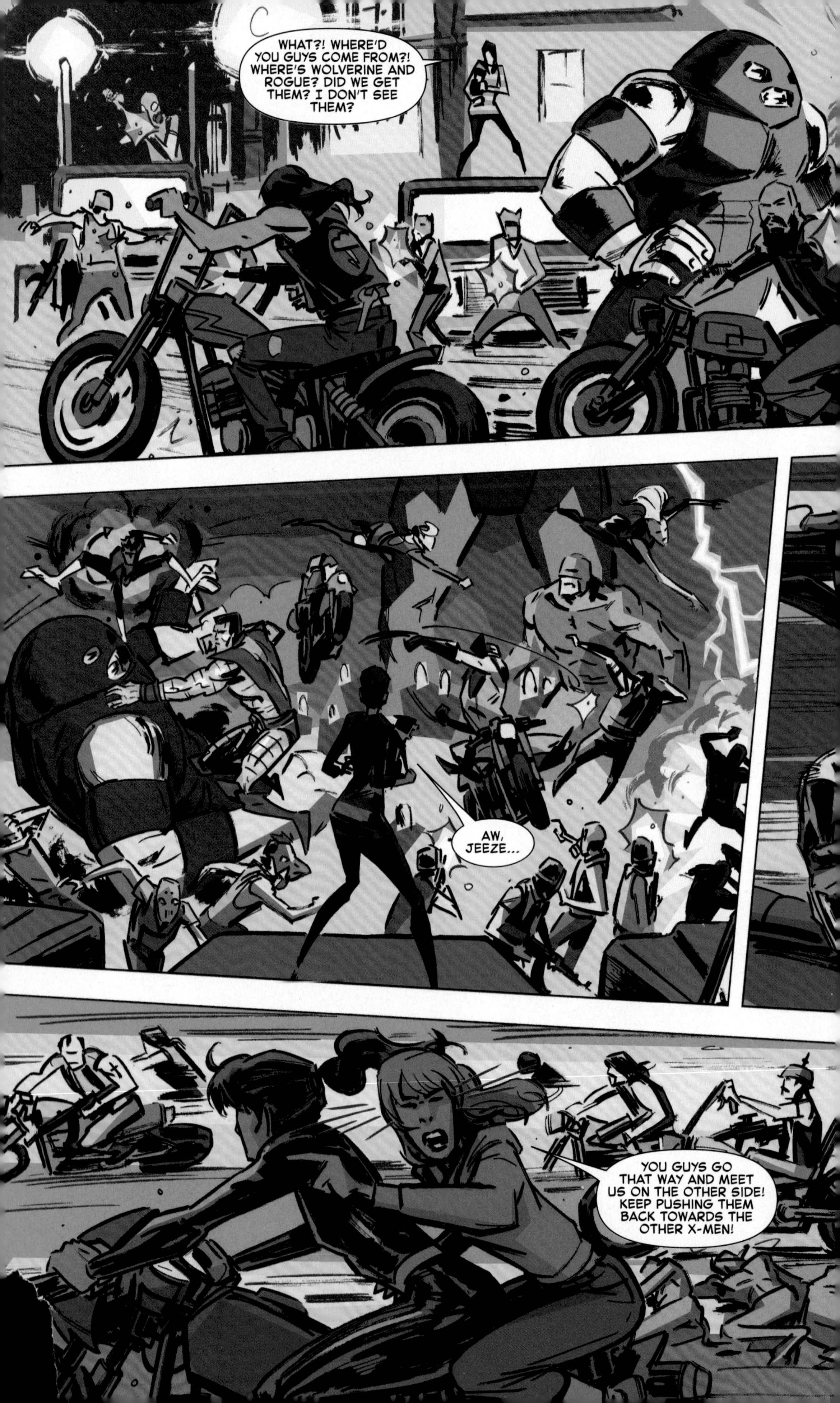
WHAT?! WHERE'D YOU GUYS COME FROM?! WHERE'S WOLVERINE AND ROGUE? DID WE GET THEM? I DON'T SEE THEM?
AW, JEEZE...
YOU GUYS GO THAT WAY AND MEET US ON THE OTHER SIDE! KEEP PUSHING THEM BACK TOWARDS THE OTHER X-MEN!

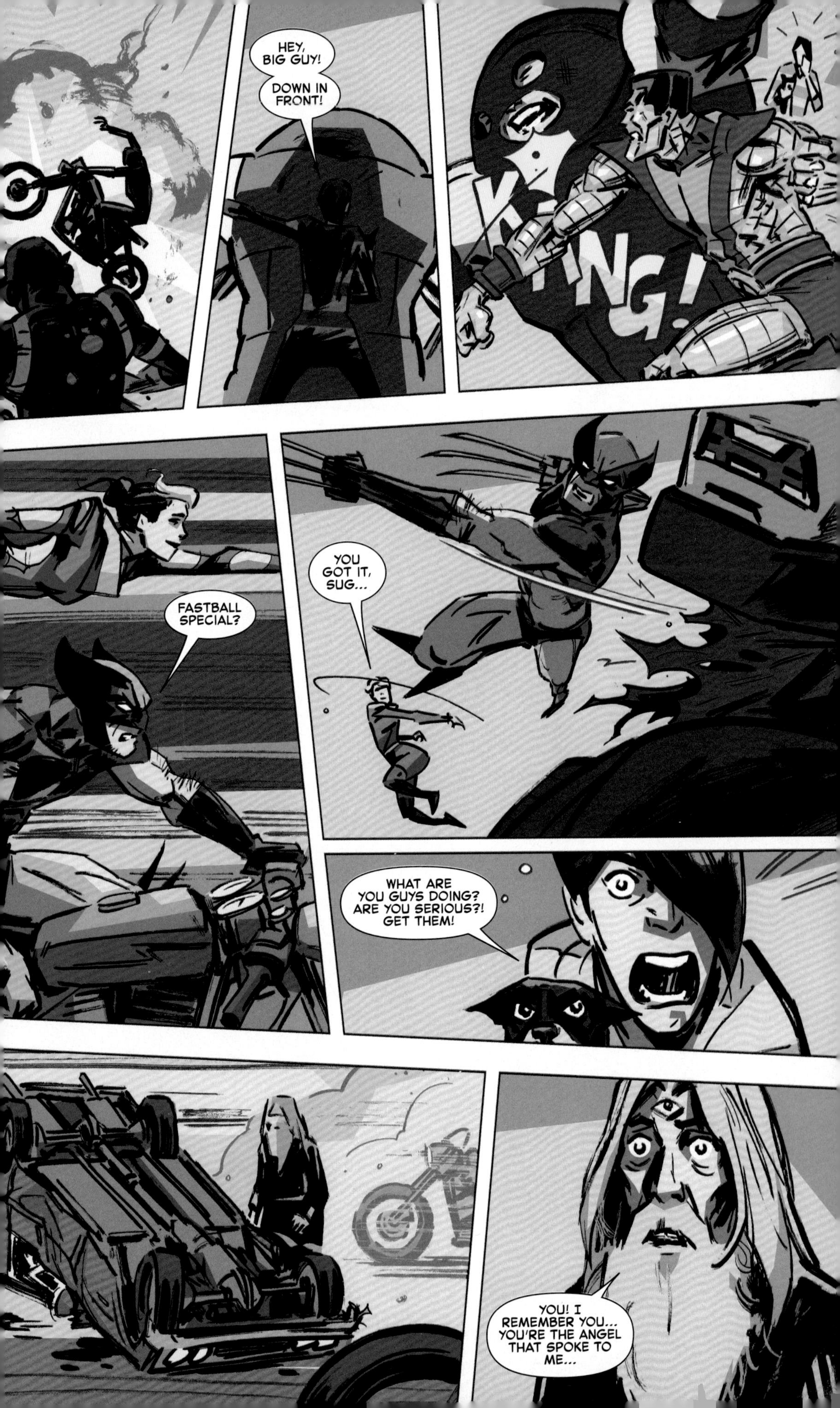
HEY, BIG GUY!
DOWN IN FRONT!
KRANG!
FASTBALL SPECIAL?
YOU GOT IT, SUG...
WHAT ARE YOU GUYS DOING? ARE YOU SERIOUS?! GET THEM!
YOU! I REMEMBER YOU... YOU'RE THE ANGEL THAT SPOKE TO ME...

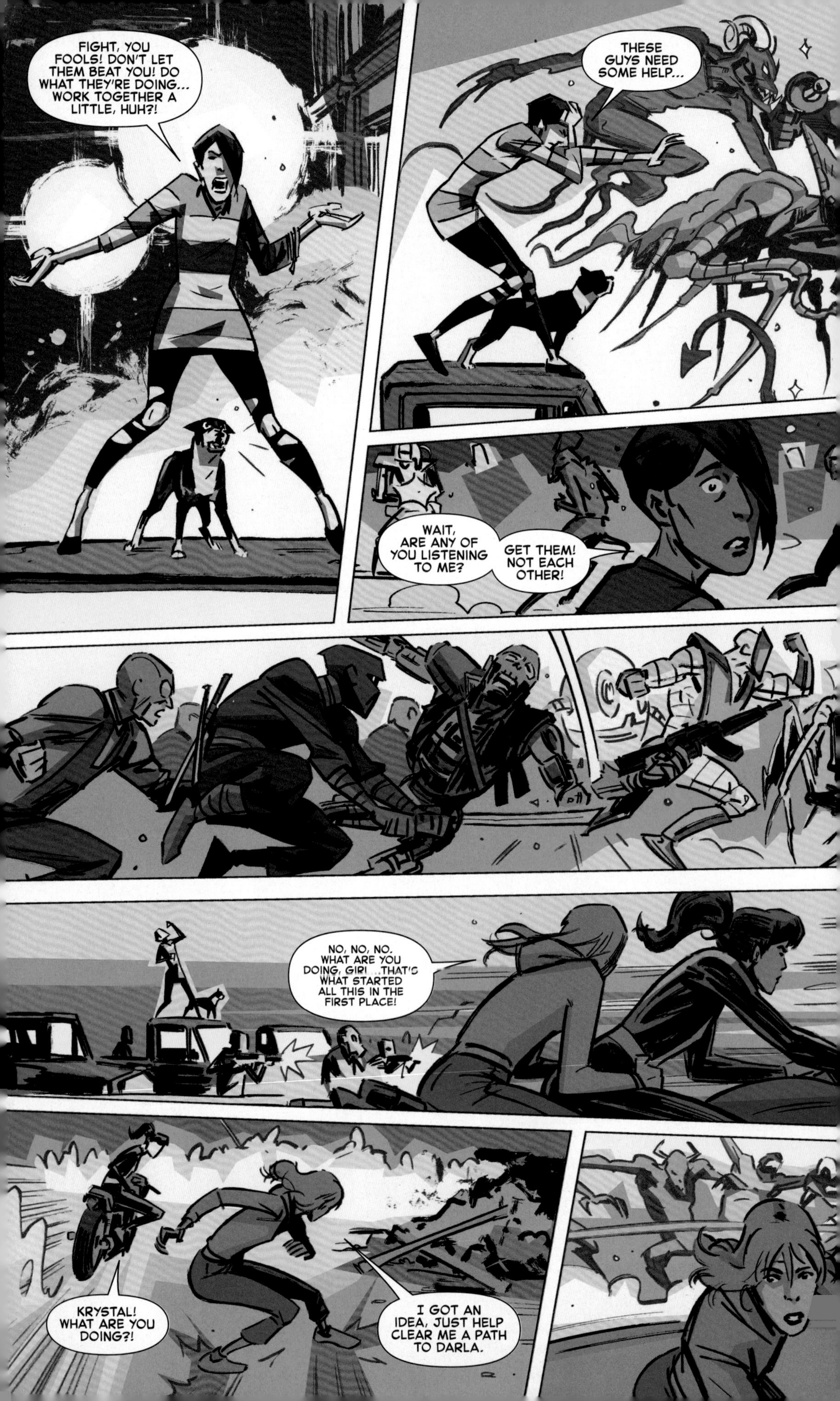
FIGHT, YOU FOOLS! DON'T LET THEM BEAT YOU! DO WHAT THEY'RE DOING... WORK TOGETHER A LITTLE, HUH?!
THESE GUYS NEED SOME HELP...
WAIT, ARE ANY OF YOU LISTENING TO ME?
GET THEM! NOT EACH OTHER!
NO, NO, NO. WHAT ARE YOU DOING, GIRL...THAT'S WHAT STARTED ALL THIS IN THE FIRST PLACE!
KRYSTAL! WHAT ARE YOU DOING?!
I GOT AN IDEA, JUST HELP CLEAR ME A PATH TO DARLA.

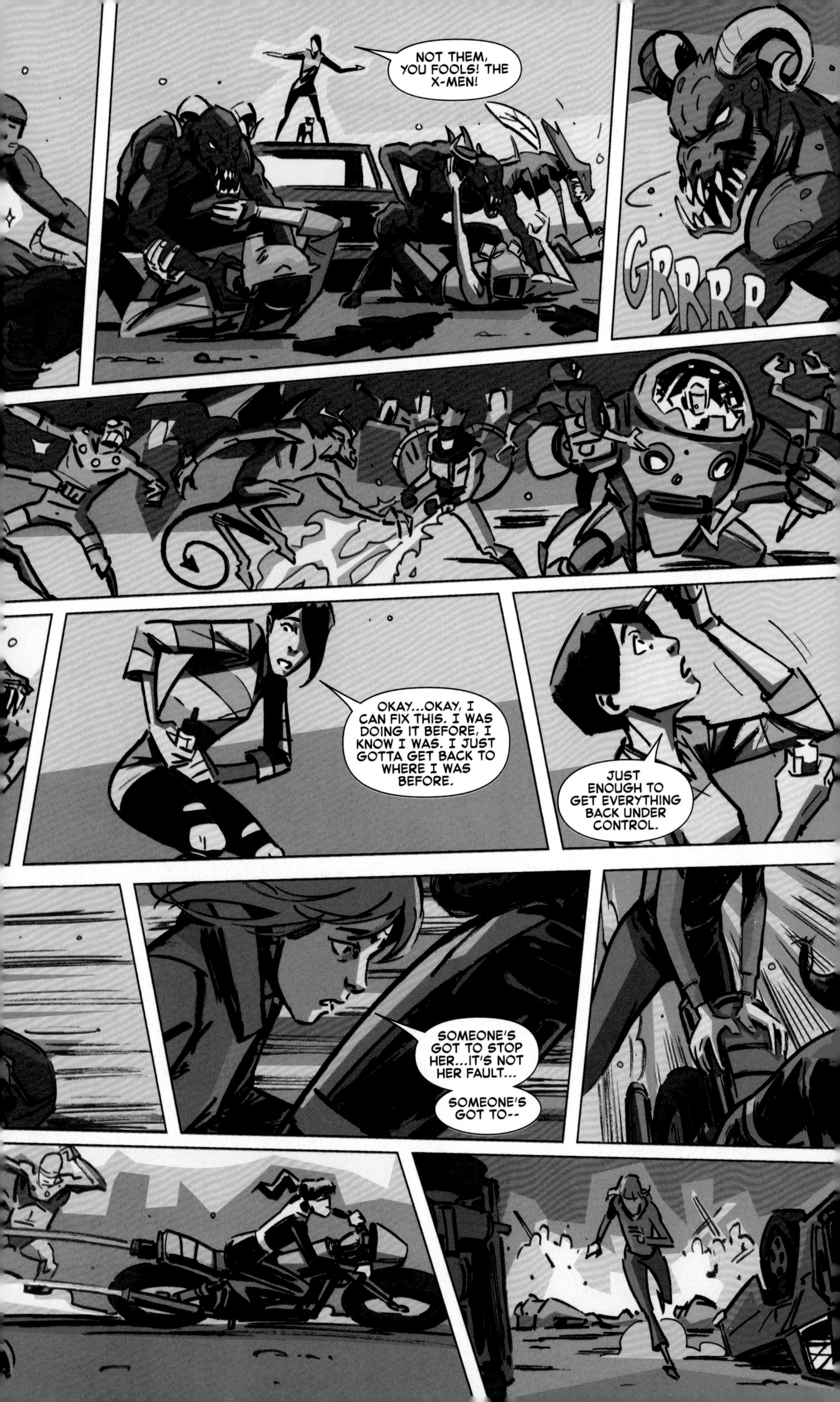

NOT THEM, YOU FOOLS! THE X-MEN!
GRRRR
OKAY...OKAY, I CAN FIX THIS. I WAS DOING IT BEFORE, I KNOW I WAS. I JUST GOTTA GET BACK TO WHERE I WAS BEFORE.
JUST ENOUGH TO GET EVERYTHING BACK UNDER CONTROL.
SOMEONE'S GOT TO STOP HER...IT'S NOT HER FAULT...
SOMEONE'S GOT TO--

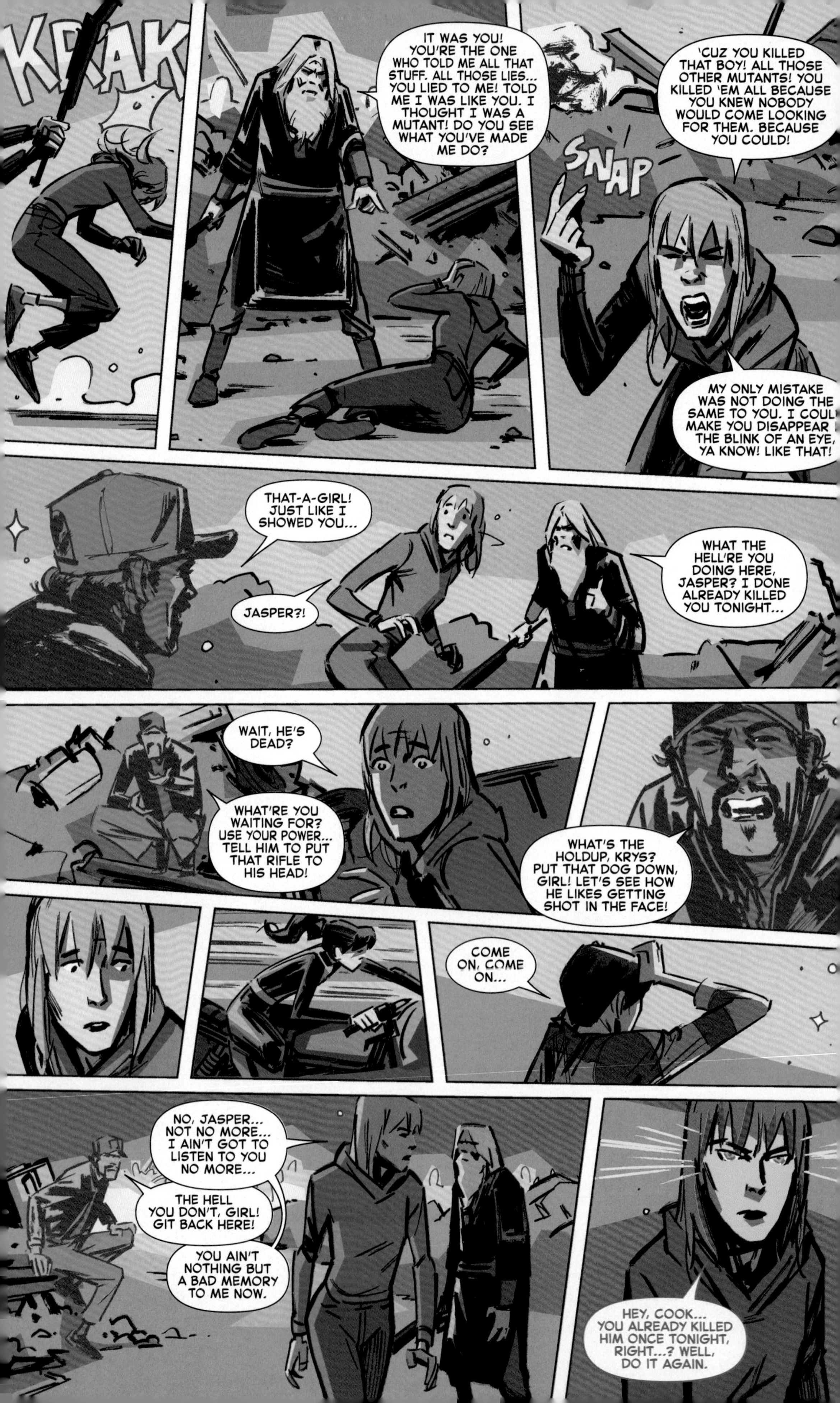
KRAK
IT WAS YOU! YOU'RE THE ONE WHO TOLD ME ALL THAT STUFF. ALL THOSE LIES... YOU LIED TO ME! TOLD ME I WAS LIKE YOU. I THOUGHT I WAS A MUTANT! DO YOU SEE WHAT YOU'VE MADE ME DO?
'CUZ YOU KILLED THAT BOY! ALL THOSE OTHER MUTANTS! YOU KILLED 'EM ALL BECAUSE YOU KNEW NOBODY WOULD COME LOOKING FOR THEM. BECAUSE YOU COULD!
SNAP
MY ONLY MISTAKE WAS NOT DOING THE SAME TO YOU. I COUL MAKE YOU DISAPPEAR THE BLINK OF AN EYE, YA KNOW! LIKE THAT!
THAT-A-GIRL! JUST LIKE I SHOWED YOU...
JASPER?!
WHAT THE HELL'RE YOU DOING HERE, JASPER? I DONE ALREADY KILLED YOU TONIGHT...
WAIT, HE'S DEAD?
WHAT'RE YOU WAITING FOR? USE YOUR POWER... TELL HIM TO PUT THAT RIFLE TO HIS HEAD!
WHAT'S THE HOLDUP, KRYS? PUT THAT DOG DOWN, GIRL! LET'S SEE HOW HE LIKES GETTING SHOT IN THE FACE!
COME ON, COME ON...
NO, JASPER... NOT NO MORE... I AIN'T GOT TO LISTEN TO YOU NO MORE...
THE HELL YOU DON'T, GIRL! GIT BACK HERE!
YOU AIN'T NOTHING BUT A BAD MEMORY TO ME NOW.
HEY, COOK... YOU ALREADY KILLED HIM ONCE TONIGHT, RIGHT...? WELL, DO IT AGAIN.

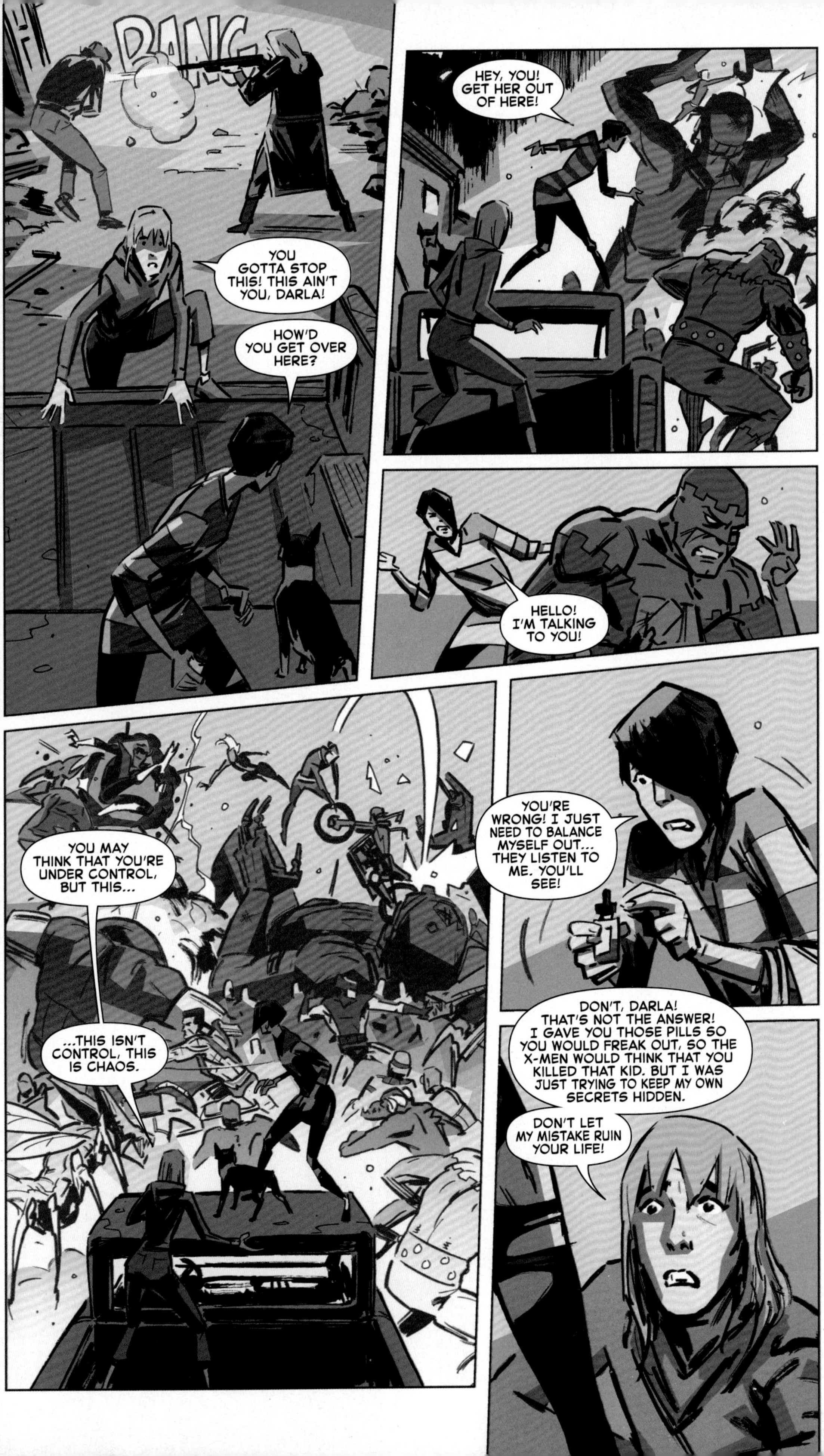
BANG
YOU GOTTA STOP THIS! THIS AIN'T YOU, DARLA!
HOW'D YOU GET OVER HERE?
HEY, YOU! GET HER OUT OF HERE!
HELLO! I'M TALKING TO YOU!
YOU MAY THINK THAT YOU'RE UNDER CONTROL, BUT THIS...
...THIS ISN'T CONTROL, THIS IS CHAOS.
YOU'RE WRONG! I JUST NEED TO BALANCE MYSELF OUT... THEY LISTEN TO ME. YOU'LL SEE!
DON'T, DARLA! THAT'S NOT THE ANSWER! I GAVE YOU THOSE PILLS SO YOU WOULD FREAK OUT, SO THE X-MEN WOULD THINK THAT YOU KILLED THAT KID. BUT I WAS JUST TRYING TO KEEP MY OWN SECRETS HIDDEN.
DON'T LET MY MISTAKE RUIN YOUR LIFE!

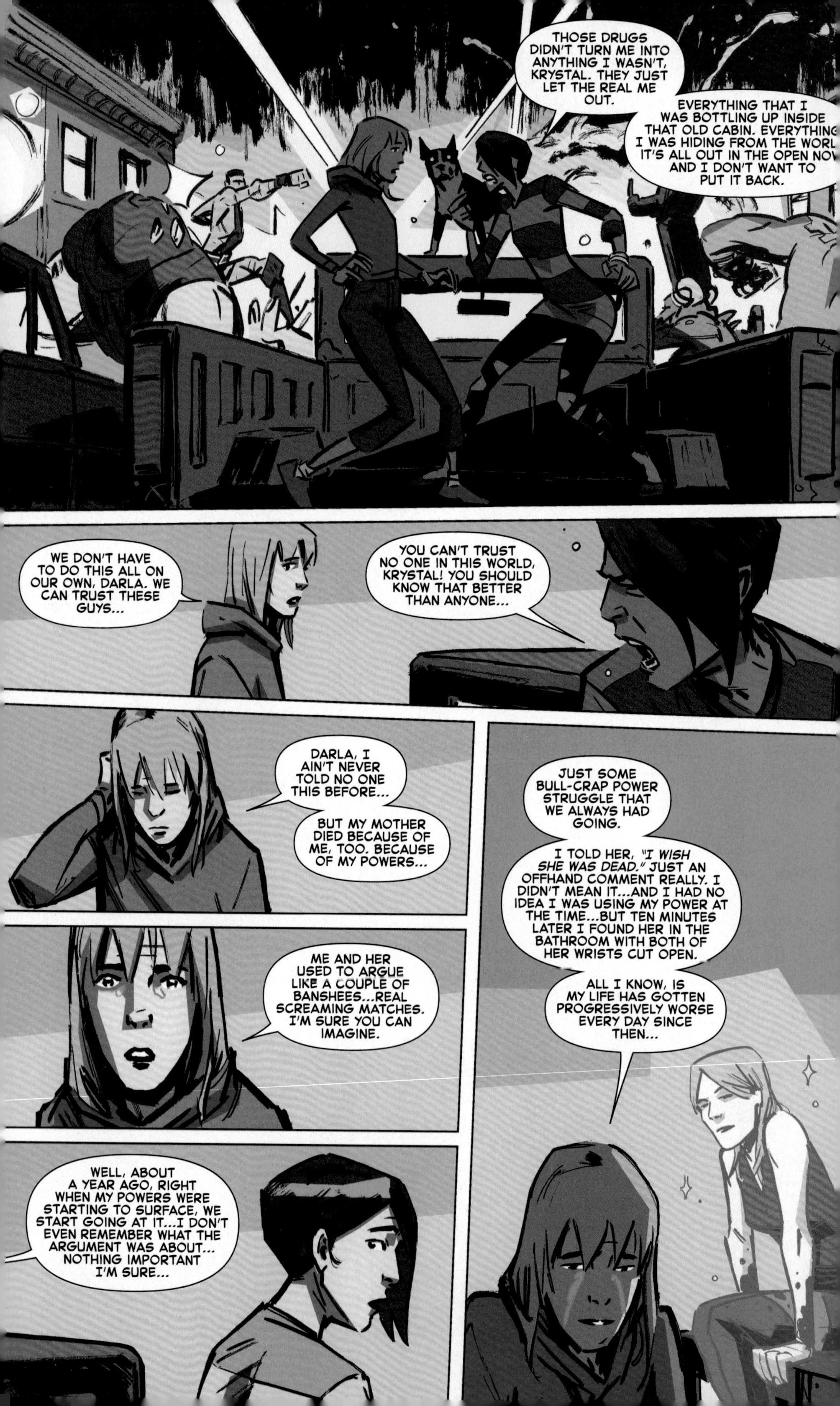
THOSE DRUGS DIDN'T TURN ME INTO ANYTHING I WASN'T, KRYSTAL. THEY JUST LET THE REAL ME OUT.
EVERYTHING THAT I WAS BOTTLING UP INSIDE THAT OLD CABIN. EVERYTHING I WAS HIDING FROM THE WORL IT'S ALL OUT IN THE OPEN NOV AND I DON'T WANT TO PUT IT BACK.
WE DON'T HAVE TO DO THIS ALL ON OUR OWN, DARLA. WE CAN TRUST THESE GUYS...
YOU CAN'T TRUST NO ONE IN THIS WORLD, KRYSTAL! YOU SHOULD KNOW THAT BETTER THAN ANYONE...
DARLA, I AIN'T NEVER TOLD NO ONE THIS BEFORE...
BUT MY MOTHER DIED BECAUSE OF ME, TOO. BECAUSE OF MY POWERS...
ME AND HER USED TO ARGUE LIKE A COUPLE OF BANSHEES...REAL SCREAMING MATCHES. I'M SURE YOU CAN IMAGINE.
WELL, ABOUT A YEAR AGO, RIGHT WHEN MY POWERS WERE STARTING TO SURFACE, WE START GOING AT IT...I DON'T EVEN REMEMBER WHAT THE ARGUMENT WAS ABOUT... NOTHING IMPORTANT I'M SURE...
JUST SOME BULL-CRAP POWER STRUGGLE THAT WE ALWAYS HAD GOING.
I TOLD HER, "I WISH SHE WAS DEAD." JUST AN OFFHAND COMMENT REALLY. I DIDN'T MEAN IT...AND I HAD NO IDEA I WAS USING MY POWER AT THE TIME...BUT TEN MINUTES LATER I FOUND HER IN THE BATHROOM WITH BOTH OF HER WRISTS CUT OPEN.
ALL I KNOW, IS MY LIFE HAS GOTTEN PROGRESSIVELY WORSE EVERY DAY SINCE THEN...

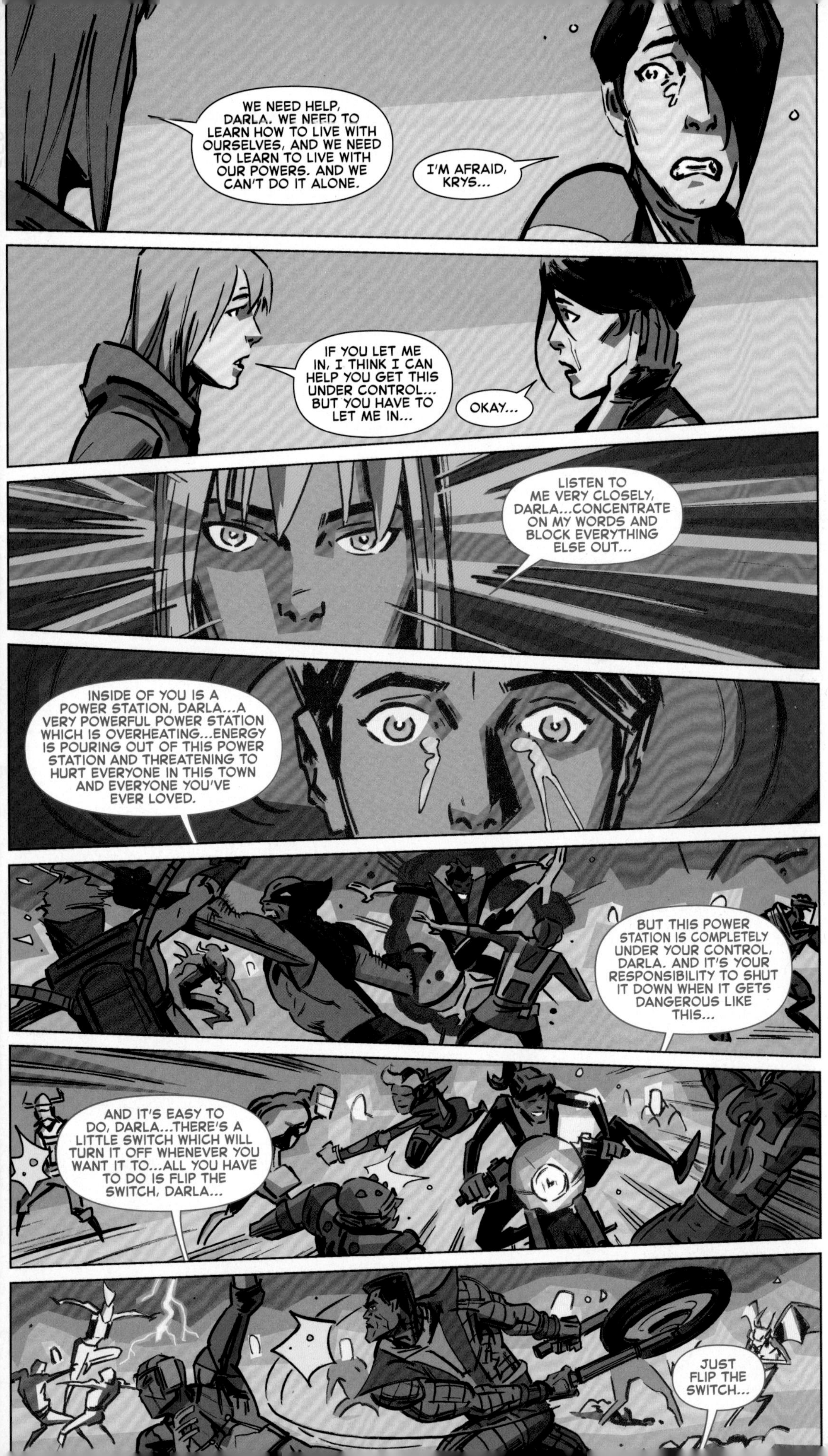
WE NEED HELP, DARLA. WE NEED TO LEARN HOW TO LIVE WITH OURSELVES, AND WE NEED TO LEARN TO LIVE WITH OUR POWERS. AND WE CAN'T DO IT ALONE.
I'M AFRAID, KRYS...
IF YOU LET ME IN, I THINK I CAN HELP YOU GET THIS UNDER CONTROL... BUT YOU HAVE TO LET ME IN...
OKAY...
LISTEN TO ME VERY CLOSELY, DARLA...CONCENTRATE ON MY WORDS AND BLOCK EVERYTHING ELSE OUT...
INSIDE OF YOU IS A POWER STATION, DARLA...A VERY POWERFUL POWER STATION WHICH IS OVERHEATING...ENERGY IS POURING OUT OF THIS POWER STATION AND THREATENING TO HURT EVERYONE IN THIS TOWN AND EVERYONE YOU'VE EVER LOVED.
BUT THIS POWER STATION IS COMPLETELY UNDER YOUR CONTROL, DARLA. AND IT'S YOUR RESPONSIBILITY TO SHUT IT DOWN WHEN IT GETS DANGEROUS LIKE THIS...
AND IT'S EASY TO DO, DARLA...THERE'S A LITTLE SWITCH WHICH WILL TURN IT OFF WHENEVER YOU WANT IT TO...ALL YOU HAVE TO DO IS FLIP THE SWITCH, DARLA...
JUST FLIP THE SWITCH...

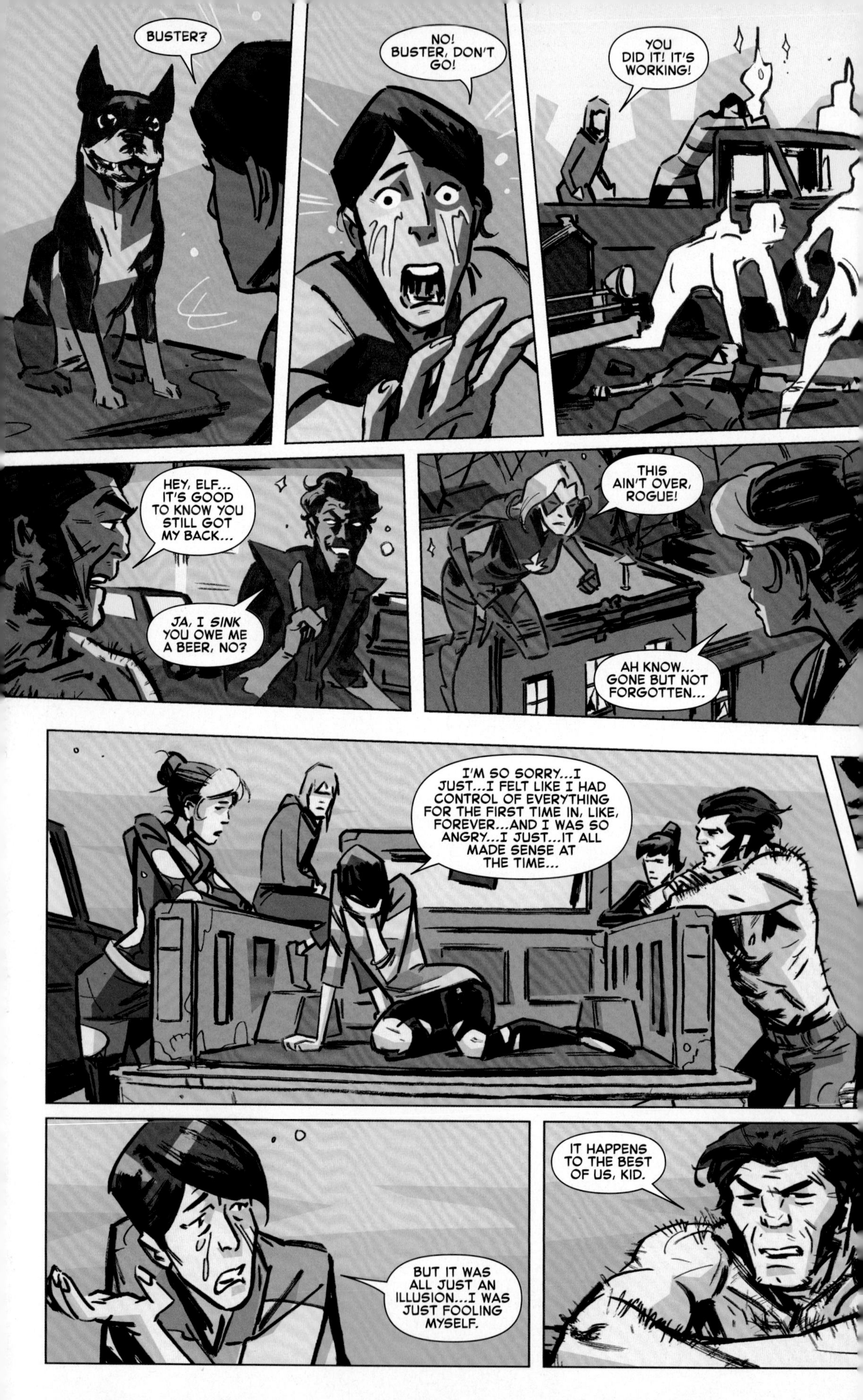
BUSTER?
NO! BUSTER, DON'T GO!
YOU DID IT! IT'S WORKING!
HEY, ELF... IT'S GOOD TO KNOW YOU STILL GOT MY BACK...
JA, I *SINK* YOU OWE ME A BEER, NO?
THIS AIN'T OVER, ROGUE!
AH KNOW... GONE BUT NOT FORGOTTEN...
I'M SO SORRY...I JUST...I FELT LIKE I HAD CONTROL OF EVERYTHING FOR THE FIRST TIME IN, LIKE, FOREVER...AND I WAS SO ANGRY...I JUST...IT ALL MADE SENSE AT THE TIME...
BUT IT WAS ALL JUST AN ILLUSION...I WAS JUST FOOLING MYSELF.
IT HAPPENS TO THE BEST OF US, KID.

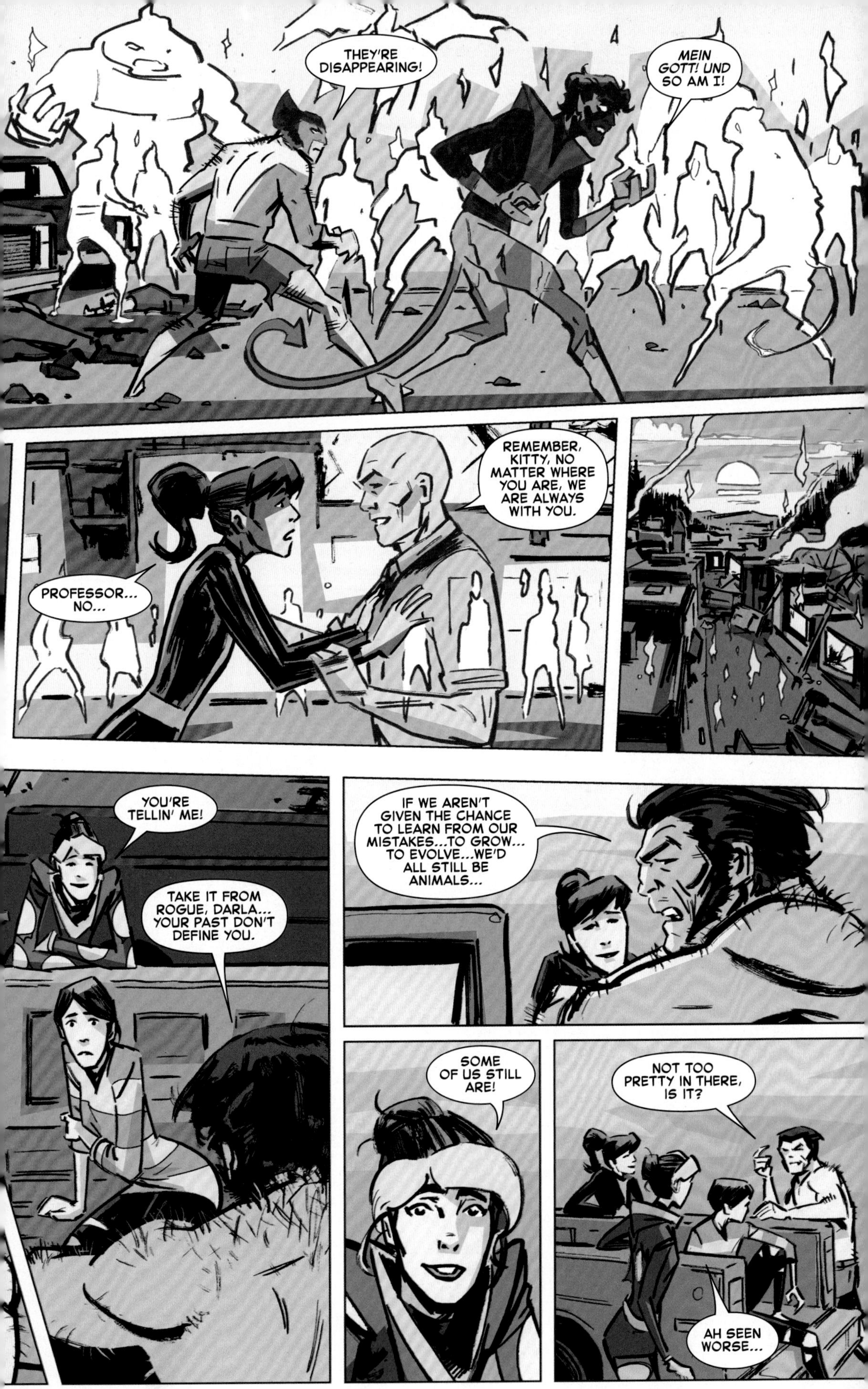
THEY'RE DISAPPEARING!
MEIN GOTT! UND SO AM I!
REMEMBER, KITTY, NO MATTER WHERE YOU ARE, WE ARE ALWAYS WITH YOU.
PROFESSOR... NO...
YOU'RE TELLIN' ME!
TAKE IT FROM ROGUE, DARLA... YOUR PAST DON'T DEFINE YOU.
IF WE AREN'T GIVEN THE CHANCE TO LEARN FROM OUR MISTAKES...TO GROW... TO EVOLVE...WE'D ALL STILL BE ANIMALS...
SOME OF US STILL ARE!
NOT TOO PRETTY IN THERE, IS IT?
AH SEEN WORSE...

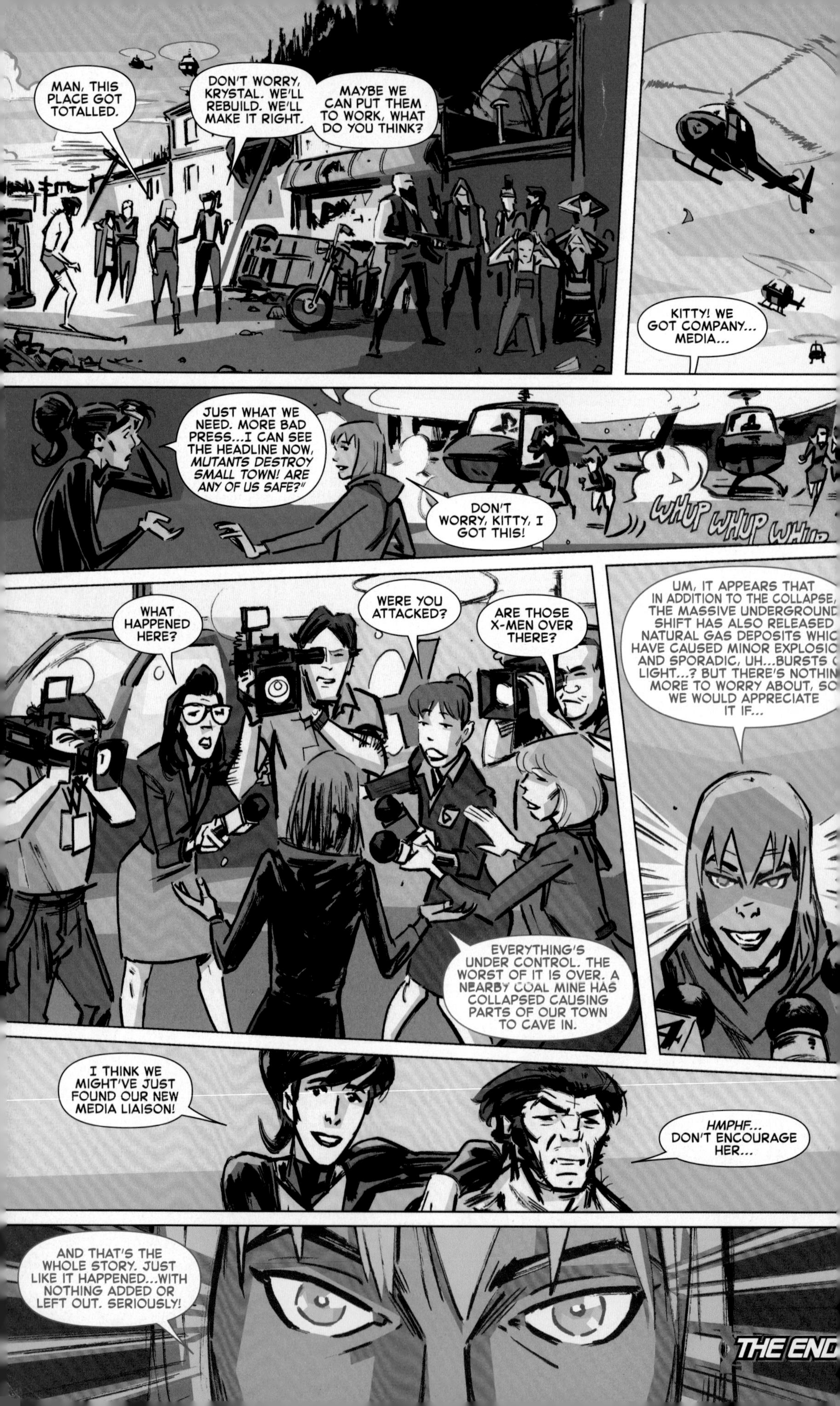
MAN, THIS PLACE GOT TOTALLED.
DON'T WORRY, KRYSTAL. WE'LL REBUILD. WE'LL MAKE IT RIGHT.
MAYBE WE CAN PUT THEM TO WORK, WHAT DO YOU THINK?
KITTY! WE GOT COMPANY... MEDIA...
JUST WHAT WE NEED. MORE BAD PRESS...I CAN SEE THE HEADLINE NOW, *MUTANTS DESTROY SMALL TOWN! ARE ANY OF US SAFE?"*
DON'T WORRY, KITTY, I GOT THIS!
WHUP WHUP WHUP
WHAT HAPPENED HERE?
WERE YOU ATTACKED?
ARE THOSE X-MEN OVER THERE?
EVERYTHING'S UNDER CONTROL. THE WORST OF IT IS OVER. A NEARBY COAL MINE HAS COLLAPSED CAUSING PARTS OF OUR TOWN TO CAVE IN.
UM, IT APPEARS THAT IN ADDITION TO THE COLLAPSE, THE MASSIVE UNDERGROUND SHIFT HAS ALSO RELEASED NATURAL GAS DEPOSITS WHIC HAVE CAUSED MINOR EXPLOSIC AND SPORADIC, UH...BURSTS LIGHT...? BUT THERE'S NOTHIN MORE TO WORRY ABOUT, SO WE WOULD APPRECIATE IT IF...
I THINK WE MIGHT'VE JUST FOUND OUR NEW MEDIA LIAISON!
HMPHF... DON'T ENCOURAGE HER...
AND THAT'S THE WHOLE STORY. JUST LIKE IT HAPPENED...WITH NOTHING ADDED OR LEFT OUT. SERIOUSLY!
THE END

A F T E R W O R D . . .

I'm not sure if a sports metaphor is really the way to go when addressing the comics community ut seeing as how spring is in the air and with spring comes the start of another of America's 'eat contributions to the world, baseball, allow me this indulgence.

When I first got the call that I was actually going to be working on this series, writing and 'awing *Marvel Knights: X-Men*, I felt like I got the call telling me I was heading from the minors the major leagues. In the comics industry Marvel is the biggest game in town, the top of the :ap, the pinnacle of the industry, and not only that, I was gonna be working on an X-Men title, ɔmething akin to signing with the Yankees (full disclosure: I am a Mets fan)! So, as I prepared yself for this potentially life-altering promotion, I tried to remind myself of all the mantras and iches that litter ESPN documentaries and sports-movie speeches. Be yourself...keep doing e same things that got you here...cuz it's the same game, there's just more people in the :ats. So that's what I tried to do.

Of course, errors were made, and it's true what they say: The game moves a lot quicker in e big leagues. But the added pressure also makes you a better player. Sure, there are things I change if I had to do it all over, but I'm also very happy with the books I produced and even bit surprised by all the nice things the fans had to say. So as I prepare to go back to the minor agues and finish my creator-owned book, GUERILLAS (plug! plug!), I know that I do so as a ɔtter artist and a better writer.

And before I go, I'd like to specifically thank Axel for giving me my shot, and Sana and all the her editors who helped me along the way!

Brahm Revel

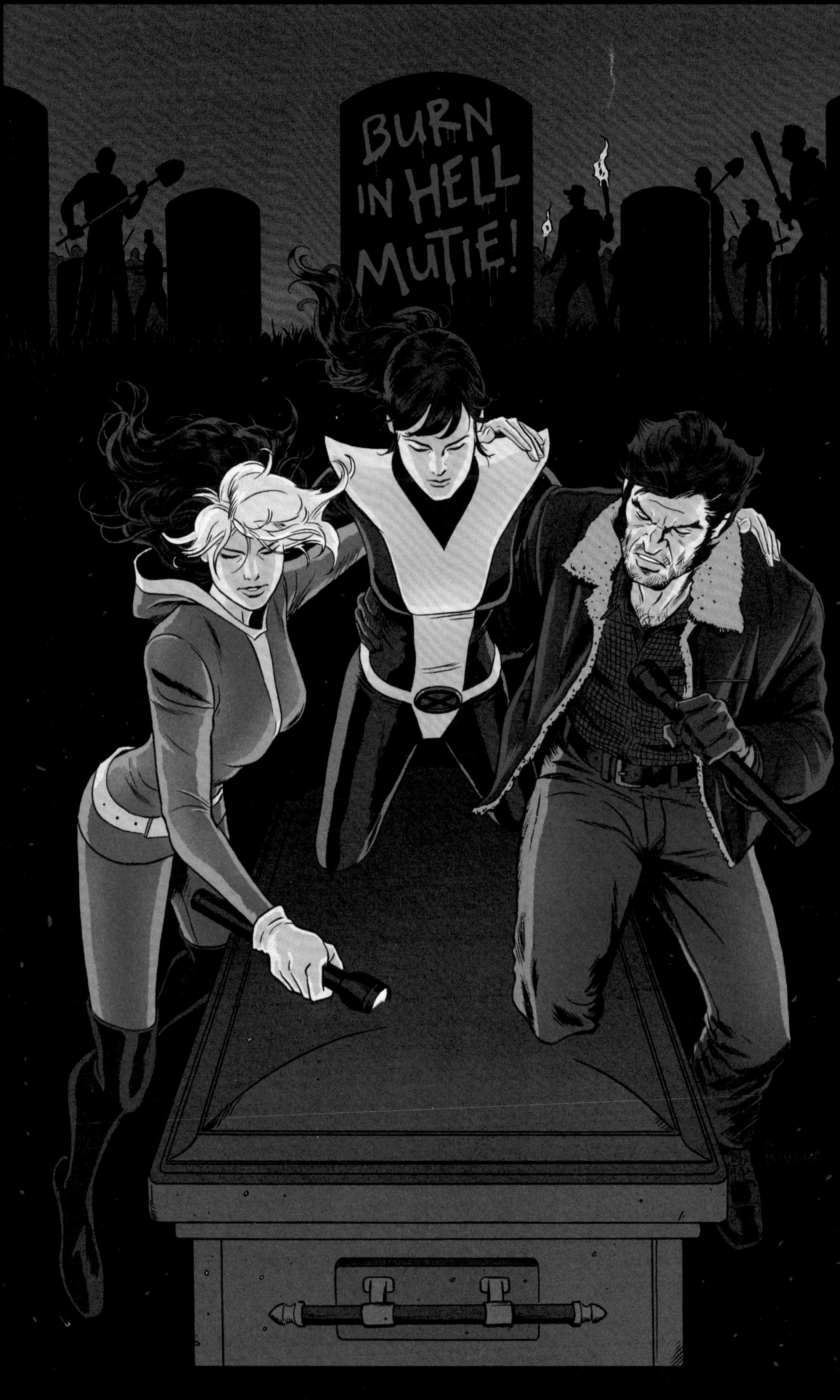
BURN
IN HELL
MUTIE!

#1 VARIANT COVER BY PAOLO RIVERA

#4 COVER SKETCH

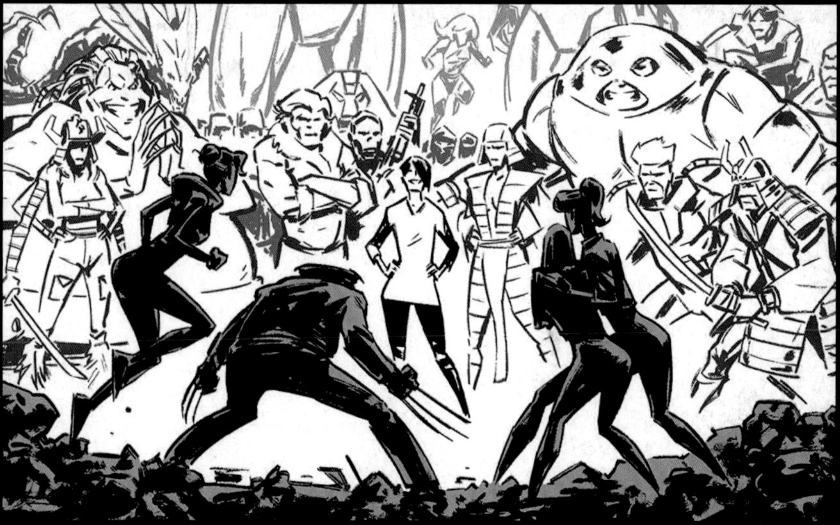

#5 COVER SKETCH

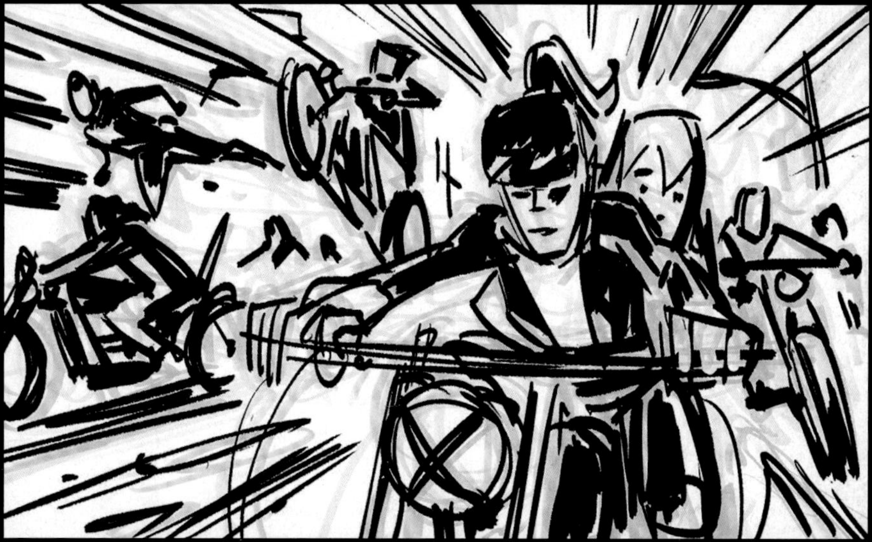

#1 THUMBNAILS

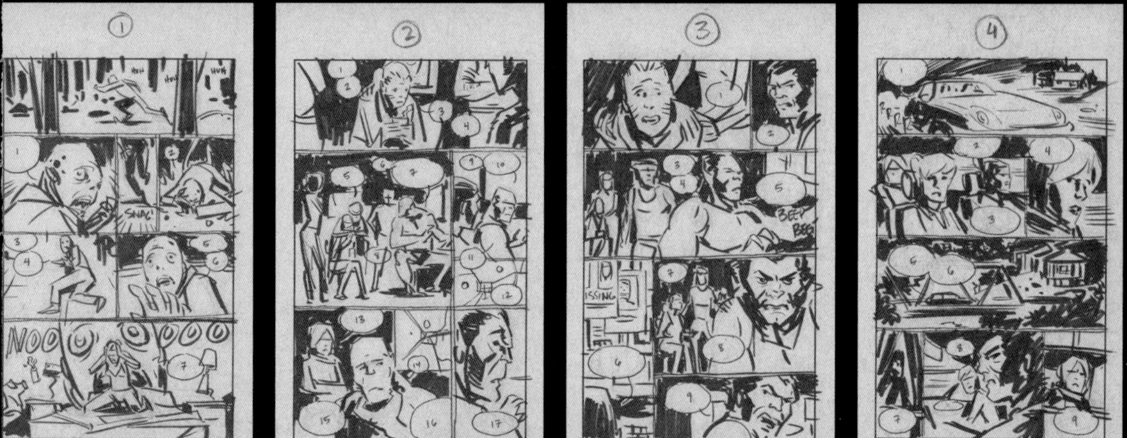

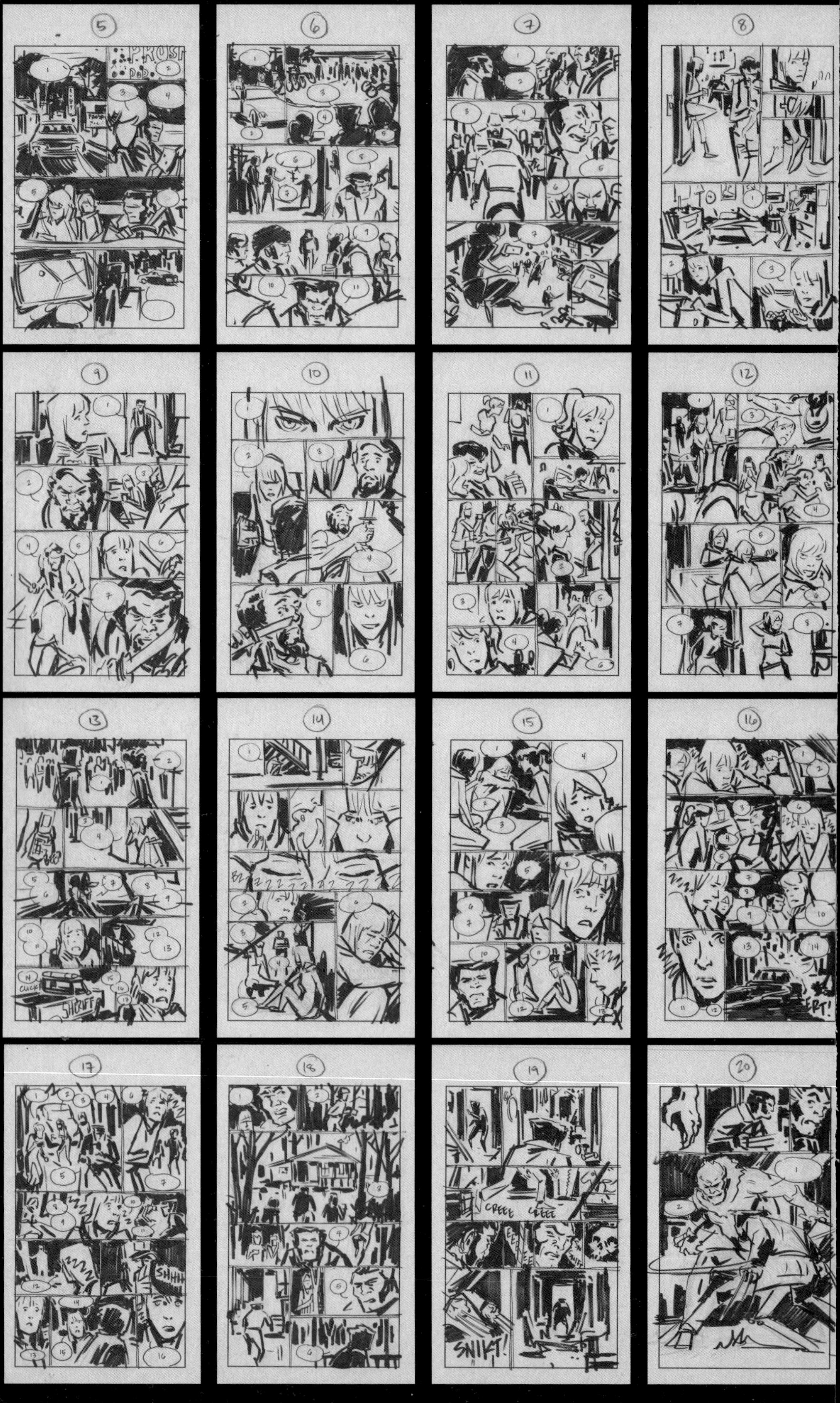

5
6
7
8
9
10
11
12
13
14
15
16
CLICK
SHERIFF
17
SHHHH
18
19
CREEE CREEE
SNIKT!
20